W9-AHN-541

SOUTH ASIAN
POLITICAL SYSTEMS

General Editor
RICHARD L. PARK

The Politics of Pakistan
A CONSTITUTIONAL QUEST
RICHARD S. WHEELER

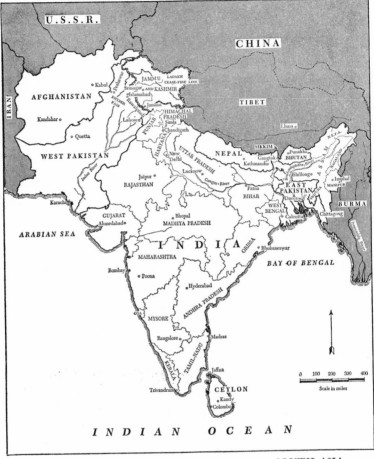

SOUTH ASIA

The Politics of Pakistan

A CONSTITUTIONAL QUEST

RICHARD S. WHEELER

Cornell University Press

ITHACA AND LONDON

099511

International Standard Book Number 0-8014-0589-0
Library of Congress Catalog Card Number 71-124728

PRINTED IN THE UNITED STATES OF AMERICA
BY VAIL-BALLOU PRESS, INC.

In memory of
Herb Heidenreich

Foreword

Serious study of modern South Asia is a relatively recent development in the United States. It began shortly after World War II, and was made possible by opportunities for language study and research in the region. Scholarly work on current South Asian themes, however, rests upon older academic traditions that emphasized principally the philosophy, religion, and classical literature of these ancient civilizations. This series, "South Asian Political Systems," is addressed to contemporary political problems, but is presented in the context of institutions and value systems that were centuries in the making.

Over the past quarter century, humanists and social scientists in Asia, Europe, the United States, and elsewhere throughout the world have worked together to study modern South Asian cultures. Their efforts have been encouraged by a recognition of the importance of the rapid rise of nationalism in Asia in the twentieth century, by the decline, hastened by the war, of Western imperial systems, and by the appearance of dozens of independent states since the founding of the United Nations. Scholars were made increasingly aware that the South Asian peoples were not anonymous masses or abstract representatives of distant traditions. They were, like us, concerned with their own political affairs, with raising families, building houses, constructing industries, educating the young, and creating better societies. They were nourished by their heritage, but they also struggled to devise political institutions, economic processes, and social organizations that were responsive to modern needs. And their needs were, and continue to be, great.

It was an awareness of these realities that encouraged private foundations and agencies of government to sponsor intensive field work in South Asia, including firsthand observation of day-to-day life and opportunities to discover and use rare source material. India has received the most attention, in part because of its size and intrinsic importance, in part because scholars have concentrated on teaching Indian languages, and research tends to be done where the languages are understood. More and more the other countries of South Asia—Pakistan, Nepal, Ceylon, and Afghanistan—have begun to attract scholarly attention. Whereas in the late 1940's one was hard pressed to find literature about the region, except in journalistic accounts or in British imperial histories, by the 1970's competent monographs and reliable periodicals are abundantly available. Today one can draw from an impressive bibliography on South Asia, including a commendable list of political works.

It remains true, however, that recent South Asian studies have been largely monographic—books that examine narrow themes in detail and that appeal to a small group of specialists who happen to be concerned with these themes. There are few broad guides to the politics of the countries of South Asia. This series has been designed to fill part of the need.

One of the problems in writing introductory works is that learning about a foreign culture is never a simple process. Experience tells us that each political system is imbedded in a broader social system, which in turn has roots in a particular history and a unique set of values. Language transmits culture, so one way to approach an unfamiliar culture is through the close study of language and literature. Knowledge of history, or of the arts, or of social organization offers another path to understanding.

The focus of this series is on political systems. Each author starts with a common organizational framework—brief history, political dynamics, political structure, continuing problems—and weaves in unique factors. For India, a complex federal organization of government and a varied and changing political party system require emphasis. For Pakistan, the constitutional dilemma is the most crucial issue. For Nepal and Afghanistan, monarchical traditions in conflict with pressures to modernize necessitate treatments that are more historically oriented. Ceylon, too, has political problems, especially ethnic and religious, not readily comparable with others. Used together the books should provide excellent opportunities for comparison and contrast.

Professor Richard S. Wheeler, of Claremont Men's College, has followed Pakistan's affairs closely—in both the Eastern and Western sectors—since the early 1950's. His book presents a clear analysis of Pakistan's political system, a subject that has received little attention heretofore. He has pin-pointed a central problem, emphasizing the difficulties of constitution-making that are continuing to be of concern to the country's political leaders.

RICHARD L. PARK

Ann Arbor, Michigan
May 1970

Preface

Anyone who attempts to analyze Pakistan's political system is confronted with the overriding importance of constitutional controversies in national politics. This study has taken the search for constitutional consensus as a theme, in hopes of making clear the nature of the problems that have caused repeated crises and constitutional upheavals. At the time of writing Pakistan is again under martial law, with a return to representative institutions and a new constitution forecast for late 1970. I have been unable, therefore, to deal with institutions and processes with the degree of finality possible in regard to political systems in which consensus on the form of executive and legislature and on the relations between central and regional authorities has been confirmed by time or by formal constitutional documents. I have sought instead to give some sense of the experience of the past and the alternatives available to those in Pakistan responsible for working out a new constitutional formula, to provide a basis for an understanding of whatever solutions are achieved in the years ahead.

Since the focus in this book is entirely on domestic constitutional issues, I have made no attempt to deal directly with Pakistan's foreign relations or with the Kashmir question. Both of these topics deserve separate studies, and although of great importance they are in my view peripheral to the primary constitutional dilemmas to which I have addressed myself. Some consideration of Muslim India's links with the rest of the Muslim world is inescapable in Chapter 1, in which I have presented the historical background essential for an understanding of how Pakistan came to be, and indeed to a degree the conflict between the Muslim League and the Congress in British India foreshadowed the difficult relations between the successor states. Chapter 2, in setting out the major social and economic characteristics of Pakistan, inevitably deals with some aspects of Pakistan's relations with India and with the United States and other aid-giving powers. Building on the foundations laid in these first chapters, Chapters 3 to 5 proceed to distinguish the areas of principal controversy and to indicate the elements both of continuity and of change in successive constitutional arrangements.

Pakistan's political history since independence has been one of tortuous and complicated maneuverings, with the role of personalities often extremely important. Chapters 6 and 7 give a generally chronological survey of political events to which some readers may wish to refer at the outset. Nevertheless, it may be well to indicate here the principal landmarks in a most confusing landscape: the death of Qaid-i-Azam Mohammed Ali Jinnah, the founder of Pakistan, on September 11, 1948; the assassination of Prime Minister Liaqat Ali Khan for unknown reasons by an Afghan on October 16, 1951; the dismissal of Prime Minister Nazimuddin by Governor General Ghulam Mohammad on April 17, 1953; Ghulam Mohammad's dissolution of the Constituent Assembly on October 24, 1954; the promulgation of the Constitution of the Islamic Republic of Pakistan on March 23, 1956; the abrogation of the 1956 Constitution and the imposition of martial law by President Iskander Mirza on the night of October 7, 1958; the termination of martial law by President Ayub Khan and the enforcement of the presidential Constitution on June 8, 1962; and the resignation of President Ayub Khan on March 24, 1969, and the abrogation of the 1962 Constitution and reimposition of martial law the following day. Chapter 8 deals with this political process, the interplay of parties, groups, and personalities, and attempts an assessment in general terms of the future political prospects of Pakistan.

My analysis has been written from the vantage point of late summer 1969. The martial-law government of President A. M. Yahya Khan has since taken a series of steps toward the establishment of a new constitutional system. On July 28, 1969, a Supreme Court judge from East Pakistan was appointed chief election commissioner, to prepare for national elections. On November 28, 1969, President Yahya Khan announced that the West Pakistan province would be dissolved and that elections for a new National Assembly on the basis of one man, one vote (resulting in an East Pakistan majority) would be held on a common electoral roll on October 5, 1970. On January 1, 1970, martial-law restrictions were relaxed, and active campaigning began. On March 28, 1970, President Yahya Khan announced that the National Assembly would have a total of 313 members: East Pakistan 162, plus 7 women; Punjab 82, plus 3 women; Sind 27, plus one woman; Baluchistan 4, plus one woman; and the Frontier Province and tribal areas 25, plus one woman. The reconstituted provinces in West Pakistan were to come into being on July 1, 1970, and provincial legislatures would be elected on October 22, 1970. Finally, the President laid down the basic principles to be enshrined in the new constitution:

(1) Islamic ideology; (2) independence, territorial unity, and national solidarity; (3) free and periodic elections on the basis of population and direct adult franchise; (4) federalism, with maximum provincial autonomy compatible with the securing of adequate powers to the federal government to discharge its responsibilities in external and internal affairs; and (5) statutory provision for the removal of economic and other disparities among the various provinces, to enable the people of all regions to have a full share in national life. The National Assembly would have 120 days to adopt a new constitution according to these guidelines, finding satisfactory solutions to the questions of Islam and federal-provincial relations, failing which it would be dissolved and another assembly election would occur.

Several points of style should be noted. The problem of the spelling of Pakistani names is a difficult one. I have attempted to use the version of a name favored by the person concerned; thus "Chaudhri Muhammad Ali" in accordance with the preference indicated in his book, rather than "Chaudhri Mohamad Ali," which was the form commonly used when he was prime minister. I have departed from the standard practice in rejecting the forms "Quaid" and "Liaquat" in the title Qaid-i-Azam and the name Liaqat Ali Khan. The elimination of the "u" is orthographically correct and indicates that the "q" is pronounced as "k." Diacritics in Arabic words have been eliminated throughout—thus Quran instead of Qur'an. I have followed Pakistani practice in my use of "government" to indicate President (or governor) and ministers, as distinguished both from the administrative bureaucracy and the legislature. I have also deliberately avoided use of terms such as "dictatorship" and "military coup" and their various combinations in dealing with martial law in Pakistan because I feel that these terms are full of misleading connotations that impede understanding of the Pakistani situation.

I have made several visits to Britain and to Pakistan which directly or indirectly have produced material for this study. I am indebted to the Ford Foundation (now the Foreign Area Fellowship Program) for supporting my stay in London in 1957–58 and in East and West Pakistan in 1958–59, and to the United States Educational Foundation in Pakistan for a Fulbright research grant enabling me to spend seven months in East Pakistan in 1965. Neither of these organizations bears any responsibility for the content of this book. I am grateful to many persons in Britain and in Pakistan for their helpful insights, and for their assistance in my exploration of various aspects of Pakistani administration, politics, and government, past and present. In particular, four good friends, Ataul, Mashuk, Makhon, and Razia, by their hospitality in Karachi and in Dacca over the years, have made me feel truly at home in Pakistan, and have nourished my interest in things Pakistani. I wish to acknowledge the cooperation of Mr. S. C. Sutton, C.B.E., and his staff in my successive visits to the India Office Library in London; of the librarian of the former Constituent Assembly Library in Karachi; of the secretaries and librarians of the Provincial Assembly libraries in Lahore and Dacca; and of Professor Gerard Friters, then head of the Political Science Department in the University of the Panjab, Lahore, for access to theses written by students in his department.

I am deeply appreciative of the perceptive comments of my friend and colleague at Claremont Men's College, P. Edward Haley, who read most of the final draft, and of Ronald N. Montaperto, then a graduate student at the University of Michigan, Ann Arbor, who was kind enough to read, criticize, and discuss an earlier version. Richard L. Park of the University of Michigan has suffered with me through successive stages in the preparation of this book, with appropriate and indispensable encouragement and criticism. Many thanks are due, too, to the editorial staff of Cornell University Press, whose sharp eyes have caught many inconsistencies and whose attention to syntax has made some of my sentences at least more comprehensible. Finally, in a study of this kind errors are inescapable, but I have done my utmost to minimize them. I particularly hope that Pakistanis will be indulgent in regard to my inadequate discussion of Islam.

RICHARD S. WHEELER

Claremont, California
July 1970

Contents

Tables

Maps

Abbreviations

ADC	Agricultural Development Corporation; also EPADC, WPADC
CML	Council Muslim League
COP	Combined Opposition Parties
CSP	Civil Service of Pakistan
DAC	Democratic Action Committee
DC	Deputy Commissioner
EBDO	Elective Bodies (Disqualification) Order
KSP	Krishak Sramik party
NAP	National Awami party
NDF	National Democratic Front
NIP	Nizam-i-Islam party
PER	Pakistan Eastern Railway
PDM	Pakistan Democratic Movement
PDP	Pakistan Democratic party
PIDC	Pakistan Industrial Development Corporation; also EPIDC, WPIDC
PPP	Pakistan People's party
PWR	Pakistan Western Railway
SDO	Subdivisional Officer
WAPDA	Water and Power Development Authority; also EPWAPDA, WPWAPDA

The Politics of Pakistan

A CONSTITUTIONAL QUEST

1. The Emergence of National Identity

Long accustomed to consider faith irrelevant to politics, the international community was startled in August 1947 to witness the birth of a state founded to provide a homeland for a nationality defined primarily in terms of religious belief. Pakistan seemed to be an anachronism in a twentieth-century world dominated by secular ideologies, its very existence offensive not only to many in the neighboring Indian Union, whose identity its creation had explicitly repudiated, but to professed liberals in Europe and America as well. Although the western world readily welcomed the establishment of a state for a religious nationality in the Middle East, the emergence of Pakistan was understood by few outside South Asia and accepted by few outside the new state itself. The roots of Pakistan were and are comprehensible only by reference to the long and complex history of Islam in the Indian subcontinent, and to the character of the faith itself. A sense of separate identity is inherent in Islam, and the challenges of the Indian environment to that identity elicited responses that gradually shaped a distinctive political community. This chapter will review the stages by which in modern times that community was led to the realization of a separate political destiny, concluding with the final achievement of the Pakistan demand. It may then be possible in subsequent chapters to attempt to understand the problems that were and are posed by the aspiration to establish a state in which Muslims may order their lives in accordance with the principles of their faith. The quest for a constitutional solution to those problems has absorbed much of the political energies of Pakistan in the years since the state was created by the partition of the British Indian Empire.

Islam in the Indian Subcontinent

Since its first arrival in force in the eleventh and twelfth centuries, Islam has been the religion of a minority in the Indian subcontinent. At first its adherents formed the ruling elite, a largely immigrant aristocracy of Turks, Afghans, Persians, and Central Asians generally which was gradually reinforced by a native-born Muslim element. By the time the British conquest in the eighteenth and nineteenth centuries wrested power from Muslim hands, the community of Islam had become primarily an indigenous one. The ruling class included numerous immigrants, but the mass of the Muslim population were ethnically Indian. Missionary activities, forced conversions, intermarriage, and the inescapable material influences of more than six centuries of Muslim rule had induced members of all classes to embrace Islam. The heaviest concentrations of Muslims were in the north, most particularly in the Indus valley and in the lower Ganges-Brahmaputra delta. In these areas they outnumbered adherents of other religions, although they remained a minority of no more than 10 or 15 per cent in other parts of the subcontinent.

As a minority and, for long, alien faith in India, Islam was faced with the continuing challenge to its separate existence posed by the powerful absorptive influences of Hindu culture. Constant recruitment in the Muslim lands to the west brought preachers and scholars as well as soldiers and administrators, enabling the Indian Muslim community to maintain its identity and even to spread the faith. The very success of proselytization created serious problems, for converts brought with them into the fold of Islam many Hinduist practices not in strict accord with the teachings of the Quran. The most successful Muslim missionaries in India were Sufi teachers, whose mystical and emotional interpretations of the faith with emphasis on a Way or Path to union with the One bore great similarities to the teachings of the Hindu bhakti (devotional) movement. The danger lay in the possibility that the Sufi pirs (saints) and their followers—often Hindus as well as Muslims—might become so obsessed with the ritual demands of their orders as to lose sight of the greater identification with the community of Islam.

Preservation of the integrity of the faith has been an ever-present problem in Islam because of its egalitarian and non-hierarchic character. The teachings of Islam are simple: there is but one God; Muhammad, to whom God's word was revealed in the Holy Quran, was the last of the Prophets; all men are equal before God and must submit themselves to His will. From these few principles the mass of Islamic doctrine was evolved in the first four centuries of the Muslim era. After the death of the Prophet (A.D. 632) there was no single authority to interpret God's will, so the responsibility devolved on the learned members of the community to read the Quran and apply its message to human affairs. Gradually the law, the Shariah, was developed: from the Quran, the revelation of truth by God; from the Hadith (traditions), embodying elaborations by the Prophet and his Companions and Followers of the principles enunciated in revelation; and from the interpretations of the former two sources by the ulama, the learned, to apply their principles to the changing needs of humanity. As differing interpretations were made, a variety of sects and schools of law arose. All those who accept the Sunnah (corpus of normative traditions) of the Prophet and the first four elected khalifas are regarded as orthodox, or Sunni. A major cleavage exists between them and the smaller of the two great sects, the Shia, who regard the Prophet's son-in-law and cousin Ali (the fourth khalifa) as his successor by divine right and therefore accept a different sunnah as the basis of their law.

Throughout the period of Muslim ascendancy in India the first obligation felt by the orthodox Sunni ulama was to defend the integrity of the community from attack. The great expansion of Islam in the subcontinent came after the overthrow of the Abbaside Khilafat by the Mongols in 1258, and many of the scholars and military adventurers who came to India were refugees from political upheavals in Central Asia. In insisting on adherence to the Shariah and emphasizing the communal aspects of religious observance, the ulama were seeking to preserve the integrity of the Islamic community in India despite its overthrow in the West. In the absence of the universal khalifa the Shariah itself, rationalized by the ulama to legitimize the political status quo of the day, was the sole unifying bond linking Muslims and separating them from nonbelievers. In India the heterodox practices of Sufiism and the occult mysteries of the Shia minority threatened the universality of the law and with it the identity of Islam as a single faith distinct from the complex of beliefs described as Hinduism. Hence the insistence of the orthodox on the enforcement of conformity and their bitter opposition to the syncretic tendencies of such as the Mughal Emperor Akbar (1556–1605) and his descendant, Prince Dara Shikoh.[1]

Despite the best efforts of the ulama, demographic realities forced Islam to come to an adjustment with Hinduism. Muslims could not isolate themselves from their Hindu neighbors; social contacts had their effects, and converts to Islam were unable to divest themselves completely of their former social attitudes. The result was that caste restrictions, saint worship, and magical beliefs appeared in the Muslim community. Islamic monotheism found its echoes in Hinduism as well, and on the borderline of the two communities there flourished sects which were as much the one as the other. This blurring of the boundaries of the community provoked the political reaction of the Emperor Aurangzeb (1658–1707), whose efforts to reassert the requirements of the Shariah in a predominantly non-Muslim society helped to precipitate the collapse of the Mughal Empire. Of more ultimate political importance was the intellectual response of such ulama as Shah Waliullah of Delhi (1703–1762), who preached a return to practices sanctioned by the life of the Prophet but a tolerant interpretation of the Shariah in order to reconcile all schools of thought within the community. The outset of the British period in India, ending the era of Muslim rule in the subcontinent, therefore saw the first stirrings of the reform movement within Islam which sought to reassert the identity of the community against their neighbors of other faiths.

---

[1] See Aziz Ahmad, *Studies in Islamic Culture in the Indian Environment* (Oxford, 1964), ch. VI, for a consideration of Akbar's religious eclecticism, and ch. V for the bhakti movement and syncretism generally.

The British Impact on Indian Islam

The overthrow of Muslim political power by the forces of the English East India Company between 1757 and 1857 profoundly transformed the role of Islam in the subcontinent. The former Muslim ruling classes were dispossessed and, in Bengal, impoverished; alienated from their conquerors, they withdrew into an isolation dominated by dreams of regaining power. Scorning service under the new rulers, Muslims left the way clear for their former Hindu subordinates, who quickly adapted to the new dispensation and flocked to the service of the Company's administration. The final blows to old-school Muslim government servants were the abandonment of Persian as the official language in 1835 and the cessation some years later of the practice of appointing *qadis* to deal with offenses under Muslim law. With missionary influences increasing among the Company's servants, both Islam and Hinduism were challenged philosophically by Christianity and the Whig morality of Victorian England. The response of Islam, already affected by the reformist teaching of Shah Waliullah and his followers, was a puritan movement to seek strength by purging the faith of Hindu influences, rather than an attempt to come to terms with a contemporary world dominated by British power.[2]

The so-called Indian Wahhabi movement, thus described because of superficial similarities with the puritan doctrines of the eighteenth-century Arab reformer Ibn Abd al Wahhab, included in fact two separate tendencies. In Bengal, peasant discontent in the early nineteenth century provided a fertile field for reform preachers who combined puritanism

[2] On Waliullah and nineteenth-century "Wahhabism" see Freeland Abbott, *Islam and Pakistan* (Ithaca, 1968), ch. 3.

with efforts to organize the community to resist oppression by the landlords and by the Company's authorities. A more overt and more formidable challenge to the Company's (and later the Crown's) government was presented by the successors of Shah Waliullah in the Delhi area, principally Sayyid Ahmad Barelvi (1786–1831). Preaching the need to reform Islam of its abuses by eliminating Hinduist practices, Sayyid Ahmad also taught that India under British rule was *dar-ul-harb* ("the abode of war," as distinguished from *dar-ul-Islam,* "the abode of peace") and that the faithful must engage in jihad for the triumph of Islam. Since revolt against the British power was impracticable, Sayyid Ahmad directed his preaching in the first instance against the Sikh kingdom in Punjab, leading his followers from a base near Peshawar in Pathan territory. After Sayyid Ahmad's death in battle in 1831, his disciples maintained the colony of *mujahidin* (the so-called Hindustani fanatics) in the mountainous area around the upper Indus until well into the twentieth century.

The Indian "Mutiny" of 1857 rallied Muslims in Awadh (modern Uttar Pradesh) and Bihar around the figure of the titular Mughal emperor in Delhi in an effort to destroy the infidel and regain lost power. Elsewhere, particularly in Punjab and on the Afghan frontier, most Muslims remained loyal to the British and helped them to crush the revolt. However, because of the Muslim color given the revolt by the prominence of the emperor and the Awadh nobility, the British tended to blame the community as a whole and to consider Muslims to be inherently untrustworthy. For their part, the ulama and the aristocracy under their influence withdrew even more from contact with the rulers and all they represented. Increasingly alienated from a society changing under the impact of western Christian ideas, the ulama seemed unable to appreciate the need to rethink the theological and political position of the Muslims if the community, no longer possessing political supremacy, were to survive.

The necessary leadership for the reform of Indian Islam and the reconciliation of the community with the British was provided by Sir Syed Ahmad Khan (1817–1898). The scion of a noble Delhi family, Syed Ahmad remained faithful to the British during the Mutiny. Recognizing that violent political action against the British was useless and that intellectual rejection of European ideas was dangerous in that it weakened the community's defenses, he resolved on a program of intellectual and educational reconstruction. This program involved three points: reconciliation with the government; adoption of the good in western ideas through English education; and abstention from politics for the foreseeable future.

Before Sir Syed's death, his goals for his community had been substantially achieved. He wrote a series of works explaining the Muslim role in the revolt of 1857 and seeking to demonstrate the essential loyalty of Muslims to the British Crown. Through interpretation of the Bible and the Quran he sought to show the similarities between Islam and Christianity, and thereby to create a more sympathetic understanding between Muslims and British. Sir Syed placed great emphasis on modern education; he founded in 1875 the Muhammadan Anglo-Oriental College at Aligarh and in 1886 the All-India Muhammadan Educational Conference. The M.A.O. College and its intellectual adherents, constituting the "Aligarh movement," disseminated Sir Syed's principles of social and intellectual uplift for the Muslim community to the rising generations of Muslims, particularly to the awakening upper middle classes of Punjab and the Northwestern Provinces (now Uttar Pradesh).

During the 1870's Sir Syed's efforts at political reconciliation bore fruit, and British officialdom began to adopt a more sympathetic attitude toward the Muslims. Thereafter Sir Syed was adamant in his insistence that Muslims should abstain from any political activity that might endanger this *rapprochement.* In 1887 he urged his fellow Muslims to remain aloof from the fledgling Indian National Congress (founded 1885), and to counter its attraction he and his colleagues founded in 1888 the United Indian Patriotic Association and in 1893 the Muhammadan Anglo-Oriental Defence Association, to oppose political agitation among the Muslims and to foster a spirit of loyalty to the Crown. Although some Muslims did join the Congress, by and large Sir Syed's viewpoint prevailed so long as he lived.

The creation of the Muslim-majority province of Eastern Bengal and Assam by Lord Curzon in 1905 marked a political turning point for Sir Syed's followers and the Aligarh movement. Theretofore content to depend on the good will of the government for the protection of their interests, the Muslims were prompted by the bitter opposition of the Hindus to the partition of Bengal to organize for defense of their gains. On October 1, 1906, a deputation of Muslim leaders organized by Sayyid Mahdi Ali (Nawab Muhsin ul-Mulk), the secretary of the Aligarh college, and led by the Aga Khan, waited upon Viceroy Lord Minto at Simla to request, and receive assurances of, special representation for Muslims in future constitutional arrangements. The following December the All-India Muhammadan Educational Conference met in Dacca, the capital of Eastern Bengal and Assam, and at the close of its sessions the leaders remained in conference to found an All-India Muslim League. Although in doing so the Muslim leaders broke with Sir Syed's advice to remain aloof from politics, the League in its early years was in fact an organized expression of his loyalism. According to the founding resolution, the League's purposes were:

a) to promote, among the Muslims of India, feelings of loyalty to the British Government, and to remove any misconception that may arise as to the intention of Government with regard to any of its measures;

b) to protect and advance the political rights and interests of the Muslims of India, and to respectfully represent their needs and aspirations to the Government;

c) to prevent the rise, among the Muslims of India, of any feeling of hostility towards other communities, without prejudice to the other aforementioned objects of the League.[3]

The loyalism emphasized in the first of the Muslim League's purposes characterized its arguments in 1906–1908 in pressing successfully to the authorities in India and in London the demand that representation for the Muslims should be provided through separate communal electorates in the forthcoming reforms of the Indian central and provincial legislatures. In this the League was following Sir Syed, who as early as 1883 had rejected the principle of straightforward election as a means of representation in India. The Muslims contended that experience had shown that without special

[3] Enclosure to demiofficial letter no. 47, Government of Indian Home Department, February 7, 1907, from Sir H. H. Risley to Sir Arthur Godley, Permanent Under Secretary of State for India (India Office Records, Judicial and Public Papers, 1907, vol. 796, file no. 614; unpublished Crown-copyright material transcribed by permission of the Secretary of State for Foreign and Commonwealth Affairs).

provision their politically unsophisticated community would be unable to elect its representatives, and that unless the situation were corrected bitterness against the Hindu majority would develop. Although the amount of separate representation provided the Muslims by the Indian Councils Act of 1909 was not as great as the League had desired, the essence of their demand was recognized in this first step toward the development of genuinely representative government in India.

Impact of the Congress on the Muslim Community

The founding in 1885 of the Indian National Congress to provide a forum for the expression of the political opinions and interests of all Indians without regard to religious or communal affiliation posed an immediate challenge to the awakening Muslim community. In seeking support from Muslims as well as other Indians, the organizers of the Congress emphasized the common interests of the new middle classes. The principal Muslim organization then in existence, Syed Ameer Ali's Calcutta-based Central National Muhammadan Association, expressed cautious approval of the first meeting of the Congress but subsequently abstained from any involvement on the ground that the Congress program aiming at democratic majority rule would "lead to the political extinction of the Mohammedans." [4] Despite this judgment and the warnings of Sir Syed Ahmad Khan, educated Muslims in the Presidency towns (Bombay, Madras, and Calcutta) responded to the Congress appeal, identifying themselves wholly with their non-Muslim colleagues. In Upper India support for the new organization came from Mus-

[4] Quoted in Ram Gopal, *Indian Muslims: A Political History (1858–1947)* (London, 1959), p. 76.

lims who were out of sympathy with the Aligarh movement and hence disinclined to follow Sir Syed's advice. Nevertheless, the Congress remained disproportionately Hindu in composition despite its efforts to achieve a national and non-communal identity.

Although loyalty to the Crown remained a basic principle of the Congress leadership throughout the thirty years of the Moderate era (1885–1915), as a focus of opposition to the status quo the organization soon attracted less conciliatory elements. During the 1890's pressures to give the Congress a more popular base increased, and under the leadership of B. G. Tilak (1856–1920) movements were launched that in time had the effect of encouraging Hindu revivalism and of challenging the liberal-constitutionalist assumptions of the Moderate leaders. In the Hindu antipartition agitation in Bengal, political and religious doctrines were blended in revolutionary terrorism directed against the government and its Indian supporters, both Hindu and Muslim. In Punjab the puritan Hindu reform teachings of the Arya Samaj (a revivalist movement founded in 1875) similarly inspired anti-Christian and anti-Muslim sentiments, and ultimately revolutionary agitation. The association of these Hindu extremist tendencies with the Congress alarmed many Muslims, particularly those of the Aligarh movement, and contributed to the decision to establish the Muslim League as a respectably loyal political body.

As a center of opposition to the British raj, the militant wing of the Congress attracted some elements in the Muslim community. In direct line of emotional and intellectual descent from that section of the ulama who had supported the revolt of 1857 to assert the supremacy of Islam and who thereafter refused to accept the imperatives of a changed world, were the traditionalists—represented theologically by the orthodox seminary at Deoband (founded in 1865)—who opposed the Aligarh movement. Repelled by Sir Syed's religious and educational doctrines and by his political loyalism, they found in the Congress allies with whom to continue the struggle against the infidel ruler. Thus, paradoxically, traditionally oriented orthodox Muslims joined forces with Congress nationalism, while the socially and educationally more advanced members of the community tended to abstain or (after 1906) to support the Muslim League.

After 1912 the broad categorization of politically conscious Muslims as either Congress nationalists or Aligarh-movement loyalists began rapidly to break down. Despite the loyalty of the Muslim League and the complete cooperation of the community with the government in an era of unrest, the repeated official declarations that the partition of Bengal was a "settled fact" were negated by the king's Delhi proclamation of December 1911. The abolition of the province of Eastern Bengal and Assam with effect from March 31, 1912, embittered the loyalists, casting doubt on the government's good faith and integrity and causing a reaction against Sir Syed's policies. At the same time, during the first two decades of the twentieth century the alienation of the orthodox from the British raj was given new emphasis by the spread of pan-Islamic ideas and an increasing concern among Indian Muslims for the political fortunes of the Turkish Empire. As Turkey tottered under the attacks of Christian powers in the Balkans and North Africa, she seemed to symbolize the fate of Islamic faith and culture. The sultan of Turkey was increasingly regarded as the khalifa of Islam, titular head of the community, and threats to his status and powers elicited prompt emotional reactions in India. This sentiment affected not only the traditionalists but also followers of the Aligarh movement, who found their loyalty to the British Crown—already shaken by the partition affair—severely strained as Turkey passed from crisis to crisis at the hands of Britain's European allies. The final complication was the outbreak of war between Turkey and the British Empire in 1914, bringing ultimately defeat and the dissolution of the Turkish Empire.

At the end of World War I pan-Islamic and nationalist sentiments in India were united in the Gandhian noncooperation movement to force concessions from the British. Indian Muslim concern for the fate of Turkey and the khalifa was expressed in 1919 in the "Khilafat" campaign. At the suggestion of M. K. Gandhi, the Khilafat committee adopted in May 1920 a program of mass action in the form of noncooperation with the government and boycott of official institutions. Subsequently the noncooperation movement was endorsed by the Congress and the Muslim League, linking the emotional Muslim pan-Islamic grievance with the postwar nationalist demand for *swaraj* ("self-government") within one year. Enthusiastic Muslim participation in the noncooperation movement gave the Congress for the first time a truly mass character and brought many Muslims firmly into the Congress fold.[5]

The Hindu-Muslim unity carefully constructed by Gandhi under the aegis of the Congress-Khilafat alliance began to collapse even before the termination of the noncooperation movement. The rebellion of the Moplahs (Muslim peasants) in Kerala in July 1921 drove a wedge between Hindu and

[5] Aziz Ahmad, *op. cit.*, "Epilogue: Modern Separatism," especially pp. 268–269 for the post-Khilafat residue of Muslim support for Congress.

Muslim Congressmen, who reacted differently to the affair. The boycott movement itself, calling for withdrawal of students from schools and colleges, caused resentment among educated Muslims when Gandhi appealed for the closure of Aligarh Muslim University and Islamia College in Lahore, seeming to undo the work of Sir Syed. Gandhi's decision to call off the movement in February 1922 was regarded as a betrayal by ardent Khilafatists, who attempted to carry on with ever-diminishing support until the futility of the movement was demonstrated by the Turks' abolition of the Khilafat in March 1924. The Muslim feeling of depression and frustration coincided with increasing Hindu-Muslim tension, culminating in the break between Gandhi and the Khilafat movement leaders Mohammed Ali and Shaukat Ali in September 1924.

The re-emergence of the Muslim League as an independent political force in 1924 marked the end of an era of close cooperation with and even subordination to the Congress. When the annulment of the partition of Bengal demonstrated the inadequacy of a policy of loyal dependence, the younger and more nationalist Muslim leaders brought about a change in the League's orientation. The League session of March 1913 adopted as its political objective "the attainment . . . of a system of self-government suitable to India." [6] Although a proposal to endorse the Congress objective of colonial (i.e., dominion) self-government was passed over, the new creed alienated conservatives such as the Aga Khan, who thereafter withdrew from the League. In subsequent years the League moved closer to the Congress, the two organizations holding their annual sessions at the same time and

[6] Sir Reginald Coupland, *The Indian Problem* (New York, 1944), I, 46.

locale from 1915 to 1920. This alliance was cemented in 1916 in the Lucknow Pact, in which the Congress for the first and only time accepted the Muslim claim for separate representation in legislative bodies, and the League, despite its past wariness of Congress politics, joined in demanding constitutional reforms and equality of status for India within the Empire. The blurring of the lines between the two organizations was encouraged by the Khilafat and noncooperation movements after 1919, and the League practically ceased to exist until the revival of communal tensions recalled Muslims to their political exclusivity and the heritage of Sir Syed Ahmad Khan.

The Muslim League's annual session of 1924 ushered in a quarter of a century of Muslim politics dominated by Mohammed Ali Jinnah (1876–1948). Jinnah, a Karachi-born Bombay barrister, began his political career as private secretary to Dadabhai Naoroji, the Parsi "grand old man" of the Congress. Strongly nationalist by conviction, Jinnah was also a dedicated constitutionalist, seeking to attain his goals through the manipulation and transformation of existing institutions. His first association with the Muslim League came in 1913 when he agreed to assist in the redefinition of its aims; he subsequently became a member on the understanding that his primary nationalist commitment was not to be compromised thereby. In 1916 Jinnah was president of the session that endorsed the Lucknow Pact. He gave evidence in London, both as a member of the Imperial Legislative Council and as a nationalist, on the constitutional proposals which eventuated in the Government of India Act of 1919. Although he favored acceptance of the reforms embodied in the 1919 Act, he resigned in March 1920 from the Legislative Council to protest the government's repression of political agitation. Later that year, disapproving of the irrational and anticonstitutional character of Gandhian mass action, he resigned from the Congress and withdrew from active politics. Following the failure of the Khilafat and non-cooperation movements and of the Gandhian experiment in Hindu-Muslim unity, Jinnah returned (in late 1923) to the central legislature and then to the platform of the Muslim League, appealing for increased constitutional safeguards for Muslims that would re-establish a sense of security and inter-communal harmony. For another ten years, despite conflicts and splits within the League, Jinnah struggled to gain acceptance of his views by the Muslims, in order to re-create, on the basis of an agreement with Congress guaranteeing minority rights, the old Hindu-Muslim nationalist alliance for constitutional advance.

Constitutional Advance

One consequence of the introduction of ministerial government in the provinces under the Government of India Act of 1919 was to increase the demands for minority safeguards. The Act itself accepted the principle, laid down in the Morley-Minto reforms of 1909, of separate communal electorates for the legislatures and extended it (in various provinces) to Sikhs, Europeans, Anglo-Indians, and Indian Christians; the allocation of seats for the Muslims was made in accordance with the principles agreed upon in the Lucknow Pact of 1916.[7] The executive at the center remained substantially unchanged, with overriding powers vested in the governor general (viceroy) and his executive council, including the power if necessary to bypass the now bicameral

[7] *Ibid.,* p. 62.

Indian legislature, but increased executive and legislative powers were devolved to the provinces. In a scheme known as "dyarchy," provincial responsibilities were divided between "reserved" and "transferred" subjects, administered by the governor in consultation respectively with appointed executive councilors and elected ministers. This was intended to allow Indians a greater share in their government, but the participation of Indian ministers, necessarily drawn from one community or another, compromised the traditional neutrality of government and led to suspicions of communal prejudice in administration. Minority community legislators soon realized that the demand for further extension of ministerial responsibility would result in provincial governments dominated by the majority (whether Hindu or Muslim) and presumably unsympathetic to the minority.

Accordingly, while demanding prompt and far-reaching constitutional advance, the Lahore Muslim League session in 1924, with Jinnah presiding, reaffirmed its insistence on separate electorates and on the Lucknow Pact rule that no bill or resolution affecting a community should be adopted if opposed by three-quarters of the representatives of that community. Further, the session resolved that a federal system with "full and complete provincial autonomy" was essential for the protection of Muslim interests. In March 1927 a meeting of Muslim leaders presided over by Jinnah elaborated this demand to include the separation of Muslim-majority Sind from Hindu-majority Bombay, reforms in Baluchistan and the North-West Frontier Province, and guarantees of a Muslim legislative majority in Bengal and Punjab. In return they agreed to accept a common electoral roll with a reservation of one-third of the seats in the central legislature for Muslims, and they promised reciprocal safeguards for minorities in the Muslim provinces. Although these proposals were accepted by the Madras Congress in December 1927, they were repudiated by the Hindu Mahasabha (the principal Hindu communal organization) and by Muslims who refused to give up separate electorates under any conditions.

The appointment of the Simon Commission by the British government in November 1927 initiated the process of constitutional discussion that led both to the collapse of Jinnah's efforts to build a new Congress-League alliance and to the official acceptance of a federation as the next stage of India's constitutional evolution. The lack of Indians on the Simon Commission outraged nationalist sentiment, and the Congress resolved to boycott its proceedings. The Muslim League split over the boycott issue, the Calcutta session under Jinnah adopting the Congress line, while the Lahore session appealed for cooperation. At this time Lord Birkenhead, Secretary of State for India, challenged Indian leaders to produce constructive constitutional suggestions. In response an All-Parties Conference, including the Jinnah section of the League in its first sessions, met and appointed a committee under Pandit Motilal Nehru to report on the principles of a constitution for India. The League soon became apprehensive about the outcome and withdrew, and consequently the Nehru Report was produced without its participation.

The Muslim reaction to the Nehru Report was generally negative, but the Jinnah faction of the League was determined to try to persuade the overwhelmingly Hindu All-Parties Convention, meeting in Calcutta in late December 1928, to modify the Report by accepting the 1927 Muslim proposals. Jinnah was the principal spokesman for the Muslim League in the Convention, but his appeals for reconciliation, generosity, and unity were in vain. The delegates, challenging his right to speak for Indian Muslims, rejected all of his proposals, and Jinnah left Calcutta depressed and disappointed: it was "the parting of the ways." [8]

The old tensions within the Muslim community between Indian nationalist and Muslim loyalist sentiments culminated, after the Nehru Report fiasco, in disillusion and disintegration. Jinnah attempted to bring about a reintegration of the League on the basis of a formula known as the "Fourteen Points," summarizing the Muslim demand for safeguards, a federal system, and—until Muslims should agree that their interests had been adequately secured—separate electorates. However, the unification meeting on March 28, 1929, was unable to reach agreement between the various factions and adjourned in failure, leaving the Muslims facing the next stage of constitutional discussions in disarray.

At the Round Table Conferences in London, convened by the British government after the Simon Commission had completed its work, the Muslim delegation was led by the Aga Khan and included the leaders of the various factions, among them Jinnah. In the absence of the Congress—then involved in a second noncooperation movement—the first conference (November 1930–January 1931) agreed that the future constitution should be federal. Civil disobedience was suspended during 1931, and the second conference (September–December 1931) was attended by Gandhi as the sole spokesman of the Congress. His refusal to accept the minorities' demands for safeguards and separate electorates angered minority leaders and forced the conference to leave the mat-

[8] Hector Bolitho, *Jinnah: Creator of Pakistan* (London, 1954), p. 95.

ter to be settled by an award of Prime Minister Ramsay Mac-Donald. Although the award (August 4, 1932) secured separate electorates for Muslims and other communities, its disproportionate allocation of legislative seats to minorities deprived Muslims of their majorities in Bengal and Punjab. The last conference (November–December 1932) again met without the Congress, which had resumed its boycott, and without Jinnah, who, apparently disillusioned by the whole course of events, had decided to abandon politics and settle in England.

The protracted constitution-making process culminated in the Government of India Act of 1935. The Act was a federal constitution, providing for government by responsible ministers in the provinces and linking the provinces with the princely states under a central government still ultimately responsible to the Secretary of State for India in London. The reaction of Indian political parties was generally negative, for not only did it fall short of responsible government at the center, but the goal of dominion status was not recognized even as an aspiration. The Congress rejected the new constitution "imposed from outside" and determined to contest the elections in the hope of "ending" the Act. The Muslim League, reunited since late 1933 under the leadership of Jinnah—who had returned from England in answer to the appeals of his colleagues—disliked the Act because of the restrictions on provincial autonomy imposed by the many reservations and special powers for the governors and the governor general. Both parties repudiated the federal part of the constitution as "fundamentally bad" because of the large voice it gave to the authoritarian Indian princes. Provincial autonomy came into effect on April 1, 1937, but the federal portion of the Act was never implemented because none of the princes agreed to accede to the federation. For that reason the central government continued to exist as constituted by the 1919 Act until the transfer of power in 1947.

The Muslim League approached the provincial elections of 1937 in a spirit of willingness to cooperate with the Congress. At Bombay in April 1936 the League resolved to work the new constitution "for what it was worth," in accordance with Jinnah's view that constitutional agitation was the proper means to secure political change. The League election manifesto outlined a social policy not greatly different from that of the Congress, and pledged League representatives to work for "democratic full self-government" in the provinces and at the center, within a framework of safeguards for the minorities. In contesting general elections for the first time, the League under Jinnah's leadership sought to bring together all Muslim factions so that their unified voice might be respected, and anticipated a policy of cooperation with the Congress "in the interests of India." [9] Congress responded to League overtures by informal "no contest" agreements, particularly in the United Provinces, and put up candidates for only 58 of the total of 482 Muslim seats.

When the election results were declared in February 1937, the Congress had won twenty-six Muslim seats (nineteen of them in the North-West Frontier Province) and a sweeping victory in the general constituencies, commanding pluralities in Bombay, Assam, and the Frontier and winning comfortably in the Hindu-majority provinces. The League won only 108 seats, losing to independents in the Muslim-minority provinces, to local parties in Bengal, Punjab, and Sind, and to the Congress-affiliated Khudai Khidmatgars in the Fron-

[9] A. A. Ravoof, *Meet Mr. Jinnah* (3d ed.; Lahore, 1955), p. 84.

tier. After some hesitation over the question of the special powers of the governors, the Congress agreed to accept ministerial office in July 1937. Emboldened by their strength and the weakness of the League, Congress leaders decided against cooperation with the League, including within the one-party governments formed in the seven Congress provinces only Muslims who accepted the Congress creed. In so acting, the Congress reflected the view its president, Jawaharlal Nehru, expressed in a public exchange with Jinnah in early 1937, that "there are only two forces in India today—British imperialism and the Congress representing Indian nationalism." This refusal to take the League seriously brought the inevitable response from Jinnah: "There is a third party in this country and that is the Muslims. We are not going to be dictated to by anybody." [10] With that the Muslim League set out on its separate course, determined to prove its right to speak on behalf of Indian Muslims as an equal of the Congress.

The two years following the Congress decision to spurn the League and to woo the Muslim masses directly saw the League begin its transformation from a small coterie of upper-middle-class politicians into a genuine popular movement. At its session in Lucknow in October 1937 the League turned its back on cooperation with the Congress and launched its own mass contact campaign. In the Congress provinces the hoisting of the Congress banner as the national flag on public buildings, the singing of "Bande Mataram" (the old Hindu nationalist song of Bengal antipartition days) as the national anthem, the quasi-religious veneration given to pictures of Gandhi in the schools, the emphasis on Hindi

[10] Gopal, *op. cit.*, p. 251, and Khalid Bin Sayeed, *Pakistan: The Formative Phase* (Karachi, 1960), p. 85.

at the expense of Urdu, plus other sorts of favoritism, fancied or real, provided the basis for League charges of Congress "atrocities" against the Muslims. Muslim members of Congress cabinets were denounced as stooges, and the governors and the governor general were attacked for failing to use their reserved powers to protect the Muslims. The charge that not only the economic position but the very existence of the Muslim minority was threatened under Congress raj found a ready response that was reflected at the polls: between January 1938 and September 1942 the Congress won not a single Muslim by-election in the Muslim-minority provinces; the League won fourteen.[11]

In the Muslim-majority provinces, where the League's electoral weakness had been most evident, its position was strengthened when provincial leaders endorsed the League at its Lucknow session. In those areas the threat of Hindu domination was not so clear as in the Muslim-minority provinces, and the traditional sense of communal identity was less pressing. There, too, the economic grievances of the peasantry rather than the aspirations of the Muslim middle class provided the basis for political action. In Punjab, Sir Sikandar Hayat Khan's Unionist party, an intercommunal alliance representing Muslim, Hindu, and Sikh rural interests, won a firm majority in 1937. The Sikandar-Jinnah Pact, bringing Muslim Unionists into the League, gave the League a foothold in Punjab while preserving the autonomy of the Unionist ministry. In Bengal, A. K. Fazlul Huq's Krishak Proja party, based on the peasantry of eastern Bengal, merged with the League to form a Muslim League coalition ministry. In landlord-dominated Sind, separated from Bom-

[11] Coupland, *op. cit.*, II, 333.

bay only in 1935, personalities rather than parties continued to determine political alignments, and it was not until 1942 that a fairly stable League ministry was achieved. In the North-West Frontier Province, where the Congress had managed to capture the Pathan peasant movement (the Khudai Khidmatgars of Khan Abdul Ghaffar Khan), the League in 1937 was the landlords' party, as in the United Provinces, facing an uphill struggle to gain popular support. The growth of the League was demonstrated in by-election victories from 1938 onward: twelve in Bengal, twelve in Punjab, three in the Frontier, and one in Sind, while the Congress secured only one Muslim seat in the Frontier and one in Sind.[12]

Like the experience of ministerial government after 1921, provincial autonomy under the 1935 Act contributed to the growing distrust between Muslims and Hindus. The inadequacy of safeguards and separate electorates had led Jinnah to the demand for a federal system, but events in 1937–1939 showed that minorities within the provinces were still at the mercy of the majority and indicated that in India as a whole the Muslim provinces would be subject to a permanently Hindu-dominated central government. Jinnah refused to countenance such a development, and early in 1938 he declared that the democratic parliamentary system of government was unsuited to India.[13] The following April, for the first time secure in the knowledge that his ascendancy in the League was undisputed, he insisted that as a prerequisite for any attempted solution of the constitutional problem the

[12] *Ibid.*

[13] At the Muslim University Union, Aligarh, February 5, 1938. In Jamil-ud-Din Ahmad, ed., *Some Recent Speeches and Writings of Mr. Jinnah* (5th ed.; Lahore, 1952), I, 41–49.

Congress must recognize that the League was the sole representative organization of the Muslims, of equal importance
with itself.[14] This the Congress refused to do, and the broad
gulf between the two was emphasized when the resignation
of the Congress ministries after the outbreak of war was welcomed by Jinnah and celebrated with thanksgiving by the
League on "Deliverance Day," December 22, 1939.

The Pakistan Demand

The concept of partnership between equals enunciated in
1939 embodied the age-old Muslim concern for the preservation of the separate identity of the community. Affirmed by
Sir Syed as the basis of his social and political teachings,
Muslim separatism was inherent in the pan-Islamic orientation of the orthodox leaders of the Khilafat movement, with
their concern for the fate of Islam in the modern world. The
obstacles impeding the re-creation of an Islamic society within
a political order dominated by non-Muslims inspired the
poet-philosopher Sir Muhammad Iqbal, addressing the Muslim League session at Allahabad on December 29, 1930, to
propose the establishment of a unified Muslim state in the
northwest as part of a new federal India. Iqbal said that the
Muslims had such distinct characteristics that they were a
nation. This concept was adopted during the Round Table
Conferences by a group of young Muslims at Cambridge to
support their advocacy of the creation of an entirely independent Muslim state for which they coined the name
"Pakistan." This proposal was dismissed by Muslim political
leaders of the time, but by 1938 the "two-nation theory" had

[14] Letter from Jinnah to J. Nehru, April 12, 1938, cited in Bolitho,
op. cit., p. 117.

become widely accepted in Muslim League circles. In October of that year the Sind Provincial League session at Karachi endorsed the principle of self-determination for both Hindus and Muslims, and recommended that the All-India Muslim League "devise a scheme of constitution under which the Muslims may attain full independence." [15]

The logic of the conception of the Muslim community as a separate nation made partnership a short-lived doctrine. A resolution of the League's working committee on September 18, 1939, endorsed the objective of a free India, but declared that the consent and approval of the League was essential for any future constitutional changes, and accordingly asked the government to "take into its confidence the Muslim League which is the only organization that can speak on behalf of Muslim India." [16] The deep-seated Muslim distrust of the Hindu majority and of the Congress gave rise during 1938–1939 to a variety of proposals for the reorganization of the subcontinent to permit the Muslim nation to coexist with Hindudom in a loosely united India, but since Congress rejected out of hand the very notion of Muslim nationhood, Muslims were driven to more uncompromising statements of their case. In so doing Muslims realized that for them Indian nationhood no longer held any meaning, and therefore the problem of agreement with the Congress had become irrelevant. In January 1940 Jinnah elaborated the "two-nation theory" in the British journal *Time and Tide,* emphasizing the unworkability of parliamentary democratic institutions when the people affected by them "represent two distinct

[15] Coupland, *op. cit.,* II, 197. See also Aziz Ahmad, *op. cit.,* pp. 271–275.

[16] Coupland, *op. cit.,* II, 216.

and separate civilisations" with different moralities and values.[17] In February he told the press that the Muslims would determine their own destiny, despite the British or the Congress, and at the Lahore session of the League in March they proceeded to do so.

On March 23, 1940, the Muslim League session at Lahore formally adopted the goal of independence for the Muslim areas of India.

Resolved that it is the considered view of this session of the All-India Muslim League that no constitutional plan would be workable in this country or acceptable to the Muslims unless it is designed on the following basic principles, *viz.*, that geographically contiguous units are demarcated into regions which should be so constituted with such territorial readjustments as may be necessary that the areas in which the Muslims are numerically in a majority, as in the north-western and eastern zones of India, should be grouped to constitute "Independent States" in which the constituent units shall be autonomous and sovereign.[18]

The Lahore Resolution made the break with the Congress and Indian nationalism complete. In his presidential address to the session Jinnah reviewed the course of events since the advent of provincial autonomy, leading inexorably to the conclusion that however well organized the Muslims might be or however justified their dissenting views, they could never prevail against the Hindu majority in India. He elaborated once more the national differences between Muslims and Hindus, and declared that the only means to enable them to live in peace and justice was for the two to achieve

[17] Jinnah's statement was republished in Jamil-ud-Din Ahmad, *op. cit.*, pp. 128–138.

[18] Full text in A. B. Rajput, *Muslim League, Yesterday and Today* (Lahore, 1948), pp. 79–80.

independence separately. After the termination of the session he replied to criticism from Congress and other quarters, explaining that while there was no question of migration *en masse,* exchange of population so far as practicable would have to be considered. The purpose of partition was to free the Muslim-majority areas only, since with or without partition the status of Muslim minorities would remain unaffected. Jinnah believed that when "the present tension created by the ambition of one community dominating over the other and establishing supremacy over all the rest is ceased [*sic*], we shall find better understanding and goodwill created all round." [19] Therefore the minorities in both homelands would find their position improved.

Having adopted the goal of Pakistan—the name was soon attached by critics to the "Muslim homeland"—Jinnah and the Muslim League set about consolidating their hold on Muslim India. The Congress still commanded the support of individual nationalist Muslims such as Abul Kalam Azad (president of the Congress, 1940–1945) and of those conservative religious elements who had consistently opposed the Aligarh movement and the Muslim League. In addition, the Khudai Khidmatgars in the Frontier maintained their alliance with the Congress, and the Punjab Unionist leaders were at best lukewarm about the prospect of a partition that might destroy their province. Asserting the League's right to be recognized as the sole voice of Muslim India, Jinnah and his working committee began to enforce a discipline over provincial Leagues very similar to that unitary control exercised by the Congress "High Command" over Congress provincial ministries before their resignations. External in-

[19] Statement on Lahore Resolution, in Jamil-ud-Din Ahmad, *op. cit.,* pp. 183–187.

terference was resented by some provincial leaders—principally Fazlul Huq of Bengal, who broke with the League in December 1941—but by virtue of his now great authority over Muslims generally, Jinnah was able to insist on rigid obedience and gradually to establish loyal League ministries in province after province. Of all the proposed Pakistan provinces, only in Punjab did the League meet a reverse. In April 1944 Premier Khizr Hayat Khan Tiwana refused to transform his cabinet into an orthodox Muslim League coalition by accepting Jinnah's authority and therewith the Pakistan objective, which was anathema to his non-Muslim colleagues in the Unionist party. The League was therefore forced into opposition, but over the next eighteen months it gradually won over the Unionist party's Muslim following.

While the strength of the League was growing among the masses as well as in the provincial legislatures, Jinnah carried on a ceaseless campaign to secure recognition by the government. The outbreak of war in September 1939, and the Congress reaction thereto, offered Jinnah and the League an opportunity they were quick to seize. Broadly, the Congress refused to cooperate in the war effort unless the British made a declaration of India's independence and transferred real power to an Indian government responsible to a constituent assembly, which would proceed to frame a constitution. In contrast, Jinnah offered official Muslim League cooperation and support of the war within the existing constitutional arrangements, provided that the League were recognized as the only spokesman of the Muslim nation—with a consequent veto on constitutional change—and were entrusted with commensurate governmental responsibilities. In the meantime he acquiesced in the wholehearted cooperation of the provincial League organizations, where the latter found it possible to form ministries. The League was able to gain British sympathy and to entrench itself politically and administratively with this strategy, and Muslim loyalty during the war—particularly during the Congress "Quit India" movement in 1942—dramatized the divergent orientations of the League and the Congress more than any number of political speeches could have done.

The Transfer of Power

Throughout the years of war and constitutional discussions Jinnah was rigid and uncompromising in his insistence that the principle of partition be accepted. The League's sweeping victory at the polls in December 1945 and the following January finally forced the British government to intervene by sending a three-man Cabinet Mission to attempt to bring about a Congress-League agreement preserving the unity of India. The Mission's twofold plan was published on May 16, 1946, after a fruitless search for agreement, and although it rejected the demand for partition the plan brought out once again the constitutionalist in Jinnah. On June 6 the League, on Jinnah's advice, accepted the plan out of a desire for a peaceful solution to the Indian problem, but stated that the ultimate objective of the Muslims continued to be the attainment of Pakistan.

The essence of the Cabinet Mission Plan was the creation of a three-tier constitution for India, with the provinces linked in two Muslim-majority groups (in the northwest: Baluchistan, the Frontier, Punjab, and Sind; in the northeast: Assam and Bengal) and one Hindu-majority group (the remaining provinces) under a central government with minimal powers. The long-term proposals were: (1) that the provinces were to be represented in a Constituent Assembly made up of members elected by the provincial legislatures on the basis of one for every million inhabitants; and (2) that the representatives of the three groups would meet separately to draw up group constitutions by majority vote before meeting in full assembly to work out a constitution for all of India. The short-term proposal was that the viceroy's executive council was to be transformed into an interim government made up of members of the Indian parties in proportions stated by the Cabinet Mission. The Congress disliked the long-term proposals intensely, on the ground that Assam and the Frontier, both Congress-ruled in 1946, should not be subjected to domination by Bengal and Punjab by being grouped against their will. Because grouping was an essential guarantee for the Muslims against the Hindu majority in India as a whole, the reservations and interpretations on this point in the Congress working committee's eventual statement of June 25 accepting the long-term plan caused much controversy. The climax came on July 10, when Congress president Jawaharlal Nehru told the press that the Constituent Assembly would be sovereign and "unfettered" and therefore no grouping was likely. This, together with Viceroy Lord Wavell's refusal to proceed to form a government after the Congress had rejected but the League had accepted the interim government scheme, led the League to a final and bitter denunciation of the Congress, the plan, and the viceroy.

The meeting of the Muslim League Council in Bombay on July 27–29, 1946, marked the destruction of the Cabinet Mission Plan. After compromising the Pakistan demand in order to achieve a peaceful solution of the political crisis, Jinnah believed himself and the League to have been betrayed by the British government in its desire to reach an

understanding with the Congress. The tradition of a lifetime was abandoned: "Never have we in the whole history
of the League done anything except by constitutional methods and constitutionalism. But now we are obliged and
forced into this position. This day we bid goodbye to constitutional methods." [20] Turning to the "tribunal of the
Muslim nation," the League rejected the plan in all its
aspects, called upon League members to renounce titles and
awards received from the government, and resolved on
"direct action" to achieve Pakistan. For the first time the
League could rely on mass support, for the general election
had shown the solidity of its popular backing. The cry of
"Islam in danger," to which the case for Pakistan had been
reduced for mass consumption, had elicited an enthusiasm
that could not in any case be limited by conference-table
decisions, and "direct action" signaled the removal of constitutionalist restraints on popular emotions. Although Jinnah
declared that its purpose was to mobilize popular support for
the leadership, Direct Action Day on August 16, 1946, was
marked by a communal holocaust in Calcutta, the capital of
Muslim League–ruled Bengal. The spread of communal
violence to other parts of India thereafter produced conditions of near civil war, rendering unity impossible. [21]

The complete collapse of intercommunal confidence was
in part occasioned by the circumstances in which an interim
government was finally formed. The League's repudiation of
the Cabinet Mission Plan was followed on August 10, 1946,
by a Congress resolution accepting the plan (as interpreted

[20] Jinnah's remarks to the League Council, quoted in Ravoof, *op.
cit.*, p. 205.

[21] See Ian Stephens, *Pakistan* (New York, 1963), chs. 7 and 8, for a
clear and graphic account by an observer of the events of 1946.

by the Congress) "in its entirety," whereupon Lord Wavell invited Nehru to form a government. This apparent demission of power by the British into the hands of Congress sharpened the communal conflict, and a veritable "war of succession" broke out. Muslim "direct action" on August 16 and later was a rejection of the projected Congress government of India. At the provincial level, it was intended to achieve *de facto* Pakistan by bolstering League ministries in Bengal and Sind and overthrowing the Congress-backed governments of Punjab and the Frontier, where minority weightages had deprived the League of power, and of Assam. After a six-week delay, during which Jinnah wrung from Nehru the admission that the League was the "authoritative representative organization of an overwhelming majority of the Muslims of India," [22] the League decided (on October 13) to join the interim government. No agreement with the Congress had been reached, but Jinnah, still convinced of the value of constitutional activity, sent his five nominees into the viceroy's executive council, both to prevent the Congress from monopolizing the administration and to carry on the battle for Pakistan from within. The League stood fast on its rejection of the Cabinet Mission Plan and the Constituent Assembly, and League members of the government used their positions to obstruct and to prevent any conventional transformation of the executive council into a cabinet (much to Nehru's outrage). The refusal of the League to participate in the Constituent Assembly when it met on December 9, 1946, finally convinced the British government that the Muslims could not be forced to accept a solution based on the unity of the subcontinent.

[22] Gopal, *op. cit.*, p. 319.

On February 20, 1947, Prime Minister Attlee announced the appointment of a new viceroy (Lord Mountbatten) and anticipated a final transfer of power to one or more successor authorities in India by June 1948. The rush of events, however, forced an acceleration of the program. Civil disobedience led by members of the Muslim League caused the fall of Sir Khizr Hayat Khan Tiwana's Unionist-Congress ministry in Punjab on March 2, 1947, and soon made it evident that Dr. Khan Sahib's Congress ministry in the Frontier Province no longer commanded popular support. Increased anti- and pro-Pakistan violence throughout the northwest was rapidly undermining all constituted authority as Muslims and non-Muslims struggled for position. The new viceroy, who had taken office on March 22, concluded that prompt partition and a transfer of power to two successor dominions was the only solution. On June 3 in London and Delhi the plan for the transfer of power was announced, and on the following day Mountbatten revealed that it would take place in little more than two months, on August 15, 1947.

The Muslim League regarded the partition plan as a "compromise" because it involved—at the insistence of the Congress—the partition of Bengal, Assam, and Punjab, producing a "moth-eaten and mutilated Pakistan." Still, the League and the awakened masses of the Muslim-majority areas had triumphed: referenda in the Sylhet district of Assam and in the North-West Frontier Province endorsed Pakistan, as did the provincial legislators of Sind, western Punjab, and eastern Bengal, and later the rulers of ten small princely states. The Congress accepted partition regretfully to preclude the possibility that princely declarations of independence might bring further disintegration in the subcontinent, but cherished the hope and belief that the parting would be short-lived. A new Constituent Assembly was elected and met in Karachi on August 10, and at midnight four days later, amid upheaval and slaughter in Punjab, Pakistan came formally into being.

Seven short years after the adoption of the Lahore Resolution a separate state had been achieved. The emergence of Muslim political separatism—the demand for separate representation, then minority safeguards, then provincial autonomy and federalism, and finally a separate state—had occurred well within an adult lifetime, and an entire population was confronted with the psychological adjustments of the transition from minority to nationality. The Pakistan movement had appealed to diverse aspirations among the urban middle classes of the provinces that were to remain Indian, the rural aristocracy of the Indus valley, and the peasant masses of eastern Bengal. There were, too, those Muslims—both traditionalist and secularist—who did not support the Pakistan idea at all, and also non-Muslims whose destinies had perforce been shaped by the surge of Muslim nationalism. This variegated people was to give institutional form to a new state, with a heritage from British India of parliamentary democracy and of autocracy, and at the same time a heritage of repudiation of both of these. From such diverse aspirations and traditions would be built a state and a society in which Islam would have definite meaning.

2. Social and Economic Setting

The task of creating a stable national political community in Pakistan out of diverse fragments of the British Indian Empire has been complicated by geographic and cultural considerations. East and West Pakistan are separated not only by 1,000 miles of Indian territory but also, broadly, by the difference between Southeast Asia and the Middle East. East Pakistan (55,000 square miles) is a rice- and jute-growing delta segment of Southeast Asia, whose linguistically homogeneous people share cultural traits with their eastern neighbors in Burma, Thailand, and Malaysia, and include a minority of non-Muslims numbering about one-fifth of the total. West Pakistan, on the other hand, is a vast (310,000 square miles) land of arid hills and plains dependent on irrigation works for the cultivation of wheat and cotton. The population is almost wholly Muslim and has much in common culturally with the Muslim peoples to the west, but includes speakers of several distinct languages. A further complication arises because of the demographic imbalance between the two parts of the country: 55 per cent of the population is crowded into East Pakistan, 15 per cent of the total area. Population pressures thus add to the problems of economic development in East Pakistan, compounding the strains inherent in cultural diversity with those arising from the conflicting claims of geography and demography in making political and economic decisions.

Demographic Context

According to the 1961 census, Pakistan's population in that year had reached 93.7 million (East Pakistan 50.8 and West Pakistan 42.9, as against 42.1 and 33.7 in 1951), and was growing at the unprecedented rate of 2.3 per cent per annum. The central government's Planning Commission believes this to have been a slight undercount and estimates 1959–60 totals at 53.9 million in East Pakistan and 45.0 million in West Pakistan, projecting 70.2 and 57.2 million respectively for 1969–70.[1] The population is very young; more than one-third is below the age of ten and well over half below the conventional voting age of twenty-one. The figures suggest that growth in the past decade has been faster in East Pakistan than in West Pakistan. This is a reversal of the trend of previous years, perhaps attributable in part to declining emigration from East Pakistan and in part to the impact of birth-control ideas in the more advanced western province. Family planning has been stressed in a high-priority program since the beginning of the Third Five Year Plan (1965–1970) in an effort to halt and then reduce the rate of increase, necessary if "future economic development is not to be submerged in a population explosion."[2] By 1968 it was

[1] Population statistics for the 1961 census are from Ministry of Home & Kashmir Affairs (Home Affairs Division), *Census of Pakistan: Population, 1961*, Vol. 1: *Pakistan* (Karachi: Manager of Publications, n.d.). The Planning Commission's estimates are from *The Third Five Year Plan (1965–70)* (rev. ed.; Karachi, 1967), pp. 19, 24. West Pakistan totals for 1961 exclude Azad Kashmir, Gilgit, and Baltistan.

[2] "Socio-economic Objectives of the Fourth Five Year Plan," para. 26. Text published in *Pakistan Times* (Lahore), November 3 and 4, 1968. (hereafter cited as "Fourth Plan Objectives").

estimated that the annual rate of increase had risen to 2.6 per cent but would have been more than 3 per cent during the Fourth Plan had there been no family planning program. It is anticipated that the rate of increase will be 2.8 per cent per annum by 1975 and will then decline.

Although the rate of urban population growth is very high, 86 per cent of the population is still rural. In this regard the difference between the two provinces is striking: East Pakistan is only 5.5 per cent urban, but West Pakistan's urban percentage is 22.5, reflecting its greater degree of industrialization. As the figures suggest, the largest cities are in West Pakistan: Karachi (1.9 million), the leading port and commercial center; Lahore (1.3 million), the capital of the province; Hyderabad (435,000) and Lyallpur (425,000),

Table 1. Population of Pakistan, 1961

Province and division	Muslims	Others	Total
East Pakistan	40,890,481	9,949,754	50,840,235
Chittagong	10,848,603	2,781,047	13,629,650
Dacca	12,669,746	2,623,850	15,293,596
Khulna	7,617,299	2,449,701	10,066,900
Rajshahi	9,754,833	2,095,256	11,850,089
West Pakistan	41,666,143 *	1,214,225 *	42,880,378
Baluchistan			
Kalat	523,723	7,170	530,893
Quetta	622,629	7,489	630,118
North-West Frontier			
Dera Ismail Khan			
Districts	726,234	1,312	727,546
Agencies	478,173 *	*	478,173
Malakand	1,536,766 *	*	1,536,766
Peshawar			
Districts	3,404,853	7,948	3,412,701
Agencies	1,423,000 *	*	1,423,000

Table 1. (continued)

Province and division	Muslims	Others	Total
Punjab			
Bahawalpur	2,543,924	30,142	2,574,066
Lahore	6,101,300	347,275	6,448,575
Multan	6,540,911	62,013	6,602,924
Rawalpindi	3,960,237	18,902	3,979,139
Sargodha	5,867,424	109,515	5,976,939
Sind			
Hyderabad	2,808,033	482,923	3,290,956
Karachi	2,073,214	61,656	2,134,870
Khairpur	3,055,732	77,980	3,133,712

Source: Ministry of Home & Kashmir Affairs (Home Affairs Division), *Census of Pakistan: Population, 1961,* Vol. 2: *East Pakistan* (Karachi: Manager of Publications, 1964), Part II, Table 5; Vol. 3: *West Pakistan* (Karachi: Manager of Publications, n.d.), Part II, Table 5, and Part VI, Table 1.

* Population figures for the tribal agencies in Peshawar, Dera Ismail Khan, and Malakand divisions are based on several methods of enumeration, including estimation. No effort was made in the census to make a separate estimate of non-Muslims in these areas, whose numbers are negligible in any case.

both industrial centers; three other cities over 200,000 and five over 100,000. In East Pakistan only Dacca (556,000), the provincial capital, and Chittagong (364,000), the chief port, exceed 200,000; with the exception of Narayanganj (the port of Dacca) and Khulna, all other cities are smaller than 100,000. Rural densities in East Pakistani districts (apart from the exceptional Chittagong Hill Tracts, with only seventy-six persons per square mile) ranged in 1961 from 526 (Khulna) to 1,768 (Dacca) persons per square mile, with an average of 922 in the province. In West Pakistan population concentrations are, apart from Karachi, in the northeastern Punjabi districts and the Peshawar valley, with densities well over 500; in the vast Quetta and Kalat divisions, most districts have fewer than fifteen people per square mile.

THE MINORITIES

The growth in the population shows wide variations among religious communities as well as between geographic regions. Although the conviction that Muslims formed a separate cultural nationality provided the basis for the creation of Pakistan, the demarcation of its boundaries included within its territory a large non-Muslim minority, and left many Muslims in India. The bloody communal upheaval in the subcontinent during the summer of 1947 brought 7.2 million Muslim refugees into the country (mostly into West Pakistan) by 1951 and sent a similar number of Hindus and Sikhs across the borders. Between the 1951 and 1961 censuses the proportion of non-Muslims fell further from 14.1 per cent to 11.9 per cent, partly from differences in fertility between Muslims and Hindus, but largely because of continued migrations to and from India. Because of tensions in East Pakistan during the 1960's a further decline in the proportion of non-Muslims by 1971 seems inevitable. Between 1962 and 1965 more than 150,000 Muslims were expelled from Assam, West Bengal, and Tripura, and others followed them into East Pakistan in subsequent years. In the tension that was generated there was renewed emigration of Hindus, and even of tribal Christians, mainly Garos, in 1964.[3] Despite professions of secularism in India and assurances in Pakistan

[3] Since Christians normally remain untouched by Hindu-Muslim tensions, the attacks on Garo Christians in 1964 were the more tragic in being completely unprecedented. Most of the Garos returned to their homes during 1965.

of the rights of non-Muslims in an Islamic state, minorities in both countries continue to feel insecure. Outbreaks of violence in either country are sufficient to renew the migrations.

The great majority of non-Muslims live in East Pakistan, distributed throughout the province. From 1951 to 1961 the Hindu community in East Pakistan increased by barely 1.5 per cent over the course of the decade, while the West Pakis-

Table 2. Non-Muslim population of Pakistan, 1961

Minority	East Pakistan	West Pakistan	Total
Scheduled Castes	4,993,046	418,011	5,411,057
Caste Hindus	4,386,623	203,794	4,590,417
Christians	148,903	583,884	732,787
Buddhists	373,867	2,445	376,312
Parsis	193	5,219	5,412
Others	47,122	872	47,994
Total	9,949,754	1,214,225	11,163,979
Percentage of total population	19.6%	2.8%	11.9%

Source: Office of the Census Commissioner, Ministry of Home Affairs, *Population Census of Pakistan, 1961,* Census Bulletin No. 2 (Karachi, Manager of Publications, 1961), Table 6.

tan Hindu population (mainly concentrated in Hyderabad division) increased by 1.7 per cent annually. The only reasonable explanation would seem to be an emigration of about two million Hindus during the decade from East Pakistan. Over half of Pakistan's Hindus are members of the so-called Scheduled Castes, formerly known as untouchables and backward castes until under the 1935 Act they were "scheduled" for special treatment. Most Christians live in West Pakistan, mainly in Lahore and Sargodha divisions, where they registered a ten-year increase of 34.9 per cent; in East Pakistan the increase was nearly 40 per cent. In both provinces Christianity has spread mainly at the expense of Hinduism, particularly among the Scheduled Castes, although in East Pakistan it has affected the Buddhist community in the Chittagong Hill Tracts and the animist tribal people of the Garo Hills in Mymensingh as well.

Formally non-Muslims have always had the same rights as Muslim citizens in Pakistan, including the rights of political participation and eligibility for government service. However, most politically active Hindus and Sikhs opposed the Pakistan movement, and after partition those who did not migrate to India were discredited and suspect. Many East Pakistan Hindus tried to maintain a foot in both camps, sending their families to Calcutta while continuing to participate in Pakistan affairs. The *bona fides* of such people naturally were in doubt, and the periodic defection to India of prominent Hindu officials—for example, a Dacca High Court judge in 1958 and the only Hindu member of the Civil Service of Pakistan in 1961—seriously compromises those who want to be accepted and regarded as loyal Pakistanis. Hindus have therefore not played a role in public life commensurate with their numerical importance. Christians are fully accepted and seem to have had little difficulty in making their mark: from 1955 to 1958 the Deputy Speaker of the National Assembly was a Christian, as was the Chief Justice of Pakistan from 1960 to 1968; others hold responsible posts in the military and public services. Since 1962 there has been increasing political criticism of foreign Christian institutions and influence, especially in West Pakistan. The tiny Parsi (Zoroastrian) community, as in India, plays a disproportionately important role in the commercial and industrial life of the country.

THE MUSLIMS

The majority community is by no means monolithic. Although the Muslim population of the two provinces is fairly evenly balanced, it is of some political significance that there are more Muslims in West Pakistan despite East Pakistan's larger total population. Most Muslims in both provinces are Sunni, but there is an important Shia element in parts of West Pakistan. Shia sects such as the Bohras, Khojas, and other Ismaili followers of the Aga Khan are tightly knit and economically active communities, prominent among the new industrial and commercial classes. Among the Sunni, the Memons form an important mercantile community. Sufi influence is particularly strong in the rural areas, the pirs and other holy men wielding political and economic as well as spiritual power over the peasant masses. In the towns the most important division among the Sunni seems to be between the followers of the rival Deobandi and Barelvi schools of ulama. Although there are occasional clashes between these groups, Sunni-Shia friction is more common and more likely—especially on festal occasions such as Muharram (the anniversary of the martyrdom of the Prophet's grandson Husain)—to break out in serious violence.

The most heterodox and controversial Muslim sect is the Ahmadi community, founded in Punjab at the end of the nineteenth century by Mirza Ghulam Ahmad (1839–1908), who claimed to be a new prophet and messiah. The Ahmadi are analogous to the Mormons in Christendom, and like the Mormons they tend to be clannish and self-reliant, and accordingly arouse the dislike if not hostility of their neighbors

on social as well as religious grounds. Because of their founder's claim to prophethood, the Ahmadis have always been
regarded as heretics by orthodox Muslims. When the debate
on the Islamic state was at its peak in 1951–1953, demands
were voiced that the Ahmadis be declared officially to be
non-Muslims and hence excluded from the Muslim electorate. The agitation was fostered by a coalition of traditionalist
and fundamentalist organizations of ulama, both Sunni and
Shia, with the aim of overawing the government on the issue
of the Islamic constitution. Large-scale rioting and disorder
in West Pakistan culminated in the imposition of martial
law in Lahore in March of 1953 and the complete suppres-
sion of the abortive Islamic coup.

The ease with which public opinion was aroused against
the Ahmadis is indicative both of the great influence of the
ulama and of the sensitivity of the Muslim population to
allegations of heresy or un-Islamic behavior. Pakistani Islam
is extremely conservative and would-be reformers—as Sir
Syed Ahmad learned by experience—must move cautiously.
Efforts to improve the status of women have been particularly controversial since they touch the very heart of the society and affect practices followed by Muslims since the time
of the Prophet. Muslim women played an active public role
for the first time in the agitation of 1946–47, and after independence the All-Pakistan Women's Association was
formed by emancipated urban women to carry on the femi-
nist struggle. Partly in response to their pressures, President
Ayub promulgated the Muslim Marriage and Family Laws
Ordinance in 1961, imposing restrictions on polygamy and
divorce and reinforcing the inheritance rights of women and
children. These changes were bitterly denounced and attacked in the legislatures in 1962–63, and as vehemently de-

fended by women inside and outside the Assemblies. Although the ulama denounced the reform as un-Islamic, with the President's support the modernist view won the day. During the agitation preceding the reimposition of martial law in 1969 the Family Laws Ordinance again became a subject of attack by the ulama and their supporters.

Language and Education

The geographic and demographic peculiarities of Pakistan are further complicated by linguistic diversities. In East Pakistan ethnic differences are minimal and nearly everyone speaks Bengali, with dialect variations most noticeable in Chittagong and Sylhet districts. In West Pakistan, there are several major ethnic groups with distinct languages. Although territorial distinctions cannot be precise, Punjabi (including its dialect variations) is spoken generally in the plain and submontane region between the Sutlej and the Indus, in Rawalpindi, Sargodha, Lahore, Multan, and Bahawalpur divisions. Sindhi is spoken in the lower Indus valley, on both banks of the river, in Hyderabad and Khairpur divisions. Pashto prevails west of the Indus along the Afghan border, in Peshawar and Dera Ismail Khan divisions and in part of Quetta division. Baluchi, Brahui, and other languages are found in the rest of Quetta, Kalat, and also in Hyderabad. Table 3 shows the relative importance of the major languages in terms of numbers of speakers and also their varying significance as vehicles of literacy. Pashto is an Iranian language, but Bengali, Urdu, Punjabi, and Sindhi are rather closely related. Barriers have developed between them, however, by virtue of the fact that Bengali uses a Sanskrit-derived script while the others use modified versions of the Arabic script. The spread of literacy therefore increases consciousness of the linguistic differences between East and West Pakistan and of their quite different literary heritages. Despite the fact that Bengali was—and is—the language

Table 3. Language and literacy, 1961

	East Pakistan			West Pakistan *		
Language	Speakers	% of popula-tion	Literacy (in % of speakers)	Speakers	% of popula-tion	Literacy (in % of speakers)
Bengali	50,321,995	98.97%	16.05%	55,808	.14%	22.00%
Urdu	679,163	1.34%	66.06%	5,859,718	14.86%	70.12%
Punjabi	(insignificant)			26,651,964	67.57%	.27%
Pashto	(insignificant)			3,526,944	8.94%	1.73%
Sindhi	(insignificant)			5,583,680	14.16%	10.15%
English	426,256	.84%	330.10% †	835,884	2.12%	119.16% †
Total population	50,840,235	100.00%	17.60%	42,880,378	100.00%	13.60%

Source: Adapted from Ministry of Home & Kashmir Affairs (Home Affairs Division), Census of Pakistan: Population, 1961, Vol. 1: Pakistan (Karachi: Manager of Publications, n.d.), Section IV, pp. 32–39.

* West Pakistan language figures do not include inhabitants of the Tribal Areas of the Frontier regions, estimated in 1961 at 3,437,939, at least 80% of whom speak Pashto; total Pashto speakers therefore would be around 6.3 million.

† At p. IV-39 of the census volume cited, the Explanatory Notes remark that English "is read and written by more people than can even speak it." Presumably persons who have studied English but either lack conversational command of the language or who "do not commonly speak English" make up this total. The actual literacy figures for English are 1,407,087 in East Pakistan and 996,012 in West Pakistan. The census definition of literacy included those able to read and write or able to read with understanding only.

of over half the population, after independence the federal government proceeded to treat Urdu as the sole state language, destined ultimately to replace English for all official purposes. Urdu developed in northern India during the

Mughal period and in the nineteenth century became the vehicle for the Muslim intellectual revival led by Sir Syed Ahmad Khan. In due course it became the *de facto* language of the Pakistan movement, and in view of its strong links with the classic languages of Islam (Arabic and Persian) was regarded as the only possible official language of the new Islamic state. Although Urdu was accepted as the lingua franca for multilingual West Pakistan, the attempt to impose it in unilingual East Pakistan evoked determined resistance. After Jinnah's death (on September 11, 1948) removed his great authority from the political scene, the already contentious language question became a paramount issue, closely related to and symbolic of the Bengali demand for an equal if not dominant voice in national affairs.

Part of the criticism that forced the withdrawal of the interim report of the Basic Principles Committee in 1950 (see p. 97) was Bengali opposition to a clause declaring Urdu to be the "State language." This opposition organized itself as the "State language movement," to secure equality of status for Bengali and Urdu. On February 22, 1952, martyrs to the cause died in police firing in Dacca, in riots precipitated by a public speech by Prime Minister Nazimuddin (a Bengali) reaffirming that Urdu was to be the sole state language. Thereafter a *sine qua non* of political influence in East Pakistan was ardent advocacy of the Bengali language demand, as the defeat of the Muslim League in the March 1954 provincial elections demonstrated.

The Bengali demand for language parity was conceded in Pakistan's first Constitution in 1956 and was confirmed in that of 1962. In 1954 the Constituent Assembly accepted a formula recognizing Urdu and Bengali as "official" languages and urging the development of a "common national language," but this was suspect as a device for securing the eventual supremacy of Urdu alone. The Bengali members of the second Constituent Assembly therefore forced the modification of the objectionable terminology, eliminating from the constitutional draft the references to a national language and describing Urdu and Bengali as "state" rather than "official" languages. The Constitution of 1962 declared Bengali and Urdu to be the "national" languages of Pakistan, "but this article shall not be construed as preventing the use of any other language." Whatever the terminology, it is unthinkable that the equality of status of the two languages can be departed from in the future.

Since independence, English has continued to be the *de facto* language of national unity, used for nearly all official purposes by provincial and central governments. Although it is spoken by only a tiny fraction of the population, that fraction includes the political, administrative, commercial, and educational elites in both provinces. As a medium of written communication English was far more important in 1969 than Urdu in East Pakistan or Bengali in West Pakistan. The 1962 Constitution provided that the use of English for official purposes would continue at least until 1972, when the President was to appoint a commission to "examine and report" on the question of its replacement. This study was anticipated by the martial-law regime in July 1969 when it announced a new educational and language policy.[4] English is to be replaced by Urdu and Bengali in the two provincial governments by 1974 and in the central government by 1975. All government servants are to acquire a working knowledge of both languages by 1973. English is to cease to

[4] *Pakistan Times,* July 4, 1969.

be the language of instruction at any educational level, but will continue to be taught as an optional language. This change is intended to help break down the barriers between the ruling elite and the mass of the population and so contribute to national integration. However, it must be recognized that unless great care is taken the abandonment of English in the universities and in the administration may seriously jeopardize interprovincial communication and damage rather than further the integration of the country.

The 1969 educational policy was intended to accomplish social and political as well as educational purposes. It outlined measures for creating an integrated educational system to help produce national consensus on the basis of Islamic values, to prevent the development and perpetuation of privilege barriers restricting social mobility, and by emphasizing technical education to make the educational process more suited to national needs. The malaise of the educational system, with its emphasis on rote and literary learning and its premium on English, has long been evident, and student dissatisfaction was an important element in the agitation against the Ayub government in 1968–69. The new policy called for administrative reorganization of primary and secondary education, increased availability of scholarships on the basis of merit for the "quality" cadet colleges and private secondary schools, the nationalization of foreign missionary institutions, and a great increase in the number of postsecondary technical and agricultural institutions. Urdu and Bengali were to be the languages of instruction at all stages, with Urdu a compulsory subject in East Pakistan and Bengali in West Pakistan. (The implications for Sindhi and Pashto, which have been the languages of instruction in their regions at the primary stage, were not explored. Urdu is already the medium of instruction in Punjabi areas.) In an effort to eliminate illiteracy and to provide universal primary education by 1980, the new policy proposed a national literacy corps to be conscripted from among students aged from eighteen to twenty-two, to be sent after six months training to teach in the rural areas for eighteen months. This program, which has been very successful in Iran, would also help deal with the immediate problem of some 200,000 educated unemployed (presumably holders of secondary and intermediate certificates).

The present distribution of literacy and higher educational attainments in different parts of Pakistan is of considerable political and economic significance. Within each province there is much regional variation, but in general, in terms of the population above five years of age, in East Pakistan in 1961 19.9 per cent could read and write, while in West Pakistan the figure was only 14.4 per cent. In urban areas the percentages were more than doubled, and literacy among males was much higher than among females. In educational terms the picture is quite different, for in East Pakistan there is a very high rate of attrition in the primary schools and a sharp drop in enrollment after grade four. In East Pakistan, 71.6 per cent of those claiming to be literate had less than four years of schooling and fewer than 4 per cent had completed secondary or higher education. In contrast, in West Pakistan the respective proportions were 44.4 per cent and 12.4 per cent. West Pakistan made great educational progress during the 1950's and in 1961 had nearly twice as many matriculates and holders of intermediate qualifications as East Pakistan, and well over twice as many persons with bachelors' and higher degrees. The number of university graduates in West Pakistan increased from 59,000 in 1951 to over 78,000 in 1961, but in East Pakistan decreased from about 50,000 to about 35,000, in part because of the emigration of educated Hindus and in part because some educated Bengalis now work and reside in West Pakistan.[5] These totals, which have considerably increased since 1961, indicate why West Pakistanis dominate the economy and administration and perhaps permit an understanding of the reason for the general sense of frustration and desperation in East Pakistan.

The educational policy of July 1969 proposed, with the replacement of the much-excoriated "University Ordinances" under which colleges and universities were administered, extensive changes to improve the status of teachers and to assure the independence of academic institutions. Of great importance to East Pakistan, private institutions were to be required to conform to general standards in regard to instructional facilities and staff salaries and benefits. There were in 1969 some 500 colleges throughout the country, with a total of about 300,000 students. It was proposed to found five more universities in each province, for a total of ten in East Pakistan and twelve in West Pakistan, three of them specializing in engineering and five in agriculture. A further much-needed reform would provide for the election of both the vice-chancellor (the administrative head) and the chancellor (the ceremonial head) of each university by that university's representative organs. If implemented, this will end the era in which the chancellorship has always been combined with the office of governor or head of state. The policy recommended that student unions be encouraged, with students represented in the management of schools and colleges

[5] Data in this paragraph from *Census of Pakistan: Population, 1961*, Vol. 1, Pt. IV, ch. 4.

and at all levels in university government. Finally, government financial support for colleges and universities was to be channelled through independent university grants commissions in each province, appointed by the governor from a panel nominated by the universities. In financial terms, these educational reforms would require an increase in educational expenditure from about 1.8 per cent of gross national product in 1968–69 (Rs 100 crore) to about 3.6 per cent in 1975 (about Rs 200 crore) and 3.3 per cent in 1980 (Rs 320 crore), which is more in line with the U.N.E.S.C.O. standard of roughly 4 per cent of G.N.P. in developing countries.[6]

The Agricultural Economy

After more than two decades of independence and extensive developmental efforts, agriculture remains the most important segment of the economy of Pakistan, although by 1965 its contribution to the gross national product had declined to less than half. Eighty-five per cent of the population is dependent directly or indirectly on the nation's farms, with most of the remainder being concerned with service activities or processing the products of the land. Because of differences in climate, topography, and soil types between East and West Pakistan, their crops and agricultural problems vary, but in a fundamental sense the agriculturalists in both parts of the country are faced with the same major concerns. The control of rivers and water resources to permit year-round cultivation and to minimize flood damage is necessary in both provinces, and in both cases this control requires agreement and cooperation with India, the upstream riparian. Further, in both provinces problems of land tenure, of land-

[6] Educational Policy Statement, ch. 7. Text published in *Pakistan Times*, July 4, 1969.

lordism, and of fragmentation of holdings have presented obstacles to the emergence of a productive and prosperous agricultural community.

WATER RESOURCE CONTROL

East Pakistan. Water is a problem in East Pakistan primarily because of its abundance, but also because of its maldistribution at certain seasons of the year. During the monsoon (June through September) much of the land is visited by often-destructive floods, but in the remainder of the year little rain falls. After the winter harvest in December and January fields are dry and uncultivated unless irrigation is available. In addition, since the slope of the land is only about three inches per mile in the south, districts along the Bay of Bengal are affected seriously by saline intrusion from the tides. Water-control projects must, therefore, be concerned with the reduction of flood damage to standing crops and to property, the extension of irrigation facilities to permit double and triple cropping during the dry season, and the protection of the fields from the sea. Because the entire Ganges-Brahmaputra delta is one interdependent system of river distributaries, any plans for improvements in one sector must consider repercussions elsewhere in the system. Since January 1959 water control has been the responsibility of the East Pakistan Water and Power Development Authority (WAPDA), a semiautonomous statutory body.

Flood control is an especially difficult and politically controversial problem. Most of the catchment area of the rivers involved is outside East Pakistan, and more water flows through the province than can be accommodated in river channels. A series of commissions and internationally sponsored experts have studied the problem, noting the inade-

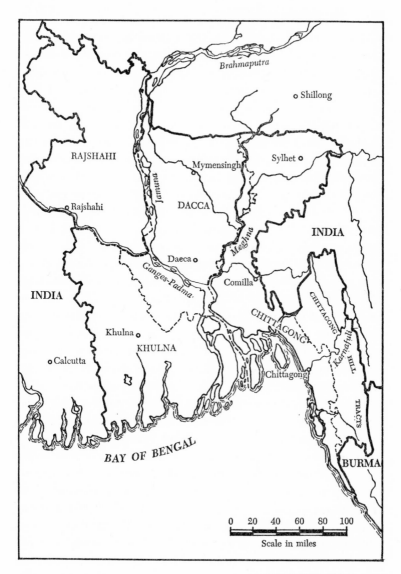

EAST PAKISTAN, 1969

quacy of systematic hydrological knowledge of the province. Although in 1964 WAPDA produced a flood-control master plan estimated to cost over $750 million and involving some 6,000 miles of embankments, uncertainties remained concerning the capacity of river channels and the impact of embankment projects on the movement of flood waters. In 1966 the International Bank for Reconstruction and Development became involved, and pending further studies a series of smaller projects were taken up and data collection continued. Loss of life, crops, and property in a series of eight devastating floods since 1954 have brought demands that the government "solve" the flood problem and make the same sort of economic and administrative effort that was so willingly devoted to the Indus basin project in West Pakistan. The International Bank's interest suggests that this may be possible in the future.

A related problem is that of the use of Ganges River waters. Since 1953 Pakistan has been developing the Ganges-Kobadak scheme, which is intended ultimately to irrigate some two million acres in the Khulna division with Ganges water and to combine flood control with measures to combat sea water intrusion in the south by building dikes and polders. The related coastal embankment project, to protect the low-lying Bay of Bengal coasts and islands, is expected to benefit some 2.2 million acres by 1970. The supply of water for the Ganges-Kobadak project in the dry season is threatened by the construction in India of a barrage at Farakka on the Ganges, ten miles upstream of the East Pakistan border, to divert water southward to reclaim the Calcutta port from siltation. India refused to delay the project, scheduled for completion in 1970, in consideration of Pakistan's interests as lower riparian, but negotiations for a settlement finally reached a serious stage in 1969. One factor affecting India's willingness to negotiate is Pakistan's projected Ganges barrage near the Hardinge Bridge, which if no agreement is reached could apparently be constructed so that the high pond level during the flood season would threaten both Farakka itself and associated canals and dikes. Settlement of this dispute may also involve large-scale, internationally underwritten expenditures to ensure that the needs of both Calcutta and the Khulna division are equitably met.

The only water storage possibilities in East Pakistan are in the Chittagong Hill Tracts district. A multipurpose hydroelectric project was completed at Kaptai on the Karnafuli River upstream of Chittagong in 1962. A similar project is under consideration for the Sangu basin, south of the Karnafuli, but the alternative interests of the tribal hill people—some of whom have already been relocated from the Kaptai lake area—and of timber preservation must be weighed. Such hydroelectric projects are of greater industrial than agricultural importance, but they permit flood control in the Chittagong area, and the power produced can be utilized in pumping and drainage installations. Electrically powered tube wells, along with low-lift diesel pumps, are the basis of an irrigation program fostered by the Agricultural Development Corporation and the Academy for Rural Development at Comilla through the union councils to add to the productive winter acreage and thus contribute to rural economic growth.

West Pakistan. Development of the arid lands in the Indus basin through modern irrigation works was begun over a century ago. Since then, a succession of great canal projects and colonization schemes have transformed desert and scrub jungle into productive and populous regions. The most easily accessible waters having been exploited during the nineteenth century, the great Triple Canal Project was completed in 1913–1915, bringing water from the Jhelum to the Chenab, and from the Chenab across the Ravi to a new canal system serving desert lands between the Ravi and the Sutlej. Thereafter further headworks were built lower down on the Sutlej, Ravi, and Chenab rivers, and more canals pushed into the deserts. In each successive area immigrant cultivators were settled in canal colonies whose prosperity became proverbial in a few years.

The Indus itself was first harnessed by the Lloyd barrage at Sukkur in the present Khairpur division, bringing perennial water supplies to existing inundation canals and opening up new desert areas. Completed in 1932, the barrage transformed the face and economy of the lower Indus valley, the annually cultivated area increasing gradually from 3.6 to around 5.5 million acres over a period of thirty years. The great success of the Sukkur barrage led to the construction of others at Kotri below Hyderabad (completed in 1956), at Taunsa in Multan division (completed in 1958), and at Guddu in the northern extremity of Khairpur division (completed in 1962). Together these barrages will command some 7.6 million culturable acres when the construction of canals has been completed. The colonization of a further 1.5 million acres of formerly desert land in the Thal, between the Indus and the lower Jhelum and Chenab, was entrusted in 1950 to the Thal Development Authority on the basis of waters drawn from the Jinnah barrage (completed in 1947) on the Indus at Kalabagh in Sargodha division.

A consequence of the extension of irrigation has been the increasingly serious menace of waterlogging and salinity,

WEST PAKISTAN, 1969

undermining the prosperity and productivity of the canal colonies. In the 1930's the danger became sufficiently serious to justify the expense of lining new canals to minimize seepage. Seepage is only one factor, however. The canals themselves interrupt the natural drainage lines and cause the accumulation of rain and flood waters and the rise of the water table. In some areas the rise of the water table toward the surface brings up salts which adversely affect fertility; elsewhere, the lack of sufficient water on the land causes the deposition of salts on the surface through too rapid evaporation. In this case, leaching through the addition of large quantities of water to wash the salts down below root level is the principal method of reclamation. The application of so much water leads in turn to the danger of waterlogging unless supplementary steps are taken to improve drainage. A further obstacle to leaching has been the lack of adequate water supplies, in the absence of storage reservoirs.

The fundamental problems of water supply and drainage in the Indus basin were compounded when in 1947 the Indo-Pakistan frontier was drawn across the existing systems of rivers, barrages, and canals.[7] About eleven million irrigated areas in Punjab fell to Pakistan, and more than five million went to India. The upper reaches of the Ravi and Sutlej rivers, including headworks commanding some 1.6 million acres in Pakistan, remained in Indian territory. On April 1, 1948, Indian authorities cut off all supplies in canals crossing the border, opening a lengthy controversy concerning water

[7] See Aloys A. Michel, *The Indus Rivers: A Study of the Effects of Partition* (New Haven and London, 1967), which is an excellent study of the problems of the Indus basin, including detailed analyses of the Indus Basin Agreement and its implementation.

rights in the basin. India insisted on her ultimate intention of utilizing the entire flow of the three eastern rivers (Ravi, Beas, and Sutlej) for irrigation works within her own territory. Pakistan protested and insisted on her legal right to continue to receive traditional supplies from those rivers, but in the meantime took up urgent construction of link canals to bring water from the Chenab and Jhelum to the canals previously dependent on Indian headworks. Nevertheless, the grave threat posed by Indian control of the three rivers, plus the upper Chenab in Indian-held Kashmir, remained.

Fortunately, in 1951 the International Bank offered to assist the two countries in working out an economic settlement of the waters dispute, and their effort finally succeeded in 1960. The basis of the Indus Waters Treaty, signed in Karachi on September 19, 1960, after long and delicate negotiations, was the division of the resources of the basin. Pakistan was allotted exclusive use of the waters of the western rivers (Indus, Jhelum, and Chenab) except for limited traditional withdrawals by India in the upper reaches. India was allotted exclusive use of the three eastern rivers, effective at the latest in 1973, by which time replacement works must be completed in Pakistan. These works include a system of link canals, with a total length of nearly 400 miles, to carry about 14 million acre-feet of water annually from the Indus and the Jhelum to the lower Ravi and Sutlej. To integrate these new canals into the earlier system, six new barrages have been built and several existing barrages and canals remodeled. Finally, two huge reservoirs in the northern mountains, at Mangla on the Jhelum (completed in 1967) and Tarbela on the Indus above Attock (estimated completion date 1976), will impound flood waters and permit the maintenance of adequate levels in the canals during the dry season.

Because the cost of the undertaking was beyond the resources of Pakistan, the Indus Waters Treaty was supplemented by the Indus Basin Development Fund Agreement, creating an internationally supported fund administered by the International Bank.[8] Originally the fund totaled $893.5 million for works in Pakistan, including $376.7 million in foreign exchange and the remainder in U.S.-held rupees, but within two years the cost estimates were revised upward to roughly $1800 million. There ensued a lengthy controversy between the Bank and Pakistan concerning the inclusion of the Tarbela project, which the Bank questioned and Pakistan insisted was essential to the Indus basin scheme. A supplementary agreement was signed in early 1964, by which an additional $315 million in foreign exchange was subscribed for works *excluding* Tarbela, as a "final" contribution to the fund. A further study of Tarbela was undertaken by the Bank, however, and the project was finally approved in 1967, at an estimated cost of some $900 million. In March 1968 a separate Tarbela Development Fund was established, including a $324-million balance from the Indus Fund and a further international contribution of $174 million, with Pakistan agreeing to pay all rupee costs from her own resources.

[8] "The Indus Waters Settlement" (London: Reference Division, Central Office of Information, August 1960), Pamphlet R 4731; Michel, *op. cit.*, pp. 251–253, 310–312; S. S. Kirmani, "The Story of Tarbela," *Pakistan Times Tarbela Supplement,* November 4, 1968. The subscribers to the Indus Basin Development Fund were Australia, Canada, Germany, New Zealand, United Kingdom, United States, and the Bank; in the Tarbela Development Fund, France and Italy replaced Australia, Germany, and New Zealand.

In addition to its primary purpose of providing West Pakistan with replacement irrigation works, the Indus basin project engendered other extremely valuable benefits. The creation of the West Pakistan Water and Power Development Authority (WAPDA) in 1958, to provide for the coordinated and integrated development of the water and power resources of the province, was one of the factors contributing to the soundness of the Indus basin scheme accepted by the International Bank and underwritten by the Indus Basin Development Fund. WAPDA designed the project to permit further development of the agricultural economy rather than merely to secure a threatened status quo. The preparation of an integrated scheme for irrigation required also a systematic attack on the related problems of waterlogging and salinity, assisted after 1961 by the Revelle panel appointed by President John F. Kennedy in connection with the U.S. aid program. The surveys and investigations necessary greatly enlarged the body of knowledge of West Pakistan's hydrology, and resulted in an extensive and successful attack on waterlogging by means of tube wells to pump excess water back into the canals, and the discovery of a vast usable ground-water reservoir underlying the northern portion of the basin. The great importance of Tarbela to the development of the basin lies in its ability to assure a dependable supply of surface water in the lower Indus valley in the dry season and to supply (along with Mangla) the power demands of tube-well drainage and irrigation schemes, which by 1975 will amount to half of West Pakistan's energy requirement. This is partly attributable to the remarkable increase in the number of privately owned tube wells installed in recent years. A final and not unimportant effect of the Indus basin project has been the economic and technical impact of vast expenditures, the development of administrative and technical infrastructures, and the creation of a pool of trained personnel.

LAND TENURE

The pattern of relationships governing the occupancy and use of land is, in Pakistan's predominantly agricultural economy, of the utmost economic and social importance. Together with natural factors, the size and nature of holdings and the extent of ownership and tenancy determine the pattern of cultivation, the crops grown, the efficiency and productivity of agriculture, and, not least, the level of well-being of the rural population. Reconstruction of the agricultural sector in the interests of national economic and social advance therefore demands the rationalization of landholdings in terms of size and the simplification of the relationships between the cultivator and the state.

East Pakistan. For over 150 years land-tenure relationships in most of what is now East Pakistan were governed by the Bengal Permanent Settlement Regulation (I of 1793). This Regulation was intended to stabilize the revenue situation in Bengal by fixing in perpetuity the land-revenue obligations of the existing proprietors and tenure holders. It gave legal sanctity to the ownership status of the zamindars (proprietors), whatever their historical origins, and by so doing effectively swept away the traditional rights and interests of the cultivators. The newly recognized proprietary rights of the zamindars were subject only to the absolutely punctual payment of the assessment, which was fixed at ten-elevenths of the prevailing rent paid at that time by the cultivators. As prices rose during the succeeding century and a half, the zamindars rack-rented their tenants, so that by 1950 only about one-tenth of the total rent paid by the cultivators was received by the state as land revenue. The remainder was appropriated by the zamindars and a host of intermediate tenure holders who had grown up by a process of subletting and fragmentation of the right to collect rents. At the same time, the lack of direct contact between the state and the peasant prevented the former from acquiring any systematic knowledge of rural conditions and left the latter to be exploited, economically and socially, by the frequently corrupt agents of the absentee tenure holders.

By the beginning of the twentieth century the evils of the Permanent Settlement had been recognized, but the first steps toward its elimination were not taken until the appointment of the Land Revenue (Flood) Commission by the Bengal government in 1938. The Commission recommended in 1940 that the system should be abolished, but because of the war and subsequent constitutional changes legislation was not proceeded with until after independence. Therefore when East Pakistan came into being, about 49,000 square miles (91 per cent of the total area) were held under the Permanent Settlement; another 2,000 square miles (3.5 per cent) were held by proprietors and their tenants under temporary settlement (subject to periodic revision); and about 3,000 square miles (5.5 per cent) were held by the cultivators directly as tenants of the state.[9]

The Permanent Settlement was finally abolished under the terms of the East Bengal State Acquisition and Tenancy Act, 1950. In brief, the Act provided for the acquisition of all intermediary rent-receiving interests with compensation

[9] Dr. A. Farouk, "Land Reforms in East Pakistan," *East Pakistan Information*, March 23, 1960, pp. 9–14.

to the persons affected, the limitation of the size of holdings, the granting of security to the cultivator through the preparation of records of rights, and the ultimate rationalization of the land revenue through a new settlement. Operations proceeded very slowly until April 1956, when all rent-receiving interests were acquired by official notification. The immense task of implementation thus thrust suddenly upon an inadequate administration, together wtih the problem of collecting rents directly from millions of tenants, completely overburdened the machinery of government. Shortly after the imposition of martial law in 1958 the Land Revenue (Mahmud) Commission was appointed to re-examine the problem.[10] On its recommendation, the revenue department was reorganized and strengthened, and plans were made for completing the assessment process by the end of 1962. The Commission also recommended that to simplify the administrative tasks as many as possible of the two million interests involved be compensated in cash rather than in forty-year bonds. By 1968, out of a total compensation of roughly Rs 360 million, Rs 210 million had been paid in cash and Rs 10 million in bonds (to nonresidents).[11] A long-term survey and settlement operation is under way to put the entire land revenue administration on a sound footing.

Land reform, in the sense of establishing permissible limits for the size of holdings, was intended to be part of the State Acquisition scheme. In 1961 the State Acquisition and Tenancy Act was amended to increase the maximum size of holdings from 100 to 375 standard bighas (approximately

[10] Report summarized in *East Pakistan Information*, July 15, 1959, pp. 6–7.

[11] Ministry of Finance, *Economy of Pakistan, 1948–68* (Islamabad, 1968), p. 35.

125 acres), in accordance with the recommendations of the Mahmud Commission, in the belief that the higher limit would permit the growth of a prosperous rural middle class. According to the 1960 agricultural census, the average farm holding is 3.5 acres, but nearly two-thirds of the holdings fall below that standard.[12] About 61 per cent of the cultivators are reported as owners, most of the remainder owning part and renting part of their holdings. Legislation has been proposed to give some security to tenants, but the problem is complicated by the need to protect the rights of those who are obliged by circumstances to rent out their lands temporarily. The small size of most holdings is further complicated in that about 90 per cent of them are fragmented. Consolidation and upgrading in size have apparently been determined to be politically and socially impossible, in view of the population pressures in East Pakistan. Limits of three and eight acres on subsistence and economic holdings, introduced in 1961 on the recommendation of the Mahmud Commission, were revoked in 1964, and a scheme for the consolidation of holdings during the Second Five Year Plan (1960–1965) was abandoned on the advice of the Land Revenue Administration Enquiry Committee of 1962 that no such involuntary program be undertaken.[13]

West Pakistan. Because of its former division into several autonomous units, the Indus valley's problems of land tenure and land reform have been in some respects more diffi-

[12] *Pakistan Census of Agriculture, 1960,* Vol. I: *Final Report—East Pakistan* (Karachi: Agricultural Census Organization, 1962), pp. 26, 29, 86.

[13] Planning Commission, *The Third Five Year Plan (1965–70),* pp. 409–410.

cult of solution than those of Bengal. The details of the revenue settlement varied from place to place, but in general involved a reassessment roughly every thirty years (the Permanent Settlement was never applied in West Pakistan areas). The traditional modes of tenure evolved somewhat differently in the several provinces and states, and far more than in East Pakistan the rural scene has been dominated by vast disproportions in landholdings. According to the 1959 Land Reforms Commission,[14] 64 per cent of the landholders owned five acres or less, and 53 per cent of the total acreage was in the hands of the 8 per cent with holdings larger than twenty-five acres. In fact, some 6,000 owners—o.1 per cent of the total—controlled about 7.5 million of the 48.6 million reported acres. In 1960, 42 per cent of all cultivators rented their entire holdings, and although the average farm size was ten acres, nearly half of the holdings were less than five acres.[15] The vast majority of tenants had no security at all, despite tenancy legislation adopted since independence.

The need for large-scale alterations in the basis of land ownership as a means of dealing with the economic, social, and political problems of the countryside was recognized by the Muslim League Agrarian Reform Committee in 1949, and also by the Planning Board in the First Five Year Plan. Landlord domination of the political parties and of the provincial and central legislatures seemed to present insurmountable obstacles to meaningful action. Not until the martial-law regime had set aside normal political pressures was the nettle grasped, with the appointment on October 31, 1958, of a Land Reforms Commission to make recommenda-

[14] West Pakistan, Land Reforms Commission, *Report* (Lahore, 1959).
[15] *Pakistan Census of Agriculture, 1960,* Vol. II: *West Pakistan Report 2* (Karachi: Agricultural Census Organization, 1964), pp. 4, 14.

tions upon which the government might base a rational land-tenure policy.

The West Pakistan Land Reforms Regulation was promulgated by President Ayub Khan under martial law on January 26, 1959. The reforms were intended to break the political and social dominance of the landlord class without subverting its economic base, and so to bring about greater equality of opportunity and a more equitable distribution of rural incomes within the existing social order. The Regulation set maximum and minimum limits to the size of holdings, provided for security of tenure for tenants, and abolished intermediate interests and jagirs (grants of the right to collect land revenue). The implementation of the reforms was entrusted to a five-member Land Commission, which during 1959 proceeded to acquire all individual holdings in excess, roughly, of 500 acres of irrigated or 1,000 acres of nonirrigated land, and to transfer the resumed lands (totaling nearly 2.4 million acres) to some 200,000 tenants and other peasant proprietors. The purchasers were to pay for their holdings over a twenty-five-year period, at a price well below the market rate but sufficient to cover compensation to the former owners, who were paid at graduated rates in transferable, four–per cent, twenty-five-year bonds. By 1968 so many purchasers had completed payment that over 70 per cent of the total value of the bonds had already been redeemed.[16] Since the owners affected by the reforms still control some 4.8 million acres, whereas only about 4 per cent of the cultivators have had their status changed, the changes were clearly far from revolutionary.

More important to the agricultural economy and to the

[16] Ministry of Finance, *Economy of Pakistan, 1948–68,* p. 43.

ordinary cultivator are the provisions in regard to minimum holdings, which apply to new lands being colonized as well as to the older cultivated areas. No holding larger than 64 acres in the Sindhi area and 50 acres elsewhere (an "economic holding") may be so subdivided as to eliminate the economic holding or to leave any sharer with less than 16 acres or 12.5 acres, respectively (a "subsistence holding"). No holding larger than a subsistence holding may be so subdivided as to leave any sharer with less than a subsistence holding (including previously owned area). These restrictions are supplemented by legislation enacted in 1960 providing for compulsory consolidation of holdings. Agricultural productivity and efficiency has been seriously compromised in the past by the widespread disintegration of small holdings through inheritance into scattered plots of land. The consolidation program pools and redemarcates the lands in every village so that each cultivator has a compact block, upgraded where possible to subsistence or economic holdings by the addition of state or other available land. By May 1968 some 11.5 million acres out of a total of 30 million had been consolidated. Steps have also been taken to unify the tenure laws and to simplify revenue procedure so that the cultivators will be better aware of their rights and obligations and thus able to obtain more prompt redress of their grievances.

AGRICULTURAL PRODUCTIVITY

In addition to changes and improvements in water supply and land tenure, modernization of the agricultural economy requires technical inputs and changes in the cultivators' attitudes. The Food and Agriculture Commission of 1960 reviewed the various agencies concerned with agricultural development—the provincial departments of agriculture, animal husbandry, cooperatives, revenue, and (in West Pakistan) irrigation, the WAPDA's, various agricultural credit institutions, the Village AID (Agricultural-Industrial Development) organization, and the new Basic Democracy councils—and concluded that none of these were capable of tackling adequately the task of providing the cultivator with the "five firsts": better seed, fertilizers, plant protection, better cultivation techniques, and credit facilities. On the Commission's recommendation, an Agricultural Development Corporation (ADC) was created in each province in 1961 to undertake these tasks in an integrated manner. The Commission had intended that each ADC would take up project areas in different parts of its province until gradually the whole province was covered, permitting experimentation and also allowing for the growth of administrative capability by the ADC. In fact the development of the ADC's in the two provinces has been rather different.

The major efforts of the WPADC are concentrated in barrage colonization projects along the Indus: the Kotri, Guddu, Taunsa, and Thal projects, plus a project for the reclamation of eroded land in the Soan valley near Rawalpindi. Much of the work is routine colonization, building roads and canal distributaries and laying out villages and towns, but in these areas an integrated approach to agricultural extension can be applied, with features such as the Guddu project's "farmers' service centers." Outside the Indus basin the most innovative undertaking is the Small Dams Organization, to provide irrigation facilities in the hill areas and also retard erosion. EPADC project areas are principally the Ganges-Kobadak project and the Chittagong Hill Tracts, with the peculiar problems of the shifting cultivation economy of the tribal people. EPADC also has a special interest in encouraging mechanization, by experimenting with small power tillers and by fostering irrigation through low-lift pump schemes (to get water onto the land from the rivers) and by encouraging the installation of tube wells. In both provinces the ADC's are responsible for the import and production of quality seeds for distribution and multiplication, and for the import and sale of chemical fertilizers at highly subsidized rates. Despite the hopes of the Food and Agriculture Commission, the direct provision of credit has remained outside the scope of the ADC's.

The problem of credit for the farmer is always present in an agricultural economy. Almost by definition the subsistence cultivator lacks the capital necessary to prepare his land and plant his crop and to sustain him until the next harvest, and must turn for support to landlord, local notable, or neighbor. In East Pakistan the predominantly Hindu landlord class was destroyed by partition and the State Acquisition legislation, and the minimal rural services they provided collapsed; in West Pakistan the land reform of 1959 concentrated attention on the need to provide alternative sources of credit and other services if the influence of the rural aristocracy was to be lessened and a more self-reliant peasantry developed. The effort to modernize agriculture requires increased investments by the farmer, and hence increased credit must be made available. Moneylenders, whether professionals, landlords, middlemen, or more affluent relatives of the borrower, provide ready loans but at terms that usually reduce the borrower to a state of permanent indebtedness. The principal institutional source of credit at reasonable terms has for many years been government loans through the department of agriculture or revenue, but tedious bureaucratic procedures make them both difficult for the bor-

rower to obtain and difficult for the lending agency to re-
cover when repayment is due. The Credit Inquiry Commission established in 1959 recommended that such loans be
eliminated; they were not, but in 1961 the Agricultural Development Bank (ADB), with broadly defined responsibilities
for rural lending, was formed by the merger of the Agricultural Development Finance Corporation and the Agricultural Bank. The ADB is somewhat limited from the small
farmer's point of view by complicated procedures and security demands, and in consequence the noninstitutional
moneylender continues to operate.

The cooperative movement has, since early in the century,
been regarded as the ideal means for mobilizing rural economic resources and freeing the cultivator from moneylenders and mortgages. Generally, the cooperative movement
in Pakistan consists of primary multipurpose societies
(mainly for credit and marketing) and secondary central
societies, backed up by cooperative banks at the subdivision
or district level and a provincial cooperative bank at the
top, all supervised by the provincial cooperatives department. Despite the best efforts of over half a century, cooperative principles have not taken hold in the context of a faction-ridden and individualistic society. Cooperatives have
been ineffective, often functioning only on paper and subject to corruption and to exploitation for personal gain by
dominant individuals and cliques. The improvement of the
cooperative system has been endorsed by successive Five Year
Plans, and was assumed to be a necessary adjunct of the Village Agricultural-Industrial Development program, which
was inaugurated in 1953 with the objective of facilitating
rural development by encouraging local cooperation and
initiative in all fields. Although the program was relatively

successful and was expanding rapidly, with trained village workers functioning as general extension agents, Village AID had some conflicts with the regular government departments. When the creation of the ADC's brought another agency into the agricultural field, the Village AID program was terminated and its functions and personnel were transferred to departments such as health, agriculture, or cooperatives, or to the ADC's. The Village AID training institutes and the two training and research academies at Peshawar and Comilla (renamed Pakistan Academies for Rural Development) were taken over by the provincial Basic Democracy departments.

In East Pakistan the Academy for Rural Development at Comilla has shown not only that economically healthy cooperatives are possible, but that they are an indispensable part of a program of agricultural modernization and social change in the rural areas.[17] The Comilla system is characterized by a complete functional integration of the cooperatives with the local administrative structure. Primary hamlet or neighborhood agricultural societies that are small enough to have a sense of mutual confidence and identity among the members are linked by a central association, which is located at the thana headquarters town in facilities—the Thana Training and Development Center—that are shared with the thana officers of government departments (agriculture, fisheries, animal husbandry, etc.) and with the thana council

[17] See Pakistan Academy for Rural Development, *A New Rural Cooperative System for Comilla Thana* (Comilla, annually from 1961), annual reports; *The Comilla District Development Project* (Comilla, 1964); *An Evaluation Report on the Progress of the Seven Thana Projects under the Comilla District Integrated Rural Development Programme (September 1967)* (Comilla, 1967).

(of which most of the officers are members). The central association provides managerial and technical support to the primary societies, conducts weekly training programs at the TTDC with the thana departmental officers as teachers, and experiments with new farming techniques at its demonstration farm and with activities such as poultry or dairy projects. Besides channeling the regular small savings of members into the association and supervising the utilization of loans by the farmers, the primary societies provide the constituency for the training programs and thus speed acceptance of otherwise controversial activities such as the family planning and women's programs. Since it was launched at the end of 1961 the Comilla experiment has demonstrated that with careful and disciplined supervision significant savings can be mobilized in a community of very small farmers, enabling them to improve their economic situation and to free themselves from the moneylender. It has also shown that cooperatives can be a means of overcoming the problems of fragmentation of holdings, and for introducing a series of mutually reinforcing innovations affecting all aspects of rural life. Since 1967 the financial and administrative backing for this program, which at the time covered eleven thanas, has been supplied by the EPADC.

In West Pakistan the closest counterpart to the Comilla cooperative and training program appears to be the WPADC scheme begun in 1966 for "farmers' service centers" in the new barrage colonization projects.[18] However, these are established at the union council level serving roughly 1,200 to 1,500 farmers, rather than at the tehsil (the equivalent of the East Pakistan thana) level. The major focus of the farmers'

[18] *Pakistan Times Agricultural Development Corporation Special Supplement,* October 21, 1968.

service center is a demonstration farm where all local crops are grown using modern techniques, under the supervision of a university graduate agricultural agent. The farm provides full-time training of a year's duration for about fifteen farmers and supports the extension services conducted throughout the union, thus integrating the technical knowledge of the union agent and his staff with the realities of local agricultural conditions. In addition to the farm, each center has a consumer cooperative society, to supply seeds, fertilizers, and implements, and also a veterinary dispensary and a forest nursery. Although the cooperative credit element is absent in this program, and there is no counterpart to the hamlet primary societies in East Pakistan, the important principle of the interrelation between local experimentation, training, and practice is common to both schemes. It is possible that in the future the tehsil may prove a convenient level to link the activities in neighboring unions.

The prospects for the effective expansion of the Comilla and WPADC schemes throughout the two parts of Pakistan are governed largely by the nature of the respective rural societies. In East Pakistan prior to independence the dominant classes, both rural and urban, were high-caste Hindus. The social and political revolution accompanying and following partition and zamindari abolition eliminated the Hindu establishment, leaving a nearly classless and predominantly Muslim rural society in which status and influence depend almost entirely upon relatively minor—and transitory —economic differentiations. The rural vested interests threatened by an egalitarian cooperative movement are relatively weak and few in number, and given the common cultural and agricultural characteristics of the province, the experience of a few thanas can be expected to apply in the remaining 400-odd. In West Pakistan, ethnic, geographic, and agricultural diversity is combined with strong hierarchical social organization and great differences in wealth. Measures of innovation and change that are workable and effective in a newly colonized tract without an established rural hierarchy may be frustrated by vested interests and traditional authorities elsewhere, and agricultural or cooperative patterns appropriate to one context may not be easily transferable to other regions. West Pakistan is likely to require a variety of rural development patterns, although the basic principles developed at Comilla and in the Guddu project would seem to be applicable anywhere. It should be borne in mind that these programs benefit principally those who already have some small landholdings and leave the landless unaffected.

An important adjunct to the cooperative and rural development efforts in the modernization of the agricultural economy is the rural works program. This program, which originated in an experiment conducted by the Comilla Academy in 1961–62, has undertaken labor-intensive improvements in the rural infrastructure—roads, bridges and culverts, drains, canals and embankments, besides community centers and schools—by the mobilization of labor through the local councils in the winter dry season. The scheme provides work during the agricultural slack season for the laborers who are little if at all benefited by the cooperative programs. Originally financed from funds engendered by the sale of wheat provided by United States aid, the program, up to the end of the Second Five Year Plan, expended in East Pakistan— where it had been most successful—a total of Rs 453 million, and some Rs 200 million in West Pakistan. The revised allocation for the Third Plan (1965–1970) was Rs 1200 million for East Pakistan and Rs 600 million for West Pakistan, but alteration in wheat-loan terms and financing difficulties in connection with cooling relations with the United States led to serious shortfalls in expenditures in 1965–1968: only Rs 375 million in East and Rs 213.2 million in West Pakistan. Extensive small-scale irrigation works projected in East Pakistan for 1968–1970 under a rural irrigation program conceived by the Academy for Rural Development at Comilla, as part of the drive for provincial self-sufficiency in rice, may make up part of this shortfall.

The remarkable success of the agricultural sector of the economy has been a notable achievement of the Second and Third Five Year Plans. The Second Plan goal of a 21 per cent increase in food crop production was surpassed, despite a setback in 1962–63 because of adverse weather conditions which threatened over-all objectives of the Plan and dramatized the key importance of agriculture. The revised Third Plan (March 1967) aimed at an additional increase of nearly 35 per cent in order to achieve the goal of self-sufficiency in food grains in 1970. Only 13 per cent of the sum invested in the public sector was allotted specifically to agriculture, but the planners argued that investment in irrigation, power, and other related sectors made the share of agriculture much higher. During the Second Plan, when the annual growth rate in agriculture was higher than 3.4 per cent, there were signs of a breakthrough in private agricultural investment in West Pakistan, particularly in the sinking of tube wells and the use of fertilizers. Among the factors that must be recognized here are the land reform of 1959 and subsequent consolidation measures, the impact of the investment and technological advances connected with the Indus basin project, and the improved infrastructure for supplying seed and fertilizer. By mid-1968 the hoped-for breakthrough in agriculture was evident, with an increase over 1967 of 15 per cent in rice production and 44.7 per cent in wheat, partly because of very favorable weather conditions but also because of extensive use of new wheat strains in West Pakistan. A similar spurt in East Pakistan is anticipated early in the Fourth Plan period with improved winter irrigation facilities as well as suitable new rice strains. The Planning Commission must now seriously consider the impact of agricultural surpluses on national economic programs.

Planning and Industrial Development

At independence, Pakistan inherited very little industry apart from plants that processed food crops for domestic consumption and prepared cash crops for export. The two zones were suppliers of agricultural raw materials to areas that fell to India and relied predominantly on those areas for finished goods. Known resources for industrial development were extremely limited, particularly in deltaic East Pakistan. In West Pakistan coal mines and a small oilfield were being exploited long before partition, and the possibilities for large-scale production of cement were evident. Subsequent exploration revealed additional reserves of coal, low-grade iron ore, and other minerals in West Pakistan, and even in East Pakistan extensive but not easily exploitable coal reserves were discovered in the 1960's in the course of the search for oil. Exploration added to the existing knowledge of oil reserves in the Punjab area, but elsewhere it revealed not oil but vast reserves of gas in Quetta division and in Chittagong division in East Pakistan. Natural gas, providing fuel for thermal power stations and raw materials for the chemical and fertilizer industries, thus became a major component of industrial development in both zones.

The partition of the subcontinent drew an international frontier between the suppliers and consumers of 1947, disrupting the traditional pattern of commerce and communications. Karachi became the sole inlet and outlet for the Indus valley with the breaking of ties between the northwest and Delhi, but fortunately the North-Western (now Pakistan Western) Railway system was preserved substantially intact. In Bengal, however, the new border cut across rivers and rail lines, and severed the port and industrial complex of Calcutta from the hinterland. East Pakistan was left with only the small port of Chittagong in the extreme southeast, and the disjointed fragments of a rail system—broad gauge in the western half of the province and meter gauge in the east—which now constitute the Pakistan Eastern Railway.

The task of building an integrated national economy out of two disparate segments of the former British Indian Empire was seriously hampered by the flight of Hindu capital and of skilled managerial and entrepreneurial personnel. In their place millions of Muslim peasants and petty artisans poured into West Pakistan, overflowing from the countryside into the cities and placing an additional burden on the weakened administration. Those few refugees who possessed exploitable talents and resources were quickly absorbed into public service or into commercial activities, filling some of the gaps left by the flight of the non-Muslims. The great majority, without training or abilities, formed an impoverished and underemployed laboring class. Somehow the chaos of 1947 was surmounted, and gradually persons who legitimately or otherwise gained control of productive resources began to lay the foundations of Pakistani industry, exploiting the cheap refugee labor and the seller's market to extract maximum profits, which were reinvested in expanding enterprises.[19]

The planning process began shortly after independence, passing through a number of phases before the planners and their organization achieved their current high status. The First Five Year Plan (1955–1960) was the result of the efforts of the National Planning Board, established in 1953. Because of the low level of planning consciousness in the administration and the confusion of jurisdictions within the planning hierarchy, the period to be covered by the Plan was well under way before the publication of the draft Plan in May 1956. The Constitution of 1956 created a National Economic Council, including representatives of the federal and provincial governments under the chairmanship of the prime minister, which approved the modified draft Plan in April 1957. When the final version of the Plan was published in May 1958, it still had not received the formal approval of either the federal or the provincial governments, although the Plan period was half over. The Plan called for a total investment of about $2.3 billion, with greatest emphasis on industry, irrigation, and power. There was a general failure to attain the goals set, largely because of political and administrative weaknesses and lack of direction.

The experience of the First Plan period and the planning orientation of the army contributed to a greater planning consciousness, and changes in the planning hierarchy were made under martial law and confirmed in the Constitution

[19] Gustav F. Papanek, *Pakistan's Development: Social Goals and Private Incentives* (Cambridge, Mass., 1967), especially ch. II, "Robber Barons' Progress."

of 1962. Broad responsibility for the formulation of policy
and the approval of national plans was vested in the National
Economic Council (NEC), including the President as chairman, the governors, the Deputy Chairman of the Planning
Commission, and central and provincial ministers concerned
with development matters. Responsibility for current supervision of policy and sanctioning of schemes lay with the
executive committee of the NEC, under the chairmanship of
the finance minister. These arrangements continued, with
appropriate personnel adjustments, after the reimposition of
martial law in 1969. The Planning Commission itself (before
October 1958 the Planning Board) is attached to the President's Secretariat with the President as chairman, enhancing
the Commission's status and ensuring that its voice is heeded
throughout the administration. The Deputy Chairman is the
operational chief. The Commission has a large staff of econ-
omists and other technical experts and wields growing influence in every ministry of the central government, and
under its encouragement the provincial planning departments are becoming increasingly sophisticated.

Guided by the new planning structure, Pakistan's economic performance during the 1960's won international recognition. The Second Plan (1960–1965) considerably exceeded its original objectives, and the Third Plan (1965–
1970), despite international and domestic problems, continued the advance. From 1960 to 1968 the gross national
product increased by 55 per cent, agricultural production by
40 per cent, and industrial production by 160 per cent; the
changing structure of the economy was reflected by the decline of the agricultural share in the G.N.P. from 53.2 per
cent to 45.8 per cent, and the increase of the industrial share
from 9.3 per cent to 12.2 per cent. In 1967–68 the annual

growth rate of the G.N.P. rose to 7.5 per cent, suggesting further over-all increases by 1970, but the domestic turmoil of 1968–69 resulted in something of a setback, to 5.2 per cent. The objective of the final year of the Plan is to reach 6.5 per cent, the intended average annual increase for the Plan period.[20] The total Plan expenditures were $5.2 billion during the Second Plan, and a projected $10.9 billion in the Third.

A major objective of the Second and Third Plans and of the long-range perspective plan for 1965–1985 is the achievement of balanced development in the two zones of Pakistan. In 1947 West Pakistan was economically more advanced than East Bengal and benefited from the influx of some immigrant skill and capital. Although the gross provincial products of the two zones were still approximately the same in 1949–50, the more favorable environment in West Pakistan encouraged both public and private investment, which in turn improved the social and economic infrastructure of the region. Since opportunities were greater there, West Pakistan received and benefited from foreign-aid projects, and foreign exchange earned by East Pakistan's jute exports was consumed in imports for the expanding economy of the western province. During the 1950's the gross provincial product in West Pakistan increased at the rate of 3.1 per cent annually, while in East Pakistan the rate was only 1.9 per cent—less than the population increase. In consequence, disparities in per capita income increased from 18 per cent in 1951 to 29 per cent in 1960, with much larger differences in

[20] "Fourth Plan Objectives," para. 3; *Economic Survey of Pakistan, 1967–68*, reported in *Dawn* (Karachi), June 4, 1968; "Annual Development Plan" (for 1969–70), *Pakistan Times*, April 29, 1969; *Economic Survey of Pakistan, 1968–69*, reported in *Pakistan Times*, June 23, 1969.

terms of purchasing power, and were increasing between 1959–60 and 1962–63 at the rate of 7.7 per cent annually.[21] These trends made the impoverishment of East Pakistan a grave political issue during the 1950's, increasing the pressures which evoked the military intervention of 1958.

The terms of the Second Plan and of the Constitution of 1962, which obligated the National Economic Council to end regional disparities in income with the least possible delay, indicated the response of the Ayub administration to the problem of unbalanced national development. The Second Plan gave much greater emphasis to East Pakistan, increasing the province's share of annual public sector investment from 36 per cent in 1959–60 to over 50 per cent in 1964–65. In absolute terms this was an increase in East Pakistan of nearly 220 per cent compared with 63 per cent in the West. The perspective plan published in 1965 proposed to eliminate disparities entirely by 1985, and to quadruple the G.N.P. and double per capita income. During the Third Plan 54 per cent of all expenditures for development in the public sector was allocated to East Pakistan, plus 66 per cent of development loans from the central government and 51 percent of project assistance. Net foreign-exchange allocations (taking into account East Pakistan's exports, imports, and foreign assistance) rose from $119 million in 1960–61 to over $210 million in 1966–67.[22] Impressive as these increased

[21] The problem is treated in considerable detail in Mahbub ul Haq, *The Strategy of Economic Planning: A Case Study of Pakistan* (Karachi, Lahore, and Dacca, 1963), ch. 4; see also text of the "Report on Inter-regional and Intra-regional Disparities," published in the *Pakistan Times*, December 19, 1967.

[22] Planning Commission, *The Third Five Year Plan (1965–70)*, pp. 12, 126; "Fourth Plan Objectives," para. 33; "Report . . . on Disparities," in *Pakistan Times*, December 19, 1967.

proportionate allocations were, in calculating them the planners left out of account the huge expenditures in West Pakistan on the Indus basin works and reclamation schemes, amounting to roughly $2 billion by 1970, which shift the balance of total expenditure decisively in West Pakistan's favor. By 1967–68, although the over-all East Pakistan economic growth rate during the Second and Third Plans had risen to 4.5 per cent, in West Pakistan it had risen to over 6 per cent, indicating that while the rate of increase in disparity had been reduced, the gap was still widening and was unlikely to be closed by 1985. In 1967–68 the gross provincial product of East Pakistan increased by more than 8 per cent because of a massive 9.5 per cent growth in the agricultural sector, surpassing the rate in West Pakistan for the first time, but this favorable portent was clouded by a drop to 2.6 per cent in 1968–69, largely caused by an agricultural setback due to flood damage. In West Pakistan the rate declined much less, to 6.8 per cent.[23]

Official strategy for growth in East Pakistan has been based on two major assumptions: (1) a higher level of investment in the public sector than in West Pakistan, involving a transfer of resources from West to East Pakistan, and the creation of an adequate development infrastructure by government action, and (2) increased investment in the private sector. Considerable success has been achieved under the first head, in terms of transfer of resources through public investment and in infrastructural improvements both physical (trans-

[23] *Economic Survey of Pakistan, 1967–68,* reported in *Dawn,* June 4, 1968; "Annual Development Plan" (for 1969–70), *Pakistan Times,* April 29, 1969; abstract of Disparities Report for 1967–68, *Pakistan Times,* December 15, 1968; budget speech by Vice-Admiral S. M. Ahsan, published in full in *Pakistan Times,* June 29, 1969.

port, communications, power) and administrative (investment facilities, tax benefits), but the private sector has not responded. In the mid-1960s only 22 per cent of all private investment was taking place in East Pakistan, a proportion which reflects the activity of the private sector in West Pakistan in both industry and agriculture, where private investment by farmers has played a most important role in recent progress. The Comilla cooperative system suggests a means by which private investment may be mobilized in rural East Pakistan with perhaps a similar effect. The Third Plan allocated 50 per cent of total private-sector investment to East Pakistan, but given the difficulties in attracting investment the political turmoil of 1968–69 assures a serious shortfall.

Each Plan thus far has anticipated that about two-fifths of total investment would be in the private sector, about half of that share in industry, and most of the remainder in housing and transport. Planning policy is officially described as "pragmatic" and oriented to a free economy, although the long-term goal of planning is to create an "Islamic welfare state." Under the industrial policy statements of April 1948 and February 1959, only munitions, hydroelectric power, railways, telecommunications, and nuclear energy have been reserved exclusively to the public sector. The normal role of the state is envisioned to be the provision of investment facilities and economic overheads in other fields, except that if the public interest requires it, or if private capital is not forthcoming for essential industries, then the state may intervene. The Pakistan Industrial Development Corporation (PIDC) was founded in 1952 to promote the industrialization of East Pakistan in view of the paucity of private investment there, but it soon became active in West Pakistan as well. By

1962 PIDC enterprises included production of cotton tex-
tiles, sugar, ships, natural gas, and chemical fertilizers in each
province, plus jute goods, paper, and newsprint in East
Pakistan and woolens, paperboard, chemicals, cement, and
coal in West Pakistan. Partly because of the vast dimensions
of these undertakings and partly to decentralize decision
making, in 1962 the PIDC was replaced by an Industrial
Development Corporation in each province. With greatly increased investment in industry by the public sector in East
Pakistan under the Third Plan, EPIDC plays an even more
dominant role in the industrial economy of the province.
Both EPIDC and WPIDC are involved in the petroleum industry in cooperation with private capital, and the country's
first steel mill is EPIDC's 150,000-ton Chittagong project
which began production in 1967. (Steel mills at Karachi and
Kalabagh in West Pakistan remain in the planning stage.)
The corporations follow a policy of disinvestment whereby
successful concerns are transferred by sale to private hands—
increasingly with special arrangements for the small-scale
investor—in order to free capital for new ventures. In 1964
indications of excessive concentrations of private wealth and
economic power and the growth of monopolistic tendencies
in some industries led to criticism of the disinvestment policy
during the preparation of the Third Plan. Despite this, increased difficulties in international financing of the public
sector in the mid-1960's made necessary additional reliance
on the private sector to achieve industrial development objectives under the Plan.

The change in the foreign-aid climate in 1965 posed unexpected challenges to Pakistan's economic vitality. The
original Third Plan estimates called for 32 per cent of the
financing from external sources, or roughly $3.8 billion. This

may be compared to the total amount of foreign debt con-
tracted by Pakistan from 1951 to December 1967: over $3.6
billion. From 1959–60 to 1967–68 foreign loans and credits
financed about 35 per cent of total developmental expenditures, and nearly half of total imports. The largest single
subscriber to Pakistan's foreign-exchange needs has been the
United States, with a total (as of December 31, 1967) of
nearly $3.6 billion in loans and grants, including Public Law
480 wheat loans; the International Bank has provided $804
million.[24] After the great success of the Second Plan there
was every expectation that the United States and other countries would provide enthusiastic support in the Aid-to-Paki-
stan consortium. However, in the summer of 1965 President
Johnson, in an apparent show of displeasure at Pakistan's
growing relations with China, obtained the indefinite post-
ponement of the consortium meeting, and in September war
broke out with India. The war was brief, but resources were
diverted to defense needs, and further blows came in the
form of natural calamities, necessitating the diversion of
foreign exchange for food imports. Supplementary resources
for the Third Plan were found through a total of about $1.4
billion in additional taxation at home. Increased export
earnings (expected to be more than double the 1959–60 level
by 1969–70) and unforeseen assistance from other countries
(principally the Soviet bloc and China) helped to make up
the foreign-exchange gap that resulted when the consortium
powers contributed little more than 60 per cent of the expected amounts in 1965–1967. In early 1967 a new order of
priorities was announced, in the hope of making up in the
remainder of the Plan period the shortfalls of the first two

[24] *Economic Survey of Pakistan, 1967–68,* reported in *Dawn,* June 4,
1968; "Fourth Plan Objectives," para. 39.

years. The following year (1968) consortium support was renewed in recognition of the continued strength and promise of the economy.

The successes of economic development during the 1960's were the result of concentration on growth, physical investment, and exports, and the relative neglect of social investment. The perspective plan for 1965–1985 set out as goals a fourfold increase in gross national product, removal of economic disparity between East and West Pakistan, full employment, universal primary education, and elimination of dependence on foreign assistance. Progress was made on the first and last of these, but the others "proved to be more complex than originally envisioned." The Planning Commission's outline of the socioeconomic objectives of the Fourth Plan admitted the impossibility of achieving all the objectives simultaneously and emphasized the necessity for a "conscious and judicious" national choice among the conflicting values involved.

We must attain a rapid pace of development to eliminate poverty, but at the same time, the nation must preserve its moral and spiritual values and strive for the creation of a just and stable society. Economic progress can give us more material goods but would not necessarily give us happiness or contentment. An adequate balance between economic and social objectives is a difficult task but we must make a beginning for the evolution of a synthesis.[25]

The Commission pointed out the failings of the development process insofar as the ordinary Pakistani was concerned —for example, in average income, diet, housing, education, and employment—whatever over-all growth rates might

[25] "Fourth Plan Objectives," para. 6.

show. "It is quite clear on the eve of the Fourth Plan that the conflict between economic dynamism and social justice has become fairly sharp." The Commission foresaw a much greater emphasis in the Fourth Plan on equality of opportunity, a more equitable return to farmers and wage earners, growing social services, and ending undue concentrations of wealth and economic power. The inherent limitations imposed by the present stage of Pakistan's economic development—"we cannot distribute poverty"—led the Commission to warn that the material rewards of the system must be supplemented by a "fair and just social system, a humane and responsive administration and cheap and speedy justice." The strains on the political system imposed by social as well as economic injustice were evident to all in late 1968. In the Commission's view the attainment of a just society "will be possible only by a change in our present legal, administrative and social system." The political and constitutional crisis of 1969 proved the Commission's diagnosis to have been painfully accurate.

3. Constitutional Dilemmas

Although the transfer of power at midnight on August 14, 1947, was in a sense a revolutionary change, it took place smoothly within the framework of the existing constitutional arrangements. The Indian Independence Act of 1947 granted dominion status to India and Pakistan, each to be governed in accordance with the federal scheme of the Government of India Act of 1935, with essential modifications. In each dominion a Constituent Assembly, elected by the provincial legislatures in the approximate ratio of one member per million inhabitants, was empowered to adopt a new constitution and to act in the interim as the federal legislature. In Pakistan, Mohammed Ali Jinnah, the Qaid-i-Azam ("Great Leader"), became governor general, the successor of the viceroy as the king's representative, but in his own view holding office as the representative of his people. His principal lieutenant, Nawabzada Liaqat Ali Khan, became his prime minister, at the head of a cabinet constitutionally responsible to the Constituent Assembly. Thus, as the result of historical circumstances, Pakistan began its quest for an appropriate national constitution as a secular, federal, and parliamentary state.

Pakistan has been faced with two major constitutional dilemmas in the years since independence. The terms of the

Independence Act preserved the federal constitutional order which had evolved painfully over many years, and with which political leaders and the politically aware were generally familiar. The history of the Muslim League and of the Muslim separatist movement itself committed Pakistani political leaders to a federal structure, tempering an overriding belief in Muslim unity with a recognition of the geographical and cultural facts of provincial diversity. In addition, the League's dedication to constitutionalism, epitomized in Jinnah's career, predisposed the leaders to seek solutions within the democratic parliamentary tradition, avoiding a radical break with the past. On the other hand, the very nature of the Pakistan demand required that a new and Islamic constitutional order, reflecting the unity of the Muslim nation, be defined. During the seven-year struggle for independence little effort had been made to detail the constitutional, political, or social implications of a Muslim-majority state. The consequent ambiguity permitted Muslims holding widely differing views to join together, each sure that Pakistan would reflect his own aspirations. Although the vast majority of these Muslims, simple and sophisticated alike, assumed that the Pakistan won through their support of the Muslim League would be an "Islamic state," the task of defining this state in generally acceptable terms proved to be far from easy. The successive political and constitutional crises of the past twenty years have arisen from a continued lack of consensus on the role of Islam in the state (the "Islamic issue") and from the even more difficult problems of reconciling the diverse interests of a geographically divided political community (the "federal issue") in a democratic constitutional order.

The Islamic-State Issue

Since it concerns the very nature and purpose of the Pakistani political community, the Islamic-state issue has been one of the two principal stumbling blocks impeding the formation of a stable Pakistani polity. The status of non-Muslim minorities and the rights of the individual are involved, in addition to the institutional forms and the ethos of the political system. How Islam is interpreted will determine whether Pakistan is to be a free society or a closed, conformist one. Apart from a small group of Western-educated secularists, Pakistani Muslims agree that Islam should provide the philosophical (or ideological) foundations of the state. Unfortunately, the approaches to Islam differ widely, and the same individual may subscribe to differing and conflicting views at different times or even at the same time.[1]

The traditionalist interpretation of Islam, propagated by the ulama (principally those of the Deobandi school, through their organization, the Jamiat-ul-Ulama-i-Islam) is reactionary in dreaming of the establishment of social harmony by a return to the practices of a mythical Golden Age. The commitment of the ulama to Islam as an indivisible supranational community presided over by a khalifa and defended by strict adherence to the traditional schools of law interpreted by themselves caused them in earlier years to reject the Aligarh contention that the Indian Muslim community was a society in itself. Their support of the Congress version of

[1] The ensuing discussion of traditionalist, fundamentalist, and modernist approaches to Islam is based in part on Leonard Binder, *Religion and Politics in Pakistan* (Berkeley and Los Angeles, 1961). There are, of course, variations on these major themes, which are presented here in a simplified form.

Indian nationalism continued until the obvious success of the Muslim League in its campaign for Pakistan led increasing numbers to change sides. In the final two years of the struggle, the influence and moral authority of the ulama over the masses were invaluable to the Muslim League in propagating the cry of "Islam in danger." In accepting the concept of a geographically restricted Islamic society, however, the ulama continued to envision a political community headed by a khalifa and guided by their own interpretations of the divine law. The Islamic state in this view, therefore, would vest political power solely in the hands of the Muslims and would entrench the leading role of the ulama in the process of implementing the requirements of the Shariah.

The fundamentalist approach to the Islamic state seeks to deal with the moral and economic problems of modern man by strict adherence to the essential truths of the Quran. It differs from the traditionalist approach primarily in finding the basis of social and political organization in the Quran and Sunnah rather than in the historical practice of the Muslim community. It appeals to those who have been sufficiently affected by modern education and ideas to scorn the passive and obscurantist attitudes of the ulama yet believe that "true" Islam has definite ideological meaning, realizable and enforceable on mankind. The Jamaat-i-Islami Pakistan, following the rigidly constructed ideology propounded by its *amir,* Maulana Abul Ala Maududi, is the foremost exemplar of fundamentalism. The Jamaat conceives of a universal state under the sovereignty of God, in which the governing power vested in the community of believers is exercised in accordance with the Shariah by an elected amir, whose interpretations are, in the final analysis, binding. This approach is supported by those who believe that in an Islamic state divine law must prevail unequivocally, and nonbelievers must be relegated to an inferior position.

The modernist view of the political meaning of Islam is, broadly, that of the Aligarh movement. Sir Syed Ahmad Khan taught that Islam, science, and democratic values were compatible; Ameer Ali and others elaborated the view that democracy and Islam were identical, rejecting the claims of the ulama to exclusive authority to interpret Islamic principles. The modernists insist that God speaks to each man through the Quran, without intermediaries; the individual Muslim conscience, not ecclesiastical authority, determines the meaning of the Quran. To them Islamic principles are flexible and adaptable to new conditions, an eternally valid message, dynamic rather than static. Pakistani political leaders have therefore argued that the Islamic state is democratic, its government based on consultation among equals and respecting the individual conscience. According to Prime Minister Liaqat Ali Khan "it means a State where the brotherhood of Islam will prevail, where there is no minority or majority and where human dignity and human equality will prevail." [2] Such an Islamic state is morally Islamic, dedicated to justice, social welfare, and community responsibility, but the institutions through which these purposes are achieved are determined by the requirements of the environment, not by divine decree.

To the controversy among the Muslims concerning the constitutional implications of Islam was added in the early years the bitter opposition of the Hindu minority to any formal link between the state structure and religion. Pointing to disagreements between the proponents of various "Islamic

[2] Constituent Assembly (Legislature) of Pakistan, *Debates* (Karachi: Manager of Publications), First Session, I, No. 5 (March 2, 1948), p. 136.

state" schemes, Hindu spokesmen protested that a dedication to Islam would permit any faction that gained the upper hand to impose its religious views on the entire society. The result, they contended, would be at best a theocracy and at worst a totalitarian state ruled by an elite of "true believers." The contention that in such a society non-Muslims would be second-class citizens, "hewers of wood and drawers of water," was elaborated with particular reference to the system of separate communal electorates that many Muslims believed to be essential in an Islamic state. These arguments were advanced at great length in the Constituent Assembly in 1949 in the debate on Liaqat Ali Khan's Objectives Resolution, but in vain.

The Objectives Resolution, adopted by the Constituent Assembly on March 12, 1949, set out the general principles upon which the constitutional order was to be based. The passages referring to Islam were as follows:

In the name of Allah, the Beneficent, the Merciful:

Whereas sovereignty over the entire universe belongs to God Almighty alone and the authority which he has delegated to the State of Pakistan through its people for being exercised within the limits prescribed by Him is a sacred trust;

This Constituent Assembly, representing the people of Pakistan, resolves to frame a Constitution for the sovereign independent State of Pakistan; . . .

Wherein the principles of democracy, freedom, equality, tolerance and social justice as enunciated by Islam shall be fully observed;

Wherein the Muslims shall be enabled to order their lives in the individual and collective spheres in accord with the teachings and requirements of Islam as set out in the Holy Quran and the Sunna; . . .[3]

[3] Full text in Constituent Assembly of Pakistan, *Debates*, V, No. 1 (March 7, 1949), p. 1.

These paragraphs did not use the expression "Islamic state" or "Islamic republic" but were sufficiently vague to win support from all Muslim factions. At a later stage, when efforts were made to give constitutional definition to these generalities, Muslim modernists began to share non-Muslim misgivings.

ISLAM IN THE CONSTITUTION OF 1956

The question of the supremacy of the Holy Quran and Sunnah and the prohibition of legislation repugnant to them has been an especially controversial issue. The interim report of the Constituent Assembly's Basic Principles Committee, presented September 28, 1950, recommended that the Objectives Resolution be included as one of the "Directive Principles of State Policy" but advised that it would be impossible to make detailed provision for Islamic matters in a constitution. The resulting outcry from traditionalists and fundamentalists caused the report to be referred back to the Committee. The final report reflected the increased traditionalist influence prevailing after Khwaja Nazimuddin had succeeded Liaqat Ali Khan in the prime ministership. It was presented on December 22, 1952, and recommended that boards of ulama be established to review impugned legislation. This, together with the recommendation that existing law should be brought into conformity with Islamic principles and that the injunctions of the Quran and Sunnah be codified, led to a further outcry of protest. Both modernists and secularists considered the proposals un-Islamic in seeming to recognize a priesthood and undemocratic in vesting powers of review in persons not responsible to the people. Concern was also expressed for the economic consequences of a rigid enforcement of the Quranic ban on interest. The ultimate result—after Mohammed Ali of Bogra had succeeded Nazimuddin as prime minister in April 1953—was new official proposals to the Constituent Assembly, in which the reference to codification was included among the "Directive Principles of State Policy," fiscal matters were exempted for a period of twenty-five years from the provision prohibiting laws repugnant to the Quran and Sunnah, and the Supreme Court was vested with power to rule on questions of repugnancy. To allay the apprehensions of minority Muslim sects the phrase "Holy Quran and Sunnah" was to have the appropriate sectarian meaning when applied to them.

Supplementing the constitutional entrenchment of the Quran and Sunnah, the Constituent Assembly recommended in 1954 that Pakistan should be an "Islamic Republic" and that the President should be a Muslim. Hindu members of the Assembly hotly opposed the first of these provisions, which they held to be emblematic of everything objectionable in the whole idea of an Islamic state, and then walked out. The second provision was therefore opposed only by a few Muslim members who felt it to be an unnecessary affront to the minority communities. In general Muslims were satisfied with the "Islamic" provisions of the constitutional draft: modernists felt that the most objectionable features of the original proposals had been eliminated, traditionalists envisioned achieving their original objectives by securing the appointment of ulama to the Supreme Court, and fundamentalists believed the draft to provide the basis for the propagation and implementation of their dogmas.

The dissolution of the first Constituent Assembly in October 1954, in connection with a crisis concerning the federal issue, made it necessary to reopen the Islamic questions when constitutional debate was resumed in early 1956. For the first time, Muslims—encouraged by the changed political climate of the months of secularist dominance—argued openly against the very attempt to define specific institutions as "Islamic." The disappearance of the political monopoly of the Muslim League contributed to the more open political atmosphere and necessitated constant negotiation and compromise between parties, all of which was reflected in the Constitution enacted on February 29, 1956.

The knotty problem of the supremacy of the principles of the Quran and Sunnah was dealt with simply by making no provision in the Constitution for the challenge of legislation on the ground of repugnancy. Constitutionally, anything approved by the legislature was by definition in accordance with the principles of Islam. As a concession to the protagonists of the Islamic constitution, the President was to appoint a commission to make recommendations to the National Assembly in regard to the bringing of existing laws into conformity with the injunctions of Islam and to compile a list of such injunctions as could be given legislative effect. The creation of the commission was severely criticized by those who felt it to be as objectionable as the former boards of ulama, but its recommendations were not to be binding on the legislature and in any case could not affect the rights of minorities or "any provision of the Constitution." As a corollary to its recognition of the right of the legislatures to interpret the principles of Islam, the Constitution provided for the establishment of an organization for Islamic research and teaching to "assist in the reconstruction of Muslim society on a truly Islamic basis." In recognition of previous non-Muslim objections, no reference was made to the propagation of the teachings of Islam among the people.

The only other Islamic provisions to arouse serious dispute were those identifying Pakistan as an Islamic Republic and requiring that the President be a Muslim. As in 1953, Hindu members insisted that such provisions negated the democratic spirit of the Constitution and were repugnant to the fundamental rights and equality of citizens. Muslim critics pointed out the dangers of confusing the principles of Islam with the constitution of a state, with the implication that matters not endorsed in it are in some sense un-Islamic and with the probable consequence of involving religion in every political controversy. The preamble (based on the Objectives Resolution) in fact softened the impact of the Islamic dedication by referring to Jinnah's declaration that Pakistan "would be a democratic State based on Islamic principles of social justice" and recognizing the people (not God, or the Muslims) as the source of the Constitution. In this way, by qualifying and compromising the references to Islam, the drafters sought to conciliate those elements who demanded an Islamic constitution without giving them real power. Final authority was left with the legislatures and the people, who—whatever the Constitution might say—remained in the vast majority Muslim and oriented to Islamic values.

SEPARATE ELECTORATES

One matter closely bound up with both traditional and fundamentalist conceptions of the Islamic state that was not dealt with in the Constitution of 1956 was the difficult question of electorates. Separate electorates had been introduced in 1909 on the insistence of the Muslim League as a political device to ensure the representation of the Muslim minority in British India. During the political struggle, separate electorates were gradually rationalized theologically in roughly the following terms. The Muslim community was united by belief in one God and one Law, which required only interpretation by qualified leaders chosen by the community. Because Islamic unity was based on knowledge of one truth, disagreement could derive only from error, which the faithful would seek to correct; parties, seeking to exploit and institutionalize disagreement, were therefore un-Islamic and blasphemous. Leaders would be chosen on the basis not of party but of their reputations as Muslims and servants of the community, by an electorate consisting of members of the community only. The Muslim League became in this view the organized expression of the community through the Muslim electorate. Any other Muslim political party was by definition the result of error and was to be condemned.

After the Pakistan demand had been articulated, the Muslim League became the national movement, basing its appeal on the theory of the national incompatibility of Muslim and Hindu ideals and values. The concepts of separate electorates and separate representation for religious communities, therefore, were for many identified with the Pakistan movement. Jinnah himself seems never to have taken a dogmatic view of the matter, and certainly on occasions before independence he had contemplated abandoning separate electorates under appropriate conditions. His great speech to the Constituent Assembly on August 11, 1947, suggests that he anticipated that all communities would be politically equal in Pakistan.

If you forget your past and work together in a spirit that everyone of you, no matter to what community he belongs, no matter what relations he had with you in the past, no matter what his colour, caste or creed, is first, second and last a citizen of this State with equal rights, privileges and obligations, there will be no end to the progress you will make. . . . You are free; you are free to go to your temples, you are free to go to your mosques or to any other places of worship in this State of Pakistan. You may belong to any religion or caste or creed—that has nothing to do with the business of the State. . . . We are starting in the days when there is no discrimination, no distinction between one community and another, no discrimination between one caste or creed or another. We are starting with this fundamental principle that we are all citizens and equal citizens of one State. . . . Now, I think we should keep that in front of us as our ideal and you will find that in course of time Hindus would cease to be Hindus and Muslims would cease to be Muslims, not in the religious sense, because that is the personal faith of each individual, but in the political sense as citizens of the State.[4]

Whatever the Qaid-i-Azam's intentions in regard to separate electorates in Pakistan, after his death strong pressures were exerted to maintain and extend the principle of separate voting and representation. The initially successful Muslim League argument was that Islam guaranteed and even demanded the full self-expression of each community, through its own representatives; by ensuring this, separate electorates freed the smaller minority communities from Hindu domination and also precluded the political use of religion in election campaigns. Furthermore, the argument insisted that a common electoral roll was contrary to the ideology of Pakistan and subversive of the integrity of the Muslim community. Other Muslims, particularly members of the Awami League party after 1955, rejected these contentions, along with the Muslim League's claim to be the

[4] Full text in Constituent Assembly of Pakistan, *Debates,* I, No. 2 (August 11, 1947), pp. 18–22. I have discussed at length the separate-electorates issue, and the development of Jinnah's position thereon, in my unpublished dissertation, "Government and Constitution-Making in Pakistan" (University of California, Berkeley, 1957), ch. 10.

national movement. They argued that separate electorates weakened society both by encouraging pressures within the Muslim community to expel the unorthodox (for example, the anti-Ahmadi movement of 1952–53) and by creating un-integrated blocs within the state—in effect, potential non-Muslim "Pakistans." They insisted that separate electorates were undemocratic and un-Islamic, that a religious sanction was being given to a political device, and that the Muslim League displayed a "colonial mentality" in forcing on the minorities an arrangement they did not want. Actually some non-Muslims—mainly Christians in West Pakistan and Scheduled Castes in East Pakistan—favored separate elec-torates as a means of preserving their political representa-tion in an essentially communal society. Caste Hindus, the most vocal minority political spokesmen, adhered to the tra-ditional Congress view that separate electorates divided and weakened the society and worked to the disadvantage of the minorities by making the government independent of and indifferent to them.

The debate over separate electorates assumed practical political importance while the compromises that ultimately resulted in the Constitution of 1956 were being hammered out. In 1950–1952 successive bills were enacted by the Con-stituent Assembly over vehement Hindu opposition to pre-pare for adult-suffrage elections for the various provincial legislatures. In addition to the Muslim electorate, these bills provided for Christian and "general" electorates in parts of West Pakistan and Christian, Buddhist, Scheduled Caste, and "general" electorates in East Pakistan, each to return its own representatives. In consequence, the East Pakistan Assembly elected in March 1954 included 72 non-Muslims in a total of 309. During the bitter political division within the majority community in 1955–1958, these non-Muslim legislators found themselves wooed from all sides. Far from being reduced to political impotence by separate electorates, or quarantined from influencing Muslim affairs, non-Muslims were in effect the arbiters of East Pakistani and of national politics, thus justifying the Awami League arguments during the constitutional debates for a common electoral roll: in the short run, a common electorate would obtain non-Muslim political support, and in the long run it would eliminate the unassimilated bloc within the provincial and national legislatures. Nevertheless, in West Pakistan, where there were only 10 non-Muslims in the 310-member Assembly of the integrated province, separate electorates were insisted upon: non-Muslims were not a significant political force, and in any case they favored separate electorates, while the "Islamic" overtones of the issue provided a ready focus for appeals to the overwhelmingly Muslim population.

Since in the Constituent Assembly it was impossible to agree whether in the future there should be separate electorates or a common electoral roll for national and provincial elections, the Constitution of 1956 left the matter undetermined, to be settled by ordinary legislation. Because to many East Pakistani leaders a common electoral roll was a necessary concomitant to equal representation of East and West Pakistan in the national legislature, while to important groups in both provinces separate electorates were essential to an Islamic state, the political struggle over the principle of electorate was as bitter as constitutional dogma could make it. Intergroup conflict increased as each party sought to achieve supremacy in order to impose its electoral principles on the country, hoping to win parliamentary control in the ensuing election and then to amend the Constitution to incorporate its views on Islamic and other matters. In October 1956 the Electorates Act provided for separate electorates for all elections in West Pakistan, and a single common electoral roll in East Pakistan, only to be amended in April 1957 to extend the latter system throughout the country. Thereafter the possibility of further amendment following changes in the balance of political forces was never excluded, until the imposition of martial law terminated the struggle.

During the Ayub years from 1958 to 1969 the electorates issue was for the most part quiescent. The Constitution Commission appointed in early 1960 considered the matter and found persuasive the arguments in favor of separate electorates to safeguard minority interests. Despite the evidence of the great influence of separately elected minority members during 1955–1958, the Commission also held it to be not "safe" to adopt a common electorate while so many Hindus remained "unreconciled" to the existence of Pakistan, and recommended accordingly.[5] Instead of accepting the Commission's advice, President Ayub followed the precedent of the union council elections of late 1959 in making no provision in the Constitution of 1962 for separate voting either at the primary or the secondary level. Indirect elections made the issue seem less important, but their results confirmed the view that a common electoral roll would practically eliminate non-Muslim representation in the legislatures. Non-Muslims in East Pakistan may have been content with voting

<hr>

[5] Cabinet Secretariat, *Report of the Constitution Commission, Pakistan 1961* (Karachi, 1962), pp. 71–76. The Commission reports that 40 per cent of the 6,269 responses to its questionnaire favored separate electorates, while 55.1 per cent favored a joint electorate.

influence only, but in West Pakistan Christian voices were raised at the end of the Ayub era for reforms guaranteeing them representation.

ISLAM IN THE CONSTITUTION OF 1962

Part of the reason for the abrogation of the "Islamic" Constitution of 1956 was the generals' disgust at what President Iskander Mirza termed the "prostitution of Islam for political ends." Martial law eliminated the Islamic trappings of the constitutional order, sweeping away the Islamic laws commission and the provisions concerning repugnancy. The Constitution of 1962 minimized the overt Islamic provisions and refrained from describing Pakistan as an "Islamic Republic," although the preamble—a modification of the Objectives Resolution of 1949—recognized the sovereignty of Allah and made clear the dedication of the state to Islamic principles in accordance with the "will of the people." This proved politically insufficient, and severe public criticism made it necessary for President Ayub Khan to accept amendments in January 1964 restoring more explicit constitutional references to Islam, including the appellation "Islamic Republic."

The principal innovation of the 1962 Constitution in matters Islamic was the creation of the Advisory Council of Islamic Ideology. Initially the Council was intended to make recommendations on the means for enabling Muslims to order their lives in accordance with the principles of Islam. It was also to advise whether a law referred to it disregarded, violated, or otherwise was not in accord with the "Principles of Law-making," a constitutional chapter of hortatory legislative guidelines mainly concerning individual rights but including the stipulation that "no law should be repugnant to

Islam." This reference to repugnancy was elaborated by the constitutional amendment of January 1964. In replacing the "Principles of Law-making" with justiciable fundamental rights, the amendment inserted into the chapter on "Principles of Policy" the declaration that "no law shall be repugnant to the teachings and requirements of Islam as set out in the Holy Quran and Sunnah, and all existing laws shall be brought in conformity" therewith. The Advisory Council, on a reference by the National Assembly or a Provincial Assembly, the President, or a governor, was to express its opinion on a question of repugnancy, but no authority was obliged either to ask for advice or to follow it if asked and given. In addition, the amendment required the Council to examine all existing laws "with a view to bringing them into conformity with the teachings and requirements of Islam," and to submit a report to the President before January 15 on its activities during the preceding year.

The Advisory Council of Islamic Ideology (which continued to exist after the imposition of martial law in 1969) is reminiscent of the abortive boards of ulama of the 1952 proposals, although its membership and functions are more broadly defined. The Council includes five to twelve persons appointed by the President for three years, on the basis of their "understanding and appreciation of Islam and of the economic, political, legal and administrative problems of Pakistan." Ordinarily among its membership have been judges, professors, and retired civil servants, besides ulama representing different schools of thought. President Ayub no doubt anticipated that such a body would interpret Islam in practical Pakistani terms, partly because its diverse membership would preclude agreement on extreme formulations of any sort. Although by 1969 several matters had been referred to the Council by the central and West Pakistan authorities—concerning, for example, the problems of interest, prohibition, gambling, and family-law legislation—and although it had begun a review of the entire Pakistan code, its views received little publicity. One exception which brought public expression of shock was the Council's recommendation that Quranic punishments by amputation of limbs for certain crimes be enforced when Islamic moral and social principles had been re-established.[6] The Council thus earned a certain amount of scorn from modernists, while more conservative elements tend to discount its qualifications to serve as a "supreme court" of Islamic principles.

Soon after he assumed power in 1958, President Ayub made clear his belief that the moral basis of society must be provided by a realistic and scientific interpretation of Islam as a living faith. To that end, in September 1959 an Institute of Islamic Research was established in Karachi, charged with the responsibility of defining and interpreting the teachings of Islam in a rational and liberal manner in the context of the modern world. Given formal sanction in the Constitution of 1962 and moved to Islamabad in 1965, the Institute is loosely linked with similar scholarly institutions in Dacca, Karachi, and Lahore. In a sense the original theological and historical research undertaken at the Institute is supplemented by educational and training programs sponsored by provincial agencies. In both provinces, governmental departments have been established to supervise and if need be to administer Muslim shrines and charitable trusts (auqaf), to prevent corruption and misappropriation of funds, and, especially in West Pakistan, to end the social and political

6 Pakistan Times (Lahore), February 19, 1966.

power of the pirs and other holy men over the masses. The funds realized by efficient administration are used to assist in the modern and systematic training of imams and other mosque functionaries, to fit them for positive roles in their local communities.

With the collapse of the presidential system introduced by President Ayub Khan and the reintroduction of martial law, the detailed constitutional arrangements in regard to Islam are subject to change. It is clear that Pakistan will be described in the future as an "Islamic Republic," that its President will be a Muslim, and that constitutional provisions will seek to forbid laws repugnant to the principles of Islam and to reconcile existing laws with those principles, through the agency of an organization similar to the Advisory Council of Islamic Ideology or its predecessor Islamic laws commission. The Institute of Islamic Research is likely to continue, either in its existing status or linked with a university, because despite controversy over some of its publications it serves a genuine and valuable scholarly purpose. Similarly, the *auqaf* departments have proved too useful to be eliminated, although their activities are resented by traditionalists who consider them and the other official agencies to be tools for un-Islamic "indoctrination" and attacks on the institutions of the faith.

The Federal Issue

The relationship between East and West Pakistan has overshadowed all other questions in practical importance, even the ideological one of the role of Islam. Two major problems are involved: the voice of each zone of the country in nationwide political institutions, and the distribution of powers between the central authority and the provinces. At independence Pakistan was made up of fifteen separate entities: four governor's provinces (East Bengal, West Punjab, Sind, North-West Frontier), ten princely states (the Indus plain states of Bahawalpur and Khairpur; the four Baluchistan states of Kalat, Kharan, Mekran and Lasbela; and the four Frontier states of Swat, Chitral, Dir, and Amb), and the centrally administered chief commissioner's province of Baluchistan. Under the 1935 Act all of these except Baluchistan had theoretically an equal constitutional status as units of the federation. All were located in the economically more advanced western zone except East Bengal, which had a greater population than all of West Pakistan in an area only one-sixth as large. While West Pakistan leaders argued that each of the units should have an equal degree of autonomy and equal representation in a federal upper house, East Pakistanis insisted that their isolated province was *sui generis* and entitled to a greater degree of autonomy than was practicable for the units of West Pakistan, and because of its population was entitled to a majority voice in national affairs. The constitutional debate until 1954 was the story of the gradual acceptance by West Pakistani leaders of the hard reality that only by the integration of their rather artificially fragmented region into one could they justifiably expect an equal voice in national affairs and an equal degree of autonomy with East Pakistan.

Although the integration of the western zone into one unit was suggested as early as 1948, local pride and, in the smaller units, jealousies and fears of the economically and numerically dominant Punjabis made acceptance of the idea a painful process of grudging concession. In September 1950 the interim report of the Basic Principles Committee proposed a federation of equal units, the federal cabinet being responsible to a joint session of a federal legislature in which the lower house would have an East Pakistan majority by virtue of population and the upper a West Pakistan majority through the equal representation of the units, with the exact size of the two houses left unclear. These proposals being entirely unacceptable in East Pakistan, in December 1952 the Committee proposed a solution abandoning the equality of units and providing equal representation for the two zones in each house, the cabinet to be responsible to the lower. This scheme was disliked in both parts of the country, and gave way in October 1953 to the so-called "Mohammed Ali formula," a compromise drawn up by the prime minister. This plan included elements of both previous plans: a West Pakistan majority in the upper house was to be exactly balanced by an East Pakistan majority in the lower, and the cabinet was to be responsible to a joint session; in addition controversial matters were to require passage by a majority including at least 30 per cent of the members from each zone. In effect, this device created a disguised unicameral system, recognizing through parity that the Federation of Pakistan consisted of two partners rather than fifteen. The same was the effect of the emerging assumption that prime minister and head of state had to be from different zones.

Despite its realism, the "Mohammed Ali formula" did not receive a warm reception in either part of the country. The grouping of the units of West Pakistan for parliamentary purposes left unaffected their separate constitutional identities and the difficult problem of the distribution of powers between the federation and the units. The constitutional proposals perpetuated a fragmentation that would presumably have enabled East Pakistan to dominate the national

scene, even without the parliamentary majority its spokesmen continued to demand, by exploiting anti-Punjabi particularisms within West Pakistan. These considerations, by
mid-1954, led many West Pakistanis (especially Punjabis) to
endorse a "One Unit" plan for the integration of all the provinces and states. When added to the long-standing dissatisfaction in East Pakistan with the work of the Constituent
Assembly, the opposition to the constitutional proposals in
West Pakistan produced a political crisis that culminated in
the dissolution of the Assembly by the governor general on
October 24, 1954. A month later the federal government announced its intention to bring about the integration of West
Pakistan in order to simplify the constitutional problems of
representation and of distribution of powers.

Although the original intention of the governor general
and his ministers was to carry through the merger of West
Pakistan by executive order, decisions of the Federal Court
(see p. 137) in a series of cases arising out of the dissolution
of the Assembly made it clear that no action could be taken
without the approval of a new Constituent Assembly. The
merger plan was therefore delayed for consideration by an
Assembly elected in June 1955 on the basis of equal representation of the two zones. To allay the fears of the smaller
units, the merger bill provided for Punjab to accept representation of 40 per cent rather than 60 per cent in the new
provincial legislature, while decentralization of the administration, guaranteed shares in the public services, and additional public expenditures in non-Punjabi areas were promised. Considerable opposition was expressed by members of
the Constituent Assembly from Sind and the Frontier, both
to the principle of merger and to the political means used by
the federal government to obtain support for it. East Paki-

stanis who regarded the scheme as a means of perpetuating Punjabi domination over the entire country were also highly critical of it. Nevertheless, the bill was passed with only one West Pakistan member among those voting against it, other critics from the new province abstaining. The unified West Pakistan came into being on October 14, 1955, but opposition from the non-Punjabi areas continued, straining the political compromises of the Constitution of 1956.

CONSTITUTIONAL PARITY

According to spokesmen for East Pakistan's Awami League, their decision to accept parity between East and West Pakistan in order to solve the federal problem was part of a bargain made in early 1955 prior to the election of the second Constituent Assembly. In that bargain East Pakistan agreed to the unification of West Pakistan and accepted equal representation with the new province in the national legislature, in return for West Pakistan's acceptance of a common electoral roll for all Pakistanis. Just as some West Pakistanis feared that the East might attempt to exploit the differences between Punjabis, Sindhis, and Pathans, East Pakistanis feared that the West would seek to exclude their large non-Muslim minority from the effective political community. Consequently, the merger of West Pakistan and the constitutional provision of parity between the two provinces in the National Assembly should have been followed by the merger of Muslims and non-Muslims into a single electorate. The omission of specific provision in the Constitution of 1956 for a common electorate was, from the Awami League viewpoint, a betrayal of the parity agreement. With equal representation of the two provinces, if separate electorates were enacted the Muslims of East Pakistan would have much smaller representation than the Muslims of West Pakistan, although their numbers were roughly the same. Instead of the majority voice that they had demanded, they would have been reduced to a minority under the guise of parliamentary parity.

Having conceded parliamentary parity, East Pakistan demanded full parity—an equal share—in the administration, military services, and economic development. In all these spheres West Pakistan was overwhelmingly predominant, and the deep-seated Bengali feeling of neglect or discrimination inspired insistence on specific guarantees that past omissions would not be repeated and that immediate efforts to equalize the provinces in all spheres would be made. Because the lack of trained Bengali personnel for the public services could not be made up over night, it was possible in the Constitution only to recognize parity of participation as one of the "Directive Principles of State Policy." Many East Pakistanis believed that complete regional autonomy including the division of national financial institutions, limiting the federal government to defense, foreign affairs, and currency, would enable their province to overcome its economic backwardness. The opposing view was that such a weakening of the responsibilities of the center would confirm the economic disparity between the two provinces by throwing East Pakistan back on its own inadequate resources. The Constituent Assembly compromised by including a distribution of powers between the federation and the provinces very similar to that in the 1935 Act, while placing several matters under joint federal-provincial control or in the hands of independent bodies. Under this arrangement, economic and administrative parity under the 1956 Constitution was very largely to be a function of the political consequences of parliamentary parity.

The presidential system under the martial law of 1958–1962 and the Constitution of 1962 significantly modified some aspects of parity while confirming others. The fundamental elements of the parity bargain were preserved: an integrated West Pakistan, a common electorate, and equal representation in the National Assembly. The constitutional commitment to parity in the public services was affirmed in the "Principles of Policy" and both the National Finance Commission (NFC) and National Economic Council (NEC), as well as the central and provincial governments, were obligated to work toward the removal of economic disparities. The President's cabinet and other national bodies—including the NFC, NEC, and the public service commission—were conventionally made up on the basis of parity. However, by eliminating the distinction between head of state and head of government, the new system made impossible the conventional sharing of these two offices, and the concentration of power in the hands of the President much reduced the significance of parity in the composition of the cabinet. The elimination of a formal federal distribution of powers also technically annulled provincial autonomy, making the provincial authorities creatures of the center. Although the residuary powers left normally to the provinces gave them greater practical legislative and executive autonomy than before, the center retained power to legislate in the provincial sphere "in the national interest" and the governors were subject to direction by the President. Hence it was possible for East Pakistanis to feel not only that they lacked a real voice in the central government, but that their provincial government in its own sphere was subject to decision makers in West Pakistan. In that context, "parity" seemed to have become a mockery.

PARITY CHALLENGED

Parity was a compromise bargain between political leaders of East and West Pakistan, and like all compromises was achieved at the cost of considerations held valuable on both sides. West Pakistanis had originally been strongly opposed to treating East Pakistan as anything other than one among several equally autonomous political units, regardless of population. Gradually the weakness of this position became evident, and it was concluded that the autonomy of the separate units in West Pakistan would have to be sacrificed in order to make possible the regional autonomy upon which East Pakistan was insistent. East Pakistanis had originally demanded preponderant representation in the central government and a greater share of autonomy than the units in West Pakistan, but ultimately they were led to abandon the former and to agree to the integration of West Pakistan in order to achieve wider autonomy for their province. During the period when this process of accommodation was under way, East Pakistan in fact held forty-four of the seventy-five seats in the Constituent Assembly (including thirteen non-Muslims), but this did not prevent the entrenchment and even the growth of disparities in administrative, economic, and other fields. East Pakistani leaders therefore were willing to give up their parliamentary majority providing a common electoral roll were adopted, in return for guarantees that inequalities in other aspects of national life would be eliminated.

Although it made a great deal of sense in federal terms, the parity compromise involved the abandonment of the cherished if somewhat contradictory political principles of Islamic universalism and provincial autonomy. Parity presupposes that Pakistan is composed of two political communities with distinct identities and that bargaining between them as equals must be the foundation of political life. This view is inconsistent with the Pakistan movement's commitment to one political community governing its affairs in accordance with the universal precepts of Islam, ideally in a unitary state. An Islamic state, based on belief in the equality of men before God, would seem to require equal representation of all, whether through separate or joint electorates, regardless of regional considerations. The East Pakistani case for a parliamentary majority was based on this straightforward plea of one man one vote, and on the assumption that political issues within the community would never simply pit representatives from one region against those from another. In West Pakistan, perhaps because of the existence of several distinct cultural groups, the political process was understood in terms of accommodation between groups, and the possibility of one group dominating others. Hence although the creation of "One Unit" signified the political acceptance of Islamic universalism with its implication of a unitary state within West Pakistan, this was somewhat qualified by the representational bias in the province in favor of non-Punjabis. The demand that West Pakistan and East Pakistan should be equally represented showed that West Pakistani universalism extended only to that region, and was an indication of distrust and exclusivity of the sort that a federal structure is intended to accommodate through the autonomy of the federal units.

Provincial autonomy also underwent a modification in the parity compromise. The Muslim League's commitment, in the Lahore Resolution of 1940, to the creation of " 'Independent States' in which the constituent units shall be autonomous and sovereign" was not only inconsistent with the universalism of Islam, but its devious terminology also produced much subsequent confusion. The Muslim League legislators' convention presided over by Jinnah in Delhi in April 1946 made it quite clear that only one "sovereign independent State" of Pakistan, comprising two zones, was envisioned.[7] Nevertheless, several factors combined to give the principle of autonomy the highest sanctity: the fact that autonomy from the center was a basic goal of the Muslim separatist movement; the historical circumstances that created local vested interests with traditional demands against the center (especially in Bengal and the Frontier); and the linguistic and cultural rivalries between Bengalis, Punjabis, Sindhis, and Pathans. In due course the practical difficulties of dealing with regional problems in West Pakistan showed the artificiality at least of the original multiplicity of autonomous units, but integration and the vesting of provincial autonomy in West Pakistan as a whole was opposed by those in both parts of the country who regarded autonomy as an attribute of major linguistic groups, not of geographic regions. The supersession of the "provincial autonomy" of Sindhis and Pathans (and presumably of Punjabis) was opposed in principle by East Pakistanis, who regarded it as an unacceptable derogation from what they conceived to be the guarantees enshrined in the Lahore Resolution. In practice, it was accepted in 1955–56 as part of the parity bargain in the interest of a larger definition of East Pakistan's autonomy, to which the universalist principles of majority rule subscribed to in East Pakistan were also secondary.

[7] Text of the resolution, which was proposed by H. S. Suhrawardy, then premier of Bengal, in G. Allana, ed., *Pakistan Movement: Historic Documents* (Karachi, 1967), pp. 297–299.

Since the intricate parity formula was entered into for the attainment of particular ends by particular leaders and political forces, it came under fire as soon as any one of its elements resulted in a grievance. The integrated West Pakistan was under attack from its conception, and its continuance in being was a lively political and constitutional issue within a year of its birth, even before its political and administrative workability could be fairly tested. The failure to provide for a common electorate in the constitution bill in 1956 provoked the Awami League to renew demands in the Constituent Assembly for majority representation for East Pakistan. The elimination of formal provincial autonomy by martial law and the Constitution of 1962 led once more to assertions of the necessity of parliamentary federalism and the principle of autonomy in Pakistan's constitutional order. The inability of successive governments to redress the disparity between East and West Pakistan became the most explosive of issues. The sense of grievance in East Pakistan took ever more emphatic political form, and was stated in demands for the severe curtailment of central powers in a redefined federal system, for the disintegration of West Pakistan, and, finally, for the replacement of parliamentary parity by an East Pakistan majority.

The Dilemmas Renewed

The drive to reopen the constitutional issues once thought settled returned Pakistan to the dilemmas with which she began in 1947. Twenty years after the adoption of the Objectives Resolution, the political and constitutional questions then dealt with so generally were still unanswered. The tension between the universalism of Islam, which had created a Pakistani nation from the diverse raw material of Indian

Muslims of many linguistic and racial backgrounds, and the particularisms of geography and culture, continued unabated. Logically, the one offered the ideal of a unitary state, based on an ideology of religious commitment and indifferent to cultural distinctions, the other the ideal of a league of linguistically defined, mutually exclusive nations indifferent to religious belief. Between these extremes were the practical possibilities of some accommodation of the Islamic commitment that gave birth to Pakistan with the facts of geographic, cultural, and economic differences and their attendant rivalries.

Geographic realities require that there be some degree of political and administrative decentralization in Pakistan. Parity provided a reasonable and practical formula, reconciling as far as possible the principles of unity and autonomy, and making possible the transfer of resources from one region to another by the central government. Its repudiation by East Pakistanis stems from political frustration at the continued disparity between East and West Pakistan in nearly all aspects of national life more than a decade after the parity bargain was struck. Within West Pakistan, Punjabis became the scapegoats for the varied political and economic grievances of Pathans, Sindhis, and others. The demand for the disintegration of West Pakistan and for an East Pakistan majority in the National Assembly was intended to overthrow the alleged Punjabi domination of the country. The proposed alternative to parity—maximizing East Pakistan's autonomy by reducing the central authority to responsibility for defense, foreign affairs, and little else—raises very serious problems for the distribution of powers in a West Pakistan reorganized into four linguistically defined units. Further, such a maximization of autonomy would make very difficult the transfer of resources from prosperous to poorer regions to eliminate disparities and achieve the Islamic social justice to which the Objectives Resolution referred. Abandonment of parliamentary parity also must inevitably reopen the electorates issue, with the likelihood that traditionalist and fundamentalist forces will renew the debate on Islamic issues.

In a broad sense Islam remains the source of ultimate values for the vast majority of the population. Islam provided the rallying point for mass support of the Pakistan movement and continues to be a powerful and evocative factor in shaping national political and economic goals. The sense of Islamic identity protects the Pakistani political community from the absurdities of secular "political religions" observable elsewhere in Asia and Africa, with their political divinities and sacred autobiographical texts. Whatever the terms of the constitutional document, Islamic principles will determine the moral tone of the political order that finally emerges, transcending the traditional social codes of Pathan, Punjabi, and Bengali. Despite its own internal schisms and doctrinal conflicts, Islam offers an ideal of unity and universality to overcome the local allegiances and centrifugal tendencies that beset Pakistan.

4. Institutional
Continuity

Throughout the years of struggle and conflict over the major constitutional dilemmas, the institutions that most closely affected the people continued to function and to fulfill the basic responsibilities of a political system. Change in the administrative or judicial systems, or in local government, came only gradually, and successive constitutions confirmed the arrangements existing at partition with at most slight modifications. Despite varying degrees of controversy concerning the effectiveness and appropriateness of the inherited structures in the circumstances of an independent Pakistan, major constitutional issues arose only when significant departures from the practices of British India were attempted. In consequence, the system continued to work smoothly in the absence of normal politics under martial law in 1969, just as it had done from 1958 to 1962.

Civil Administration

The administrative structure of Pakistan continues to be essentially colonial. In the course of the extension of British control over the subcontinent, the countryside was divided for purposes of revenue collection into districts, which in due course became the basic units for all administrative purposes. Each district is in the charge of a generalist administrative officer, now known throughout Pakistan as the deputy commissioner (DC). Technically the modern DC, like his predecessor of fifty or seventy-five years ago, is responsible for all that goes on in his district and is the "father and mother" of his people. He has preventive powers as a magistrate and punitive powers in criminal matters as a judge, controls the police, collects the land revenue, and supervises the administration generally. The subdivisional officer (SDO) and tehsildar in charge of portions of a district have comparable powers and responsibilities in their more limited jurisdictions, subject to the supervision of the DC. The latter, in turn, is guided and supervised by the commissioner of the division, a senior officer with primarily coordinative and appeal powers, particularly for revenue matters. Commissioners, DC's, and field officers of other departments working in the districts are responsible to the provincial government through a provincial secretariat headed by a chief secretary, which formulates policy alternatives for the political authority and transmits policy decisions to the field. The central secretariat plays an analogous role in regard to central functional departments.

In such a highly centralized system the problem of bureaucratic inertia and red tape is a serious one. Paperwork has become so important with the multiplication of government activities that it is increasingly difficult for the territorial officer to "tour" and maintain contact with actual developments within his jurisdiction. One remedy is to increase the number of districts and other jurisdictions, but this raises additional problems of finance and coordination. Further, in an era of positive government, of technical specialization in operating departments, the interposition of generalist supervisors athwart the lines of command, at the district and divisional levels and most importantly in the provincial and central secretariats, can cause quite unwarranted and costly delay. During the Ayub martial law of 1958–1962 efforts were made to decentralize decision making and to simplify the administrative process in both provinces (and in the central government) but to little apparent effect.

EAST PAKISTAN

The administration of Bengal was proverbial in British times for overcentralization, overregulation, lack of initiative, and delay. The districts were huge in population and, because of the terrain, physically difficult to administer, and at the same time the provincial secretariat was inclined to deal directly and closely with the district authorities. Since independence, communications within the districts have improved but the general pattern of centralization of decision making in the provincial capital remains unchanged. The four present commissioner's divisions roughly correspond to the major geographic regions of the province: Dacca (central), Chittagong (eastern), Khulna (southwestern), and Rajshahi (northern). They include (in 1969) nineteen districts, which in turn comprise some sixty subdivisions, each in the charge of an SDO. The smallest administrative jurisdiction, each under a circle officer, is the thana, of which there are over 400. Zamindari abolition forced the creation of a state hierarchy for revenue collection at the thana level for the first time, and the expansion of rural development activities further increases the supervisorial burdens on the present district administrations. The huge Mymensingh district in Dacca division, with a 1961 population of over seven million, presented an apparently intractable administrative problem: for nearly a century proposals to divide it were made peri-

odically but with no result. In 1960 the Provincial Administration Commission recommended the partition of the district into three, but local "patriotism," among other things,
blocked action until 1969.[1] One proposed solution is to make
Mymensingh a division, with each of its six subdivisions
raised to district status. Although the utility of the division
as an administrative entity has been challenged since before
independence, many officials feel that a considerable increase
in the number of districts is necessary if the administrations
are to be effective and responsive to the needs of a rapidly
growing population.[2] Dissatisfaction with the system that has
prevailed thus far is reflected in the expressions of grievance
against the provincial government in Rajshahi division and
occasional demands for a separate province of North Bengal.

WEST PAKISTAN

The administrative diversity that characterized West Pakistan at independence was somewhat lessened after integration in 1955, but the unified province was still more varied
than East Pakistan. By region, the province included thirteen commissioner's divisions: Karachi, Hyderabad, and
Khairpur (incorporating the old Khairpur state) in Sind;
Multan, Bahawalpur (the former state), Lahore, Rawalpindi,
and Sargodha in Punjab; Peshawar, Malakand, and Dera

[1] The report was not published, but its recommendations were made
public on June 29, 1960, and reported in the *Pakistan Times,* June 30,
July 1, 1960. On the Commission's recommendation, Khulna division
was created by the partition of Rajshahi in 1960, Patuakhali district
was formed by the partition of Bakarganj in 1968, and in late 1969
Tangail district was carved out of Mymensingh.

[2] I have discussed this in my monograph, *Divisional Councils in East
Pakistan, 1960–1965: An Evaluation* (South Asia Monograph Series, no.
4; Durham, 1967).

Ismail Khan in the Frontier; and Quetta and Kalat (incorporating the former Baluchistan states) in Baluchistan. These include a total of 46 districts divided into some 200 tehsils (in certain districts tehsils are ranked or grouped as subdivisions, but this jurisdiction does not have the same significance as in East Pakistan). In Peshawar and Dera Ismail Khan divisions, besides the special tribal areas attached to the regular districts, there are five tribal agencies under political agents whose main concern is the preservation of peace and security. The Malakand division, created in 1969, includes one tribal agency and the former Frontier States of Dir, Swat, and Chitral. In addition to the tribal territories in these three divisions, extending along the border with Afghanistan, parts of Quetta and Kalat and of one district of Multan are also classified as "tribal areas." Central and provincial laws do not apply in these areas unless specifically extended to them by the central government (or provincial government, with the former's approval) with such modifications as may be appropriate. The long-term goal is the gradual integration of these areas when social and economic conditions in them become stabilized and more similar to those prevailing in the districts, and from time to time small areas are merged with adjoining districts.

At the time of the integration of West Pakistan much emphasis was laid on the need for decentralization and for the development of an orientation toward social welfare rather than toward law and order in the administration. This was a response to fears that the affairs of the former provinces would suffer in an overcentralized and overburdened government in distant Lahore, and that the government would become even more remote and indifferent to public needs. Decentralization of some powers to the divisional level took place, but this was effected by regulations and standing orders that over time tended to become rigid and inflexible. Further, the growth of central planning increased the number of controls, and necessary references to higher authorities. The result seemed to confirm the predictions of the opponents of "One Unit," and increased the appeal of political groups demanding its disintegration. The vehemence of the attacks on the West Pakistan administration in early 1969 led in mid-February to the appointment by the provincial government of a committee under former Chief Justice Fazle Akbar (an East Pakistani), to review the administrative problems arising out of integration and to make recommendations for remedying them.[3]

THE NATIONAL CAPITAL

The capital of Pakistan is Islamabad, a new city on the northern outskirts of Rawalpindi in West Pakistan. Under the 1962 Constitution, Dacca in East Pakistan was designated the second capital and the seat of the National Assembly. Under the 1962 Constitution, both capital territories were within the administrative jurisdiction of the province concerned, with no special autonomous status. The reintroduction of a federal constitution will require that federal territories be demarcated. Until 1960 Karachi was the national capital, and a centrally administered territory from 1948 until 1961. The decision of the Ayub martial-law regime to shift the capital and then to incorporate Karachi into West Pakistan was a source of grievance in East Pakistan. This resentment stemmed, in part, from the feeling that East Pakistan had been deprived without compensation of an equity

[3] *Pakistan Times,* February 17, 1969. The creation of the Malakand division was one consequence of the work of this committee.

built up in Karachi over twelve years, and in part from the effects on the West Pakistan economy of the huge investment of the central government in building Islamabad. Among the East Pakistani demands in early 1969 was the transfer of the capital to Dacca, so that central government expenditures could be channeled through the East Pakistani economy. However, because of the expenditures already made in Islamabad it is unlikely that the capital will be shifted again.

THE PUBLIC SERVICES

Pakistan has retained the British Indian pattern of administration by an elite corps of specially recruited public services. The Civil Service of Pakistan (CSP) is the premier service, in succession to the old Indian Civil Service (ICS), with a total strength that has increased gradually from slightly more than 100 in 1948 to 512 in 1968. At present young men are recruited into the CSP by examination at the rate of twenty-five to thirty-five each year, and undergo two years of training, primarily at the Civil Service Academy in Lahore but with short periods at other institutions including the Pakistan Academy for Rural Development at Comilla. The new CSP officer begins his career as an assistant at a district headquarters, usually in his home province. After demonstrating his ability he is given an independent post in a subdivision and begins his upward move. CSP officers hold most of the posts of commissioner and DC, predominate in the key positions (secretary, joint secretary, deputy secretary) in the central and provincial secretariats, and hold some judicial posts. The provinces have their own civil and judicial services, but their members can only exceptionally rise to the heights that the CSP regards as normal career prospects. Such exceptions have been evident in East Pakistan, where the paucity of senior Bengali CSP officers has necessitated the filling of top posts with provincial service officers. Besides the CSP, the most prestigious all-Pakistan services are the foreign service, the police service, and the various finance services.

In view of the great power and prestige of the central services, the matter of the equitable representation of the provinces in them has been an important political factor in the relations between East and West Pakistan. Bengali Muslims were very poorly represented in both all-India and provincial services before independence, and consequently the new Pakistani services were dominated by West Pakistanis (especially Punjabis) and refugee Muslim officers from India. A quota system for recruitment to the central services was instituted, but the continued deficiency in numbers of Bengalis made the question of parity in the services a matter of heated debate in 1956. Demands for *ad hoc* recruitment were rebuffed, and the government was willing to concede only the constitutional pledge that "steps should be taken to achieve parity" in the administration. Although this pledge was confirmed in the chapter on "Principles of Policy" in the 1962 Constitution, its implementation was painfully slow from the point of view of East Pakistanis. By 1968 East Pakistanis were 186 out of 512 in the CSP, 73 of 177 in the foreign service, 82 of 210 in the police service, 208 of 606 in the various finance services, and 19 of 68 in the newly created information service.[4] Apparently in response to the establishment of a National Assembly special committee on parity in

[4] Statement by Khwaja Shahabuddin, minister of information, in the National Assembly on June 18, 1968 (*Dawn*, June 19, 1968). The finance services included are: Taxation, Customs and Excise, Railway Accounts, Audit and Accounts, and Military Accounts.

1968, the government, to speed the achievement of parity in the central services, modified the quota system to assign 50 per cent of the vacancies to East Pakistan and 30 per cent to West Pakistan, retaining merit recruitment for the remaining 20 per cent.[5] Under the new martial-law government in 1969, an equal number of East Pakistani secretaries to the central government were appointed for the first time, and the first East Pakistani CSP officer became chief secretary (permanent head) of the provincial administration. This is an indication that East Pakistani officers recruited since independence have now achieved sufficient seniority to attain the most important and powerful administrative positions.

The great powers vested in officialdom have made the services for many years the subject of political attack and criticism, and have at the same time made public service the most desirable of careers. To protect the administration from the consequences of possible political interference or manipulation, strong constitutional safeguards were developed during the British period. These have been retained since independence, although the 1962 Constitution slightly moderated them to make it easier to remove officials from service while preserving the right of the accused to be heard and to appeal against an injurious order. A central and two provincial public service commissions, appointed by the President and the governors respectively, conduct examinations and advise the executive on matters such as recruitment, qualifications, ap-

[5] Reported in *Pakistan News Digest* (Karachi), March 15, 1969, p. 7. Previously the 80 per cent was divided equally. The first 20 per cent of vacancies are filled by the names highest on the merit list, regardless of province; thereafter, provincial quotas must be filled no matter how low on the merit list it is necessary to go, and regardless of the availability of candidates of higher merit from elsewhere.

pointments, promotion, and discipline. To protect them from political pressures, the commissioners (at least half of whom must have been in the public service) have security of tenure for their three-year terms. Under the 1962 Constitution each commission submitted an annual report for presentation to the appropriate Assembly, indicating to what degree its advice had or had not been accepted by the government concerned.

Since the administrative structure and the elite services were developed in a prepolitical era, the bureaucracy is quite capable of running the country without politicians. It is not an undue exaggeration to say that the dedication and *esprit de corps* of the public services enabled Pakistan to survive the first chaotic months of post-partition confusion. Thereafter, the services were called upon to run nonpolitical administrations in the various provinces when they came successively under governor's rule (see p. 182). The traditional administrator's scorn for meddlesome politicians could not but be reinforced by the course of events, and in areas of political weakness officers inevitably encroached on the policy maker's sphere of responsibility. The services would have been more than human if some of their members had not on occasion yielded to political pressures or exploited their official positions for personal advantage. The martial-law regime of 1958–1962, while completely freeing the administration from political tutelage, also tightened discipline and punished or compulsorily retired many officers for corruption or malfeasance in office. The 1962 Constitution sought to strike a new balance between the bureaucracy and the political world by curtailing the privileges of the former while limiting the scope for pressures or "interference" by the latter. The result was to decrease the bureaucracy's responsibility to the public, increase its dependence on its official superiors, and heighten the sense of political frustration among those who felt that only through corruption could the administration be successfully influenced. Hence the return of martial law in 1969 was accompanied by renewed calls for administrative housecleaning and reform, along with the familiar reliance on the services to carry on with the process of government in the meantime.

The major focus of challenge to the existing administrative system in Pakistan in 1969 was the report of the Pay and Services Commission appointed by President Ayub in 1959 under the chairmanship of A. R. Cornelius (Chief Justice of Pakistan 1960–1968), a former ICS officer.[6] The Cornelius Report severely criticized the elite "governing corporation" role of the CSP, monopolizing for administrative generalists the most important posts in the regular administrative line and increasingly in the new public corporations as well, to the exclusion of members of specialist services and of the provincial civil services. The report recommended a revolutionary reorganization of the administration to replace the multitude of self-contained services by a functional hierarchy of seven inclusive classes, with provision for interclass promotion on merit. The sixth class would include all officers of all specialties at the district and divisional levels and equivalent secretariat posts and would be designated the Civil Executive Service, and the seventh would be a Pakistan Administrative Service including department heads, directors of organizations, and the highest secretariat officers, with

[6] The Commission's report was submitted in 1962, and finally made public in 1969. Pakistan, Pay and Services Commission, *Report, 1959–1962* (Karachi, 1969).

selection based on merit. In complement to these changes, the specialist departments would be freed from the supervision of the DC's and commissioners, who would lose their all-inclusive responsibilities to become coordinators of development activities and guardians—through district and divisional administrative tribunals—of the rule of law. Finally, secretariat officers would cease to be policy makers and would become instead administrative assistants to the minister in charge, with no jurisdiction over executive departments.

These proposals were so far-reaching that they were considered impracticable and were not accepted by the central government, and the report remained unpublished until 1969. However, knowledge of the Cornelius recommendations, especially their strictures on the competence of the CSP and the latter's questionable claim—given the vagaries of the quota recruitment system—to superiority over other services, became widespread. In the agitation of early 1969 the frustrations and sense of grievance of less privileged elements in the bureaucracy joined with the long-standing antipathy to the CSP in political circles to produce a great outcry for the acceptance and implementation of the Cornelius Report, and especially for the abolition of the CSP. It is not likely that the report will be accepted in its entirety, but steps taken even before the imposition of martial law on March 25, 1969, indicate that at least the complicated structure of services and classes will be simplified. The report's insistence on the essential conflict between the authoritarian and aristocratic "good government" traditions of the ICS and CSP and the egalitarian principles of democracy and the rule of law upon which the state was founded, make its proposals especially persuasive.

The Courts and the Law

From the British and Islamic traditions Pakistan has inherited a profound concern for justice and a great respect for those who dispense it. This has not prevented the corruption and manipulation of the judicial process, particularly at the lower levels, in order to further personal interests and to ruin enemies. The adversary proceedings of the common law as embodied in the great Anglo-Indian codes of the nineteenth century have very little relevance to the social environment of the vast majority of the population, and family and tribal obligations make nonsense of conventional procedures and rules of evidence.

Under the forms of law the greatest travesty of justice and fairness occurs. There are good grounds therefore for believing that in our conditions the whole elaborate machinery of English law is not suitable. The Magistrates keep on recording word for word the evidence of illiterate peasants and gentlemen of cities knowing full well that 90% of it is false. It is common knowledge that even if the events described had actually occurred, the eyewitnesses had not seen them. Even where the accused is guilty, it is perjury which proved his guilt. False evidence is always in demand, as much to prove what is true as it is to establish what is false. Against innocent and guilty alike it is equally necessary.[7]

These abuses are made possible in part by the slowness of the judicial process, which both facilitates tampering with evidence and places ruinous financial burdens on litigants.

[7] Dr. Nasim Hasan Shah, "Separation of Judiciary from Executive," *Pakistan Times*, April 24, 1964, p. 6. The passage is almost word-for-word that appearing in Sir Penderel Moon, *Strangers in India* (London, 1944), p. 51. Dr. Shah was editor of the Pakistan *Supreme Court Reports* and is now (1969) a judge of the West Pakistan High Court.

Acting on the premise that justice delayed is justice denied, the Ayub martial-law regime utilized the newly created union councils to institute a system of village courts. The Conciliation Courts Ordinance, 1961 (enforced from March 1, 1962), empowers the chairman of a union and two members nominated by each of the parties to a dispute to sit as a conciliation court, to try to reach a settlement without lawyers or formal procedures. These courts are intended to deal with particular disputes within the over-all village setting, with the aim of eliminating the basic cause of conflict without delay or expense. The regular courts become involved only if conciliation fails or if the matter is so serious that a normal trial is required. Unfortunately the conciliation courts like other institutions can be misused, their very informality and accessibility providing still another forum where false and harassing proceedings can be initiated.

For the rural population the DC in his capacity as district magistrate has traditionally been the fount of justice. He and his subordinates, combining executive authority with powers of a criminal judge, were in earlier days able to redress grievances and to deal with minor offenders with a minimum of complication and delay. In the present day most judicial work is delegated to officers who are full-time judges, and their courts suffer from the faults already described. Still, the formal combination of executive and judicial functions is open to abuse and can be used to oppress as well as to defend. There has been a consistent demand for many years for the separation of the judiciary from the executive. A few steps were taken in that direction before 1958, but were later reversed. Additional powers were vested in the district magistrate to supervise the conciliation courts, and in West Pakistan under the Criminal Law Amendment Act of 1963 (repealed in 1969) he was empowered to refer certain "heinous offences" to a tribunal which was not bound by normal procedures, if he was of the opinion that justice would not be done in a regular court. In April 1969 the West Pakistan government renewed efforts to provide sufficient officers so that it would be possible for judicial work to be handled entirely by magistrates with no executive responsibilities, and thus to speed the disposal of criminal cases.

Although the failings of the present courts as dispensers of justice are generally recognized, efforts to simplify trial procedures have always been vigorously resisted by lawyers and politicians (most of whom have legal training). The legal profession is trained in the common law tradition, and its guiding values and precedents are found in the decisions of English and Commonwealth courts. The spirit of the law as interpreted in Pakistan is overwhelmingly English, with emphasis on the "principles of natural justice" embodied in common law procedures. Any departure from the common law pattern will, it is contended, permit even greater abuses and denial of the rights of the accused. The practical result is to give more importance to the abstract "principles of justice" than to the achievement of justice for the individual in Pakistan.

THE COURTS

The deficiencies of lower-court procedures have not affected the reputation of the judiciary itself. The judges of the higher courts have great prestige and status, and a "judicial investigation" of any sort of problem is universally respected and accepted. The basic judicial unit, from which appeals are taken to the provincial High Court and thence to

the Supreme Court, is the district court for civil matters and
the sessions court for serious criminal matters. The district
and sessions judge is usually a member of a provincial judicial service, but he may be a CSP officer. Judges of the High
Courts and of the Supreme Court are recruited directly from
the bar or by promotion from lower courts. There are five
judges on the Supreme Court, about fifteen on the Dacca
High Court, and about twenty-five on the Lahore High
Court. They are appointed by the President in consultation
with the Chief Justice of Pakistan and (where appropriate)
the governor and Chief Justice of the province concerned,
and now serve until sixty-two on a High Court and until
sixty-five on the Supreme Court. Constitutional arrangements have always provided strict controls over the removal
of judges for misconduct, and only one or two instances have
ever occurred. The 1962 Constitution created a Supreme Judicial Council, consisting of the three Chief Justices and the
next two senior Supreme Court judges, whose recommendation is necessary before a judge can be removed. Normally
judges succeed to the chief justiceship in order of seniority.
After retirement a judge cannot accept another official appointment for two years, except to a judicial or quasi-judicial
post, and may not practice before the court of which he was
a member nor any court subordinate to it.

The independence and stature of the judges has enabled
them to play an extremely important role as the guardians
of constitutionalism and individual rights. In 1955 the Federal Court (the predecessor of the Supreme Court) in a series
of decisions based on English and Commonwealth precedent
preserved the constitutional order of the 1935 Act from collapse and compelled the governor general to summon a new

Constituent Assembly, after his invocation of the prerogative of the Crown to dissolve the first Assembly.[8] Again in 1958 the Supreme Court recognized the effect of the "revolution" of October 7 in abrogating the 1956 Constitution and replacing it with a new constitutional order and enabled the courts to maintain their authority under martial law.[9] Thereafter judicial interpretation defined and restricted the powers of martial-law tribunals and helped develop a martial-law "constitutionalism." During this period the function of the courts was to interpret existing law, to which all were subject unless and until the competent authority—the President—changed it.

The original scheme of the 1962 Constitution was intended to continue unaltered the status of the courts as defined under martial law. The independence of the judiciary was assured, even to the creation of the Supreme Judicial Council to replace the National Assembly as the body responsible for recommending the removal of judges. The jurisdiction of the courts was limited to that expressly conferred by the Constitution or law, and the power to declare a law unconstitutional on the ground that the legislature concerned had no power to enact it was specifically denied in order to ensure that judicial intervention could not be invoked to prevent the execution of policies approved by the national or provincial legislatures. In 1963 the Supreme

[8] Federation of Pakistan v. Tamizuddin Khan [1955] 1 FCR 155; Special Reference No. 1 of 1955 [1955] 1 FCR 439; Usif Patel v. The Crown [1955] 1 FCR 360; Federation of Pakistan v. Ali Ahmad Hussain Shah [1955] 1 FCR 566 (Federal Court Reports; Karachi, Manager of Publications).

[9] The State v. Dosso (1958), 2 PSCR 180 (Pakistan Supreme Court Reports; Karachi, Manager of Publications).

Court asserted its jurisdiction to rule unconstitutional an order of the President seeking to "adapt" constitutional provisions, on the ground that it was an amendment, which he had no power to make.[10] Subsequently, in response to public pressures, the Constitution was amended to restrict the powers of both legislative and executive branches by incorporating justiciable fundamental rights. After some vicissitudes these restrictions were again eliminated by the reimposition of martial law on March 25, 1969, limiting the courts once again to the interpretation of existing law, which was binding on all until altered by the President and Chief Martial Law Administrator.

FUNDAMENTAL RIGHTS

The power of the Supreme Court and High Courts to protect individual liberties has been limited for most of the years since independence to upholding the "principles of natural justice" in criminal appeals and asserting a broad common law view of the rights of the subject in interpreting legislation. Apart from normal civil and criminal appellate procedures, the major weapon used by the High Courts to check executive action has been the issue of writs, particularly habeas corpus, but even this power was statutory rather than constitutional until 1955. From March 1956 until October 1958, constitutionally specified fundamental rights limited both executive and legislature, and an injured individual could go directly to the High Court or Supreme Court for relief through writ proceedings. The jurisdiction of the High Courts was so broadly stated in the 1956 Constitution

[10] Fazlul Quader Choudhury v. Mohammed Abdul Haque, PLD 1963 SC 486 (Pakistan Legal Decisions; Lahore, All-Pakistan Legal Decisions).

that the High Courts found themselves involved in a vast number of cases relating to administrative matters such as promotion and discipline in government service, in addition to cases dealing with personal freedom. In reaction, the martial-law system of 1958–1962 returned to the pre-1956 status quo by eliminating the fundamental rights, and simply empowered the Supreme Court and High Courts to issue writs of habeas corpus, mandamus, prohibition, quo warranto, and certiorari—except against martial-law authorities—for the enforcement of rights established under the ordinary law.

The Constitution of 1962 provided, in Article 2, that "to enjoy the protection of the law, and to be treated in accordance with law, and only in accordance with law, is the inalienable right" of every individual in Pakistan. The assumption further spelled out in the article was that personal liberty is inherent, and that restrictions on it must be justified by law. Initially the responsibility for preventing encroachments on personal liberties was entrusted to the legislatures, guided by a series of "Principles of Law-making" defining fundamental rights. The rule here was that once the political decision was made through legislation that an encroachment on liberty was necessary, no challenge in the courts was possible. The intention of this provision was to prevent socially desirable legislation from being thwarted by vested interests, and to safeguard the land reforms and other reform measures of the martial-law regime of 1958–1962. However, the political commitment to the principle of judicially enforceable fundamental rights was so universal that President Ayub in January 1964 accepted a constitutional amendment to restore the jurisdiction of the courts as it had existed under the 1956 Constitution.

The new fundamental rights chapter "conferred," in substantially the same terms as in the previous Constitution, a broad range of rights on individuals or groups, subject in most cases to "reasonable" restrictions in the public interest. They included: security of person; freedom of movement, assembly, association, speech, and religion; the right to property; and guarantees against discrimination. The rights were enforceable through judicial review of legislation and executive acts, and the individual could go directly to the High Court for an appropriate order (the Constitution referred in Article 98 to "orders" rather than to the traditional writs) to any public authority to protect his rights. Laws inconsistent with the fundamental rights were void, although at the central government's insistence a special clause exempted from challenge a number of laws enacted since 1959 (including the West Pakistan Land Reforms Regulation of 1959 and Criminal Law Amendment Act of 1963, and the Muslim Marriage and Family Laws Ordinance). The rights were not enforceable by the High Court in the tribal areas of West Pakistan, where the Court under successive constitutions has had no jurisdiction because normal law does not apply. The chapter also provided that during an emergency the right to apply to the High Court for the enforcement of the fundamental rights could be suspended.

These constitutional guarantees remained available in full only until September 6, 1965, with a brief return in the five weeks prior to the reimposition of martial law in 1969. Under the emergency proclaimed during the conflict with India, only the guarantees against deprivation of life or liberty save in accordance with law, retrospective punishment, discrimination, and untouchability, and of freedom of religion, language, and culture remained in force. Long after the Tashkent Agreement of January 1966 had formally ter-

minated the conflict, political bitterness continued to increase, owing to the perpetuation of the emergency and the
attendant deprivation of personal liberties under the sweeping provisions of the Defence of Pakistan Ordinance and
Rules. Finally, in the face of the revolutionary upsurge that
began in November 1968, President Ayub yielded and revoked the proclamation. The jurisdiction that the courts
regained with the termination of the emergency on February
17, 1969, however, was largely nullified with the imposition
of martial law. The Provisional Constitution Order of April
4, 1969, while confirming the jurisdiction of the courts,
specifically abrogated all fundamental rights except the guarantees against deprivation of life or liberty save in accordance with law, slavery or forced labor, discrimination, and
untouchability, and of freedom of religion, language, and
culture. The ability of the High Courts—and, by appeal, the
Supreme Court—to enforce these rights or others under the
ordinary law by means of Article 98 of the 1962 Constitution
was limited by the exclusion of the martial-law authorities
from their jurisdiction.[11]

Preventive Detention. By far the most important qualifica-
tion on fundamental rights, whether defined in a constitutional document or not, is the power vested in public authorities to detain persons without trial. A variety of laws em-
power the central and provincial governments respectively
to detain persons without trial in the interest, broadly defined, of the security of Pakistan or of public safety. All suc-

[11] Text of the Provisional Constitution Order in *Pakistan Times,*
April 5, 1969. An order published on June 30 reiterated the ouster of
the jurisdiction of the courts, to eliminate any uncertainty (*Pakistan
Times,* July 1, 1969).

cessive Pakistani governments, like the British Indian government before them, have considered preventive powers indispensable in view of the volatile nature of the population and the existence of elements against whom the normal punitive law would be ineffective. Preventive detention can easily be abused for political purposes, and its use has always been attacked by parties out of power. A major basis of the attack on the emergency of 1965–1969 was the use of detention or restriction under the Defence of Pakistan Rules for purposes unconnected with the ostensible reason for the emergency. In order to check the executive, the review of detentions by an advisory board, ordinarily prescribed in the law itself, became an obligation under the 1956 Constitution and was confirmed in the 1962 Constitution. This provision, requiring that each case be reviewed within three months by a board consisting of a judge and a senior official, was unenforceable during the emergency. Under martial law in 1969 the requirement for board review was annulled, as it was in 1958–1962. In any case, such review does not touch the problem of brief detentions of a few days or weeks which can be politically or personally just as damaging as longer imprisonment.

An arsenal of other preventive powers is also available to public authorities for use under defined conditions subject to review and challenge in the courts. The most commonly used is Section 144 of the Criminal Procedure Code, empowering the district magistrate to prohibit certain actions—meetings or processions, for example—for up to two months. The security and public-safety laws permit a variety of preventive restrictions on movement, association, speech, and publication. The Press and Publications Ordinances of 1963, consolidating previous press legislation, permit further controls over the dissemination of printed matter. In view of the ease with which violence and riot can be precipitated, there is no doubt about the need for preventive powers. That they are sometimes abused is unfortunate but probably inescapable. In 1956–58 and 1964–65, their exercise was subject to judicial review to ensure that the orders concerned were "reasonable" in terms of the fundamental rights guarantees. Under martial law, the still-applicable guarantees of treatment in accordance with law in Article 2 and in the first fundamental right of the 1962 Constitution, and the High Court jurisdiction to issue orders and directions under Article 98, provide the courts with the means of ensuring at least that actions taken are those contemplated by the law. The extensive and effective use of their powers by the courts during the emergency of 1965–1969 to strike down government actions, despite the ostensibly unchallengeable authority of the executive, demonstrates the vitality and resourcefulness of the judiciary in keeping strict rein on overzealous officials.

The Armed Forces

The use of armed force in support of the civil power is always a latent possibility in Pakistan. The police themselves are organized and trained on a semimilitary pattern, under the supreme control in each province of an inspector-general of police. The rank and file are recruited into the provincial police service, but most officers are members of the elite Police Service of Pakistan. In the districts, the police, commanded by a superintendent, are under the control of the DC. In cases of riots or similar disturbances armed police can be authorized by the DC or another magistrate to fire upon crowds. Such action is strictly controlled, must be justified by the officer ordering it, and is usually followed by an investigation into the circumstances. If a situation is uncontrollable by the civil authorities, the DC may call in the army to restore order. Occupying a position midway between the regular police and the army are the West Pakistan Rangers and the East Pakistan Rifles, which are responsible for border patrol and antismuggling activities. In the tribal areas, locally raised levies and disciplined units such as the Khyber Rifles combine police with defense functions. Since 1964 a "Mujahid Force" has been created as a sort of home guard, to provide villagers with basic instruction in military procedures and the use of modern weapons.

The Pakistan army is the senior and most important of the regular military services. The navy and air force are of high quality but are relatively small. All three services are still predominantly Punjabi and Pathan in composition, although the air force and navy have a higher proportion (around 30 per cent) of Bengalis than does the army (probably 5 to 10 per cent). Because the British Indian army recruited heavily in the northern areas of modern West Pakistan (and Azad Kashmir), that part of the country inherited a population with a strong tradition of military service. Bengal, on the other hand, was considered "nonmartial" by the British, and the stereotype influences both Bengalis and West Pakistanis even today. Although East Pakistani soldiers distinguished themselves on the West Pakistan front in 1965, Bengali youths normally do not think in terms of a military career. In 1948 an entirely Bengali unit, the Bengal Regiment, was formed, consisting by early 1969 of six battalions with another four to be raised. Recruiting efforts in East Pakistan have been much criticized by Bengali politicians, but the army insists that despite the political outcry suitable volunteers are not forthcoming, particularly educated youth for the officer corps.[12] In 1969 the National Assembly was informed that physical standards had been relaxed to take account of the smaller stature of Bengali youth, and later in the year the martial-law regime announced that recruitment in East Pakistan would be doubled.

The East Pakistani demand for an equitable share in the defense services was sharpened by the feeling of defenselessness experienced in 1965. Military strategy has been to rely on a strong force in West Pakistan to defend East Pakistan's interests by a thrust at Delhi, but this was shown to be completely unsatisfactory from an East Pakistani point of view in 1965. Hence more vehement demands were made for greater mobilization of East Pakistani manpower and the construction of ordnance factories in the province. East Pakistanis have long demanded the transfer of naval headquarters to Chittagong from Karachi, both for symbolic reasons and to counter some of the impact of defense spending concentrated in the army establishments in northern West Pakistan.

In keeping with the British Indian tradition, the military services are completely professional. British influence, in terms of regimental tradition and organization, is strong, but the alliance with the United States beginning in the mid-1950's provided Pakistan with much American equipment and advice, with consequent effects on training patterns. The officer corps is highly westernized and modern, and at the same time almost by definition is one of the most nationally-conscious elements in the society. It has also been a very homogeneous group, drawn predominantly from the land-holding classes of Punjabi and Pathan districts, with close

[12] For example, the debate in the National Assembly on East Pakistani representation in the defense services, on June 22, 1963.

ties to the civil services and to the West Pakistani political class.

The military is in principle nonpolitical, its role being to defend the country under the guidance of the government of the day, whatever its complexion. Still, the first overt challenge to the constitutional system was an abortive plot by a few army officers in 1951, the so-called Rawalpindi conspiracy. Later, the political instability of the mid-1950's forced the army increasingly into the position of providing a continuing stabilizing force. The ineffectiveness of the civil authority contrasted sharply with army efficiency in suppressing the anti-Ahmadi disturbances in West Pakistan in 1953. The following year General Ayub, the commander in chief, supported the governor general's coup in dissolving the Constituent Assembly in the hope that a new start would be made, but he refused the latter's invitation to take over supreme power and only reluctantly served as titular minister of defense in the cabinet of 1954–55.[13] In late 1957 the army and navy were called upon to conduct the short-lived "Operation Closed Door" against smuggling in East Pakistan, and experienced not only the sweet taste of their own effectiveness but also the bitterness of frustration through political intrigue. The imposition of martial law in 1958 was in large part a preventive action on the part of General Ayub and his colleagues to stop the process of political decay before it could undermine the integrity of the army itself.

Having once played an overtly political role, the armed forces will never fully regain their former neutral status. The fear that the military might be contaminated by political power led to its withdrawal from administrative activities in

[13] See Mohammed Ahmad, *My Chief* (Lahore, 1960), pp. i–5.

late 1958, as soon as the martial-law regime was securely established, and officers who assumed political roles were obliged to retire. Even so, the army remained the basis of the strength of the regime, and after 1962, opposition politicians (particularly those from East Pakistan) were openly suspicious of the military elite. The 1962 Constitution sought to minimize nonmilitary considerations in defense matters by requiring that for a period of twenty years the defense minister was to be a retired officer of the rank of lieutenant general or higher, if the President had not held such a rank. President Ayub accordingly retained charge of the ministry until October 1966, when he assigned it to the retiring commander in chief of the navy, perhaps to strengthen his links with that service. The 1965 war both increased the prestige of the services and made them more controversial by giving renewed political emphasis to national military policy in regard to East Pakistan. The so-called Agartala conspiracy of 1968, in which Bengali military and civil personnel were implicated in an alleged separatist plot, tended to pit the prestige of the service commands against the East Pakistani critics of the Ayub constitutional system. In late 1968, however, several retired officers, most notably the former commander in chief of the air force, gave their support to the campaign for constitutional change.

The initiative for the reimposition of martial law in 1969 apparently came from President Ayub. The military commanders remained carefully out of the political controversy of 1968–69, except for the supply of forces to support the civil power against rioting when the anti-Ayub campaign gained in intensity, but the political possibility of military intervention was common talk. Some allegations appeared from opposition sources to the effect that the government itself was encouraging the disorder of February and March in order to justify a return to martial law. It appears, however, that President Ayub made every effort to reach a constitutional solution, until at last he became convinced that "all civil administrative and constitutional authority in the country has become ineffective" and that Pakistan's survival as a state was jeopardized; "I am left with no option but to step aside and leave it to the defence forces of Pakistan which today represents the only effective and legal instrument, to take over full control of the affairs of this country." [14] In so doing, Ayub again placed the destiny of Pakistan in the hands of a power structure in which East Pakistan had little share, but the army commander in chief, General A. M. Yahya Khan, had no alternative but to assume power "to bring back sanity." Although General Yahya asserted that they had "no political ambitions," he recognized that by default the armed forces of Pakistan had once more been vested with responsibility for the "creation of conditions conducive to the establishment of a constitutional government." [15]

Basic Democracy

The system of Basic Democracies is an institutional innovation that Ayub hoped would be the basis of a stable Pakistani constitutional government. The "Basic Democracy" properly speaking is the union council, consisting of about ten to twelve elected members exercising local government functions in a jurisdiction comprising about 10,000–12,000 people. Unions are grouped under councils in each

[14] President Ayub Khan's letter to General Yahya Khan, dated March 24, 1969, in *Pakistan Times*, March 26, 1969.

[15] Address to the nation by General A. M. Yahya Khan on March 26, 1969, in *Pakistan Times*, March 27, 1969.

tehsil (in West Pakistan) or thana (in East Pakistan) as co-ordinating bodies. Matters of broader interest are dealt with in councils at the district and divisional levels. These councils were first established after general elections in December 1959 and January 1960, under the terms of the Basic Democracies Order of October 27, 1959. They were designed both to replace the former miscellany of local government bodies by a uniform and integrated pattern of institutions throughout Pakistan, and to associate public representatives with the administration at all important levels. In the absence of political parties under martial law, the Basic Democracy hierarchy was intended to link the people with the government, providing a channel for the expression of grievances and a means for social and political mobilization.

Political and constitutional developments between 1960 and 1965 produced broad changes in the role and structure of the Basic Democracies. They were originally envisioned as nonpolitical and locally oriented, so that community responsibility could develop free of the extraneous influences that had exploited and corrupted the previous union and district boards and municipalities. The transformation of local councilors into electors for the President and members of Assemblies under the 1962 Constitution compromised their local orientation, and the revival of political parties rang the death knell for nonpartisanship in the unions. The original scheme provided for varying proportions of appointed nonofficial members in councils at all levels, in order to ensure the representation of interests such as minorities or women, or to make special local talent available to the council. Dislike of appointment was widespread, and the power was used cautiously; in 1962 the law was amended to eliminate appointments at all levels and to provide a system of indirect elections for the nonofficial membership of the district and divisional councils.

Under these arrangements all councils have been politically affected even if not politically organized. The union councils (4,032 in East Pakistan and 3,414 in West Pakistan), made up of councilors returned by adult suffrage, each elect a chairman who is ex officio a member of the tehsil or thana council. In small urban areas the equivalent of the union council is the town committee (222 in West Pakistan, 38 in East Pakistan), and larger urban areas include a number of union committees (810 and 216 respectively) whose elected chairmen along with official members comprise the municipal committee (or municipal corporation, in Karachi and Lahore) under an official chairman and elected vice-chairman. In 1965 provision was made for the election by each urban body of special representatives for women, minorities, and labor–social welfare, in the proportion of one additional representative to ten ordinary members; in 1968 this provision was extended to district and divisional councils as well. The chairmen of union councils, union committees, and town committees within the district elect the nonofficial members of the district council, and the elected members of the district councils and of the municipal committees within the division elect the nonofficial members of the divisional council. Depending on population, there are between thirty and sixty elected members in both district and divisional councils. Simultaneous membership in a district and a divisional council is not permitted. The "Basic Democrats" elected in October–November 1964, having fulfilled their electoral function, were installed as union councilors in East Pakistan in August 1965 and in West Pakistan (after a delay because of the war emergency) in January 1966. The higher councils were then elected in West Pakistan during spring 1966, but in East Pakistan legal proceedings delayed elections until October. In the West Pakistan tribal areas there are 112 union councils and 15 agency councils, established by the political agent without formal elections.

Local government in the conventional sense is primarily the concern of the union councils and of the town and municipal committees. These bodies have taxing powers and definite responsibilities for local amenities and services. The district council can also tax, and is responsible for matters of more than local significance, such as public health, water supply, and rural roads and bridges. Unions also have administrative duties in connection with agricultural and community development and the preservation of law and order. An increasingly important responsibility of the union council is the implementation of the rural public works program, which was initiated as a province-wide activity in East Pakistan in 1962–63 and in West Pakistan in 1963–64. This program has for the first time brought significant funds to the rural areas, to be utilized in labor-intensive road building, irrigation, and reclamation, and simple construction projects. The rural public works program was instrumental in vitalizing the unions and, by making council membership important and desirable, heightening popular interest and involvement in the 1964 elections.

The higher councils all have official chairmen and include official members (not more than half the total) representing government departments at that level. The commissioner presides over the divisional council, which provides a useful forum for keeping officials and public representatives alike informed about departmental activities. In East Pakistan it has yet to become a vital institution for the expression of regional interests, although it seems more successful in that regard in West Pakistan. The district council, under the DC and an elected vice-chairman, is much more important, with definite statutory responsibilities and a large budget and staff with which to implement them. Below the district, the tehsil council under the tehsildar or the thana council under the subdivisional officer was given a statutory coordinative role without definite powers. In East Pakistan the rural works program has given the thana council unexpected significance. Under the *de facto* chairmanship of the circle officer the thana council has proved to be an effective agency for the coordination and direction of development programs in its dozen or so unions. As the experimental intensive development program begun at the Pakistan Academy for Rural Development, Comilla, spreads throughout the province, the thana council will increasingly emerge as the key unit in the rural council structure.

An unusual feature of the Basic Democracy system has been the continuing emphasis on training and consultation. Since the new institutions were expected to make possible a political, social, and economic renaissance in the countryside, every effort was made in 1960 and again in 1965–66 to smooth the way. An extensive training program sought to orient all those concerned—officials as well as elected members—to the objectives and functions of the Basic Democracies, the organization of the "nation-building" departments of government, the purposes of economic planning (with special reference to the Five Year Plans), and the significance of the rural development program. Since the completion of the initial training, there have been periodic district, divisional, and provincial conventions to permit further discussion of progress and problems, to recommend changes, and to hear messages of encouragement from senior officials, ministers, the governor or the President. Repeated high-level statements and admonitions have reminded officialdom of the importance of the system and the need both to encourage local initiative and to abstain from any sort of pressures on the councilors. The regular meetings of the councils also provide training of a sort, familiarizing the members with the problems of government and acquainting them with the rudiments of parliamentary procedure.

The success of the union councils as institutions of local government has been largely dependent on the character of the leadership they secure. With leadership that is too strong they are unlikely to be democratic, but without strong leadership unions are likely to atrophy, particularly if faced with an indifferent or hostile tehsildar or circle officer. The greater financial resources available to the unions, including the rural works program funds, increased local interest in the councils and made them characteristically the objects of struggle between rival factions. Most councilors are literate (99 per cent in East Pakistan in 1965, and probably around 80 per cent in West Pakistan), and the chairmen are generally among the more prosperous in the community. Unfortunately, one consequence of the regular association of the Basic Democrats with officialdom and the constant attention to and flattery of them by the Ayub government was their development of a castelike sense of self-importance. This was manifested in demands for various kinds of special privileges for chairmen or members generally, which attenuated the sense of neighborly responsibility that was supposed to motivate the entire system. Some councilors apparently also used their positions blatantly for their own enrichment. That antipathies did develop between councilors and public was tragically evident in early 1969 when in a sort of *jacquerie* in parts of East Pakistan unpopular Basic Democrats were attacked, their property was destroyed, and in some instances they and their families were killed. The result of such attacks and of the widespread political condemnation of the councils because of the elite electoral role of the councilors under the 1962 Constitution was the near collapse of the system and a decision by the East Pakistan government after the imposition of martial law to take the council structure under study.

From its inception the Basic Democracy structure was criticized for the very faults it had been introduced to alleviate, namely its involvement in national politics and consequent exploitation for purposes other than local government. There was little real quarrel with the local self-government or administrative coordination functions of the various councils, although the originality of the system was denied. There had been, after all, union boards in Bengal since 1919 and district boards in most parts of the country since the 1880's; only the tehsil-thana and divisional councils, and the articulated nature of the system, could be considered innovations. Political spokesmen firmly objected to the large official role in the councils, particularly to official presiding officers of municipal and district councils where previously there had been elected mayors and chairmen. Given the prestige and authority of commissioners and DC's and even of their subordinates, the attitude of the official chairman makes the difference between vigor and passivity in the council concerned. Even so, the frequent charge that official members constitute a bloc with some kind of official "party line" to impose on nonofficial members seems exaggerated. On the whole, the combination of officials and nonofficials has provided a link between representative institutions and the district and divisional administrative structure that will continue to be desirable so long as that structure remains unchanged.

The constitutional arrangements that emerge from martial law are likely to confirm the council system for purposes of local government and administrative coordination. Local government functions must be carried out, and the councils are sensible units and generally have been at least as effective as the institutions they replaced. It is probable that direct election to the district councils and to the municipalities will be restored, and official membership will be confined to a definite minority if not to an advisory capacity. Whether divisional councils will be retained is more questionable. Granted that there has been some corruption of councilors and some manipulation by officials, the union council system has been successful in articulating rural interests independently of the urban political class, and in politicizing the remotest corners of the country. It did not satisfy the urban population, who were successful in making the Basic Democrats the scapegoats for the general ills and grievances of the society. Although the result was the collapse of the constitutional order based on the Basic Democracy structure, the councils themselves have survived except in a few areas in East Pakistan. In the nonpolitical context of martial law, the councils, the administration, and the judiciary continue to function, while solutions are being sought to the problem of the organization and distribution of political power.

5. Institutional Experimentation

The elaboration of an appropriate institutional distribution of political power in the Islamic constitutional order has continuously engaged the attention of the Pakistani political community. The pattern of executive and legislative institutions and of central-provincial relations has been the subject of constant experimentation and adjustment. Essentially there has been a struggle between partially conflicting traditions derived from British ideals and British Indian practice, with some supplementary appeals to Islamic tradition. The ideal of parliamentary democracy—collegial government by ministers drawn from a technically unlimited "sovereign" parliament in a unitary state—derives from Britain. From the British Indian past Pakistan draws the tradition of constitutionally limited institutions, with an independent and authoritarian single executive and a relatively weak legislature, in a pseudo-federal but ultimately centrally controlled state. Despite differing features, both these traditions exalt the executive over the legislature and emphasize central rather than local power.

Parliamentary democracy was engrafted onto the British Indian viceregal tradition in 1947 in the interim constitutional order defined by the Government of India Act of 1935 and the Independence Act of 1947. The result was a curious amalgam of federal, unitary, parliamentary, and viceregal principles. The effort in the 1956 Constitution to legitimize parliamentary democracy and federalism and to counter the evident strength of the unitary and viceregal traditions was unsuccessful for two reasons. First, the Constitution perpetuated the confusion over the ultimate locus of executive authority, and, second, it did not prevent the political erosion of the federal distinction between center and provinces. In 1958 the martial-law regime attempted to re-establish unity of authority by returning to the viceregal tradition in a presidential and nonfederal system. The 1962 Constitution confirmed the abandonment of parliamentary federalism, providing an independent executive and unlimited central powers. This decision was the result, according to President Ayub Khan, of "mature and honest assessment of the lessons of our past, the experience of the last 3½ years and the requirements of the future." [1] It was an attempt to respond to the experience of political instability under the parliamentary system by emphasizing authority and unity. Ayub believed that the Constitution embodied "a blending of democracy with discipline, the true prerequisite to running a free society with stable government and sound administration." In fact, authority and discipline seemed to smother the sense of democratic participation. The resulting frustration contributed to the collapse of the presidential system in 1969, ushering in another martial-law regime and foreshadowing further constitutional adjustments.

[1] President Ayub's speech in promulgating the Constitution, March 1, 1962 (*Pakistan Times,* March 2, 1962). The next quotation in the text is also from this source.

The Central Government

THE EXECUTIVE

From independence until October 1958 constitutional arrangements in Pakistan, following the British parliamentary tradition, envisioned a purely titular role for the head of state. Prior to March 23, 1956, this office was held by a governor general appointed by the queen on the advice of the prime minister of Pakistan. The republican Constitution of 1956 replaced the governor general with a President, to be elected by the members of the National and Provincial Assemblies. Effective executive powers were to be exercised by the prime minister, while the head of state, in whom power was formally vested, was to reign but not to rule. The prime minister was to govern with the aid of ministerial colleagues drawn from and responsible to the Assembly, the cabinet controlling through its parliamentary majority the powers of the legislature as well as the executive. These relationships, implicit in the modified Government of India Act of 1935, were spelled out in the Constitution of 1956 in articles limiting the discretion of the President to the dismissal of the prime minister if he were satisfied that the latter "does not command the confidence" of a legislative majority.

Pakistan completely lacked the political and constitutional tradition necessary to support an executive who would be responsible to parliament. Under the Government of India Act of 1919, which defined the central government until independence, the governor general of British India was a strong and independent executive, governing with the assistance of councilors responsible to him rather than to the legislature. Even the 1935 Act, in anticipating a federal council of ministers drawn from the legislature, carefully retained special powers for the governor general. When this Act was adapted in 1947 to serve as the interim constitution of Pakistan, all specific references to discretion, individual judgment, and special responsibilities were eliminated, but the basic pattern of the document remained unchanged. It was quite possible to assume, on reading the amended 1935 Act, that the governor general of Pakistan was, like his viceregal predecessors, to be the functioning head of the administration. Finally, so long as Pakistan retained the monarchical constitution, the governor general was vested with the indeterminate prerogative powers of the Crown.

The viceregal background was reinforced by personality considerations. The first governor general, Qaid-i-Azam Mohammed Ali Jinnah, brought to the office his tremendous prestige as "Father of the Nation." So long as he lived, Jinnah was, whether he wished to be or not, the real head of the central government, presiding—while his health permitted—over cabinet meetings and obliged by his ministers to make top-level decisions. The Qaid-i-Azam's immediate successor, Khwaja Nazimuddin (1948–1951), a leading Bengali politician, was content to conform to the conventional image of the dominion governor general, leaving political leadership to Prime Minister Liaqat Ali Khan (1947–1951). Governor Generals Ghulam Mohammad (1951–1955) and Iskander Mirza (1955–1958), on the other hand, were both professional administrators who followed Jinnah's example in regarding their office to have active responsibilities. Ghulam Mohammad dismissed Prime Minister Nazimuddin (1951–1953) in April 1953 and appointed Mohammed Ali of Bogra (1953–1955) in his stead without significant political challenge, and eighteen months later invoked the inherent powers of the Crown to dissolve the Constituent Assembly and reorganize Mohammed Ali's cabinet. Iskander Mirza as governor general and for his first few months as provisional president was checked by Prime Minister Chaudhri Muhammad Ali (1955–1956), another former professional administrator, but made no secret of his impatience with politicians and his conviction that the executive should be independent of legislative majorities.

During the thirty months following the promulgation of the republican Constitution on March 23, 1956, viceregal tradition gradually outweighed the limitations on the President embodied in its letter and spirit. The result was the increasing involvement of President Mirza in the making and unmaking of the cabinets of Prime Ministers H. S. Suhrawardy (1956–57), I. I. Chundrigar (October–December 1957), and Malik Feroz Khan Noon (1957–58), culminating in his dismissal of the latter, abrogation of the Constitution, and proclamation of martial law on October 7, 1958. Three weeks later Mirza was forced to resign and was succeeded by General Mohammad Ayub Khan (President, 1958–1969), the then commander in chief of the army and Chief Martial Law Administrator. The confusion of authority in the dual executive was then terminated with the formal abolition of the office of prime minister. Ministers thereafter were appointed to advise the President in the discharge of his functions and were responsible solely to him. This arrangement was roughly comparable to the position of the viceroy and his council before 1946, although the latter always had to deal with a legislature while the martial-law regime did not.

The 1962 Constitution retained the independent presidential executive, for which there was ample precedent in

British Indian practice and in the classic Muslim amirate. The President was required to be a Muslim, thirty-five years of age and qualified for election to the National Assembly, and was elected for a five-year term. The supreme command of the armed forces was vested in him, and the executive authority of the republic was to be exercised by him directly or indirectly. The President was assisted by ministers in charge of cabinet portfolios, who served during his pleasure and were responsible to him alone. Ministerial office was constitutionally incompatible with membership in the National Assembly, but ministers were authorized to attend the Assembly and to speak in order to provide leadership and liaison between the President and the legislature. During the first year of the Constitution the distinction from the parliamentary system was blurred, because President Ayub was prevailed upon in June 1962 to issue an order under the transitional clause of the Constitution (Article 224-3) waiving the incompatibility rule. A majority of the central (and provincial) ministers therefore retained seats in the Assemblies, with an eye to the voting support each could bring to the government. This experiment in quasi parliamentarism was terminated in May 1963 when the Supreme Court ruled that the adaptation was unconstitutional, and ministers then in office forfeited their Assembly seats. Most of President Ayub's subsequent ministerial appointments were made from outside the Assembly; any legislators given cabinet posts automatically ceased to be members of the Assembly concerned. A further link between the President's cabinet and the Assembly was provided by parliamentary secretaries, members of the Assembly appointed to assist ministers (or the President) in legislative business, one for each of the divisions into which the ministries were subdivided. President Ayub retained ministerial responsibility for the cabinet secretariat and the President's secretariat, which were represented in the National Assembly by parliamentary secretaries.

The presidential system made it impossible to apply the principle of parity of participation in the national executive. After Jinnah's death it had been conventionally agreed that the offices of head of state and head of government under the parliamentary system should be shared between East and West Pakistan. This "zonal convention" was strained during the period of cabinet instability from August 1955 to October 1958 while Mirza was head of state, his successive prime ministers including three from West Pakistan and one (Suhrawardy) from East Pakistan; Mirza himself was from an aristocratic West Bengal family but was born in Bombay and was generally identified with West Pakistan. Since parliamentary cabinets normally were formed on the basis of parity, each province was assured a full voice in political decision making, subject of course to party considerations and to the allocation of portfolios. This was not true under the presidential system, for although parity was observed ministers were advisors only and decision making ultimately was vested in one man: President Ayub, who was a Pathan from West Pakistan. There was a symbolic retention of the zonal convention in regard to the Speaker of the National Assembly, who under the Constitution became Acting President in the absence or illness of the incumbent. The hollowness of this provision was demonstrated in early 1968 during President Ayub's serious illness, when Speaker Abdul Jabbar Khan was not permitted to exercise the role constitutionally prescribed for him in that eventuality.

The presidential system was successful in bringing governmental stability and firm direction to policy, in great contrast to the last years of the parliamentary era. It was designed to free the government from the burden of constant concern with the preservation of a parliamentary majority that had exhausted its predecessors, but its very stability made it seem remote and unresponsive to public pressures except when bargaining for the passage of government legislation became necessary. To convinced parliamentarians, a system in which ministers were not responsible to and controllable by the legislature was by definition undemocratic. It meant nothing that they were responsible to an elected President, for in the Pakistani context he inevitably was identified with the authoritarian and irremovable viceroys of the past. Hence the insistence of the opponents of the Ayub Constitution on a return to a parliamentary responsible executive, despite the drawbacks of the latter demonstrated in the disastrous political experience of the 1950's.

The presumably transitional martial-law regime of 1969 retained the presidential executive of the 1962 Constitution "for operational necessities." Full powers were assumed by General Yahya Khan in the capacity of Chief Martial Law Administrator when he proclaimed martial law upon President Ayub's resignation on March 25. On March 31, in order to regularize his role as *de facto* head of state and government, General Yahya assumed the office of President. On April 3 he created a "council of administration" made up of the three Deputy Chief Martial Law Administrators (Lt. General Abdul Hamid Khan, Vice-Admiral S. M. Ahsan, and Air Marshal M. Nur Khan, the three service heads), to coordinate the work of the martial-law and civil administrations. Initially the members of the council performed ministerial functions as well, but in August 1969 a cabinet of civilian ministers (including one retired general, a former ambassador) was appointed. To enable the administration to be carried on normally, President Yahya issued a Provisional Constitution Order on April 4, preserving the distribution of powers and functions under the 1962 Constitution subject to modification by the President and to his overriding powers as Chief Martial Law Administrator under the proclamation of March 25.

THE LEGISLATURE

The central legislature of Pakistan has under all constitutional arrangements consisted of the head of state and a single representative chamber. This unicameral legislative body has inherited the practice and procedure of the old Indian central assembly and, more remotely, of the House of Commons. The Indian parliamentary tradition was one formed by a representative body confronted with an irremovable executive, in contrast to the House of Commons model of a chamber upon whose favor the government's existence depends. After independence the British style was cultivated, in the pretense of legislative supremacy made under the parliamentary constitutions in effect from 1947 to 1958. The 1962 Constitution reverted to the separation of the legislature from the executive familiar before independence. During both periods the Assembly was effectively subordinated to the executive. While the parliamentary system prevailed, the Assembly was controlled, in accordance with British constitutional principles, by the cabinet, and for much of that time the cabinet was dominated by the head of state. Under the 1962 Constitution the Assembly was once more placed in a junior but independent position vis-à-vis a powerful head of state, but became even weaker than before because of its failure to exploit the potentialities inherent in its own constitutional powers.

Before independence, when the central government was not dependent on a legislative majority, it was established that the Speaker should be an impartial chairman on the British model rather than an active politician as in the United States. The ideal continued to prevail from 1947 to 1958, although the presiding officers did not divorce themselves completely from party politics either before or after the adoption of the 1956 Constitution. The Constitution of 1962 provided for the election by the Assembly of a Speaker and two Deputy Speakers, to hold office for the life of the Assembly unless removed by an absolute majority vote. It was an open question whether they could with propriety involve themselves in political controversy in their private capacities as individuals and members of the Assembly, although when in the chair they were expected to be "above party." Basically, Assembly procedures were those of the House of Commons unless specifically altered by rule, and the Speaker followed Commonwealth (including British Indian) precedent in governing the house. The 1962 Constitution, in an effort to strengthen the Speaker's hand, empowered him to refer a case of "gross misconduct" by a member to the Supreme Court; a verdict of guilty would have deprived the member of his seat. Under both the republican constitutions the Speaker occasionally served as Acting President during the President's absences abroad; under the 1962 Constitution he was thus head of the government, which presumably compromised his nonpartisan status in the eyes of the opposition. On these occasions a Deputy Speaker served as Acting Speaker. All of the three Speakers elected under the Constitution were, because of the "zonal convention," East Pakistanis; [2] the successive senior Deputy Speakers were from West Pakistan and the junior Deputy Speakers in turn from East Pakistan. All of these posts were filled by unopposed election in both 1962 and 1965 with the single exception of the senior deputy speakership in 1962.

Under both the parliamentary and presidential systems Assembly business was arranged in the House of Commons fashion between the whips of the government and opposition parties. Most of the time was taken up with official business, only about one day each week being left to private members. The system of standing committees for various departments, dating from before independence, was retained even during the parliamentary years, although the committees were generally neglected and ineffective. After 1962 they were reestablished and showed more life. From 1962 to 1969 there were sixteen such committees, plus committees for rules of procedure and privileges and for unspecified matters, all with three members from each province and the minister and parliamentary secretary for the department concerned. In 1962 and again in 1965 the membership of the committees was settled informally by the party whips (ensuring a majority for the government party) so that elections were unanimous. The rules after 1962 provided for all bills to be referred to the appropriate committee unless dealt with in all stages on the floor of the house, but there was a tendency to

[2] With the exception of Qaid-i-Azam M. A. Jinnah, the first president (mainly titular—he presided only seven or eight times) of the Constituent Assembly, all other Speakers have been East Pakistanis: Tamizuddin Khan (1948–1954), Abdul Wahab Khan (1955–1958), Tamizuddin Khan (re-elected 1962, died 1963), A. K. Fazlul Quader Choudhury (1963–1965), Abdul Jabbar Khan (1965–1969).

suspend the rules and follow the parliamentary-era practice of appointing *ad hoc* select committees including more members. The Public Accounts Committee, recently including ten members under the chairmanship of the finance minister, was originally established in India in 1921 on the British model to review the central government's accounts for any improprieties or illegalities, but was not able to establish a vigorous identity in Pakistan under either parliamentary or presidential circumstances. The usual parliamentary privileges, including freedom of speech and immunity from judicial process in committees and in the Assembly, were guaranteed to members by all constitutions, subject to further elaboration by law.

The Assembly has normally met for at least two sessions each year, for a total of sixty to ninety working days. During the parliamentary years, when the fiscal year began on April 1, there was a budget session in the spring and a second session in the late fall. Under the 1962 Constitution the practice was to have three annual sessions: in midsummer for the budget (the fiscal year having been altered to begin on July 1), in the late fall, and in the spring. The 1956 Constitution required at least one annual session in Dacca, which the 1962 Constitution designated the principal seat of the legislature. Nevertheless, since the headquarters of the central government was in Rawalpindi during the 1960's, the budget session and one other were usually held there. Both the republican constitutions provided that the Assembly should be summoned and prorogued by the President. In addition, to give the Assembly control over its own meetings, the 1962 Constitution provided that a summons could be issued by the Speaker at the request of one-third of the members, and that such a session could not be prorogued by the President.

The normal legislative term has been envisioned as five years, but no Assembly has yet served such a term. The first Constituent Assembly had no fixed term and was dissolved under the governor general's proclamation of emergency after seven years, in 1954; the second, elected in 1955, became the National Assembly under the 1956 Constitution and was dissolved under martial law after three years, in 1958; the National Assembly elected in 1962 served out its special short three-year term and was dissolved in 1965; its successor was dissolved under martial law after less than four years, in 1969.

Table 4. Composition of Assemblies

	East Pakistan		West Pakistan		
Assembly	Muslims	Non-Muslims	Muslims	Non-Muslims	Total
Constituent Assembly, 1947–54	31	13	29	2	75
Constituent/National Assembly, 1955–58	31	9	38	2	80
National Assembly, 1962–69	78 *		78 *		156

* Including three women.

The total membership of the successive central Assemblies has gradually increased, and since 1955 has been on the basis of equal representation of East and West Pakistan. The small size of the two Constituent Assemblies (seventy-five and eighty) from 1947 to 1956 was further reduced and their effectiveness diminished by the practice of appointing members to executive posts such as ambassadorships and governorships, by the duplication of membership between national and provincial legislatures, by the fact that a proportion of the members were central and provincial ministers, and by a general neglect to fill vacancies promptly. All this suggested a contempt for the Assembly by the executive, which is apparently confirmed in that out of some fifty persons given ministerial appointments prior to March 23, 1956, half (including two prime ministers) were not members of the Assembly at the time, and some remained as ministers for well over a year without being elected. This practice ceased in 1956 because, with the holding by members of non-ministerial executive appointments constitutionally forbidden, ministerial appointments had to be conserved for patronage purposes to mobilize parliamentary majorities. Such parliamentary "management," possible in a house of eighty, would have been impossible had there been elections under the 1956 Constitution, which prescribed a house of 300 plus ten separately elected women. The 1962 Constitution compromised on a house of 156, including six women, but sought to preclude the constant scramble for ministerial appointments by the incompatibility rule. By a constitutional amendment of December 1967 the National Assembly was to increase at the 1970 election to a total of 200 regularly elected members, eight women, and a new special category of ten persons of professional or intellectual eminence to be elected by the Assembly itself. The special provision for non-Muslim representation in the two Constituent Assemblies was not continued when election by territorial constituency was introduced in 1962, and no non-Muslims were elected in that year or in 1965.

LEGISLATIVE-EXECUTIVE RELATIONS

The critical distinction between a parliamentary and a presidential system lies in the very different relationships between the executive and the representative body. In both systems there is a formal separation between executive and legislative authority, but the way in which the gap is bridged determines the character of the system. In a parliamentary system executive power is vested in the head of state but is exercised by ministers who hold office because they command the support of a majority in the representative body and hence can obtain from it the finances necessary for the purposes of the government. Ministers combine the powers of the executive with those of the legislature, which is powerless except to overthrow one set of ministers and replace them with another. Legislative procedures are structured to maintain ministerial control, while permitting constant challenge and harassment to keep ministers sensitive to political trends. If the political system cannot sustain majorities, ministries will be unstable and government will become ineffective, since the task of retaining office will eclipse the tasks of governing. In a presidential system executive and legislative powers remain relatively distinct: the executive does not control the representative body, and the latter cannot overthrow the former. The executive is secure in its tenure and can govern, but must bargain to create majorities in the representative body for the necessary legislation and finance. Legislative procedures are structured to enable the representative body to challenge the executive and if necessary to defeat its policies since it cannot defeat the executive itself.

It has already been suggested that after 1962 the general pattern of legislative organization remained that in effect under the parliamentary system. The President's ministers were entitled to sit and speak in the Assembly, and a senior minister was accepted as leader of the house and of the government parliamentary party. A Leader of the Opposition was recognized, although the title was a hollow honor compared with its significance from 1955 to 1958, when its holder was presumptive prime minister. A parliamentary Question Hour on the British pattern, inherited from the preindependence Indian legislature, was a vigorous feature of the parliamentary era that was retained after 1962. Adjournment motions permitted more extensive criticism of the government, but were not even the symbolic threat to it that they had been before 1958.

A major change in parliamentary procedure under the 1962 Constitution dealt with financial matters. Under the parliamentary system, the Assembly's theoretical control over the budget provided the most important occasion for review of ministerial policy and for formal challenges to the cabinet, although no central cabinet was ever defeated on the budget. The Assembly did not at any time exercise any genuine control over appropriations and taxation, for votes were entirely on broader policy matters. The 1962 Constitution, having freed the government from dependence on an Assembly majority, sought to preclude the occurrence of a financial crisis arising from the refusal of the Assembly to pass the budget. The Constitution required the budget (presented by the finance minister in June each year) to distinguish between charged expenditure (salaries of the President, judges, officers of the National Assembly, debt charges, and so forth), recurring and other old expenditures, and new expenditures. The Assembly could debate but not vote on charged expenditures and appropriations under old headings. Appropriations for new expenditures (including increases of more than 10 per cent under old headings) and for proposed expenditures for projects extending over several years required Assembly approval. Such long-term appropriations did not have to be voted again in subsequent years, unless the original amounts were exceeded by more than 10 per cent. Through these rather complex provisions the government was sure of at least the amount of the previous year's budget, whatever its relations with the Assembly, and could confidently plan long-term projects. The negative aspect was that the Assembly was deprived of its major weapon against the government, although its absolute control over any increases in expenditures was not a meaningless power in an age of constantly increasing budgets. Tax measures continued to require Assembly approval, but the retention of the requirement that all money bills and appropriations had to be recommended by the President precluded the sort of fiscal bargaining between legislature and executive characteristic of the American system.

The financial restrictions in the Constitution enraged those brought up in the tradition of the "sovereign" parliament and were among the earliest points of attack on the presidential system. The provisions were a massive sign of distrust of the members of the Assembly, in that President Ayub was afraid to risk a financial deadlock, and in retrospect they must be judged a serious fault in the 1962 Constitution. In 1966 the President agreed in principle to an increase in the fiscal powers of the Assemblies, but no final agreement was reached and no change was made. Even so, the Assembly failed to make use of its existing powers, which would have enabled it to exercise genuine control over the votable portions of the budget had it chosen to do so, in contrast to the total abdication of fiscal powers by Assemblies under the parliamentary system. Instead the Assembly permitted itself to be organized in such a fashion that it was subject to ministerial control and no more capable of forming its own judgments on matters presented to it than previous Assemblies. The powers of the Assembly in financial matters were less than was appropriate to an independent and coequal legislature in a presidential system, but its weakness was more a function of party majorities and party control than an institutional failing.

The myth of the "sovereign" parliament in Pakistan is traceable—apart from the British model—to the Constituent Assembly of 1947–1956. Vested by the Indian Independence Act with the authority to adopt a permanent constitution, the Assembly had unlimited legislative powers, despite the federal character of the interim constitution (the 1935 Act). Until the authoritative constitutional interpretations of the Federal Court in 1955, the Constituent Assembly was even considered "sovereign" in the sense that it was believed that its constitutional bills did not require the assent of the head of state to become law. That belief was struck down, although the Governor-General-in-Parliament was every bit as "sovereign" as the Queen-in-Parliament in Britain and could enact laws on any subject whatever. The enactment of the 1956 Constitution imposed limits on the National Assembly in the form of fundamental rights guarantees, the exclusive provincial list of powers, and special provisions concerning constitutional amendments, but by faulty analogy with the House of Commons it continued to be considered "sovereign" in its supposed power to control the executive. By contrast, the National Assembly under the 1962 Constitution, even after the reintroduction of fundamental rights, was subject to fewer restrictions on its power to make laws, but was considered "powerless" and not "sovereign" because the tenure of the executive was not subject to its support.

By the nature of things the resolution of conflicts between

the executive and the legislature must be more complex in a presidential than in a parliamentary system. Only legislation acceptable to the government can be passed in a parliamentary system, and the assent of the head of state follows as a matter of course. The 1956 Constitution contained provision for the repassage of a bill after the President had withheld assent, but it is difficult to conceive how the situation could have arisen without a change of ministers occurring. Under the 1962 Constitution the President's assent was assumed unless within thirty days it was withheld or the bill returned for alterations. The President's negative could be overridden by a two-thirds majority, except for constitutional amendments which required initial passage by two-thirds and three-fourths to override. A bill repassed despite the President's negative would become law unless within ten days the President called for a referendum or dissolved the Assembly, by either method referring the matter to the electorate. Dissolution, of course, is a possible means of resolving conflicts in a parliamentary system, and the dissolution of the Constituent Assembly in 1954 seems to fit into this category. The referendum device was an innovation of the 1962 Constitution and was never used. Since the result of a referendum might still leave the President and the Assembly at loggerheads, a new election would probably have been preferable. Dissolution was intended to be a serious matter, resorted to only after all other means of reconciliation had failed, since with it the President's own term of office was to end, requiring him to seek re-election as well. It was possible for the Assembly to move the impeachment of the President, in which case he was debarred from resorting to dissolution while the motion was pending. Severe restrictions on impeachment motions—including the unseating of the movers if the resolution received the votes of fewer than half the members—were intended to preclude the frivolous abuse of the procedure. A similar procedure for removal on medical grounds existed but was not invoked during President Ayub's serious illness in 1968. The success of either an impeachment or a medical removal motion would have necessitated an immediate presidential election, pending which the Speaker would have been Acting President.

From British Indian constitutional arrangements Pakistan retained the practice of vesting in the head of state the power to promulgate ordinances with the effect of acts of the central legislature. Such ordinances could be promulgated when the Assembly was dissolved or not in session, and were valid until six months from the date of promulgation or six weeks after the next meeting of the Assembly, whichever period was shorter, unless sooner repealed or disapproved by the Assembly. If approved by the Assembly the ordinance became an act of the central legislature. The relevant provision of the 1962 Constitution was interpreted to mean that the Assembly was limited to approval or disapproval without amendment. Under the 1935 and 1956 constitutions the Assembly had enjoyed the right to amend an ordinance in the process of approving it, so in 1966 the 1962 Constitution was amended to restore that right. The ordinance power has been very extensively used in Pakistan despite repeated promises from successive governments that it would be used sparingly. Both ministers ostensibly responsible to the Assembly and the presidential executive independent of it have found it useful to enact legislation without the embarrassment of debate and then to present the Assembly at some later time with a *fait accompli*.

In case of national emergency the head of state in Pakistan

has under successive constitutions been vested with even greater legislative powers. Under the 1935 and 1956 parliamentary constitutions a proclamation of emergency removed all restrictions on central executive and legislative powers and by implication permitted the latter to be exercised by the head of state (through responsible ministers) by ordinance if the Assembly were not in session. The 1962 Constitution set no limits to central executive and legislative power, but since executive and legislature were no longer interdependent it was thought necessary to permit the President to issue ordinances during an emergency even if the Assembly were in session. The Constitution (Article 30) empowered the President, if he were satisfied that a grave emergency existed "(a) in which Pakistan, or any part of Pakistan, is (or is in imminent danger of being) threatened by war or external aggression; or (b) in which the security or economic life of Pakistan is threatened by internal disturbances beyond the power of a Provincial Government to control," to issue a proclamation of emergency which was to be laid before the National Assembly as soon as practicable. The Assembly, which could be summoned by the Speaker if necessary, had no power to disapprove either the proclamation or ordinances issued under it, but any such ordinance approved by the Assembly became an act of the central legislature. All other emergency ordinances, unless already repealed, were to be automatically repealed with the revocation of the proclamation of emergency. Such an emergency was proclaimed on September 6, 1965, and under it the Defence of Pakistan Ordinance vested the central government with sweeping additional powers to issue rules and regulations affecting many aspects of national life. With the revocation of the proclamation on February 17, 1969, six ordinances were issued to preserve for the central government powers assumed during the emergency over matters such as enemy property, requisition of land, and the supply of essential commodities.

The imposition of martial law and the formal abrogation of the existing constitution on two occasions has perforce resulted in the vesting of all legislative powers in the President, in the absence of a representative body, for the duration of the extraconstitutional regime. During both periods of martial law the President's ordinance power under the abrogated constitution, no longer bound by limits as to duration, has been the normal method of enacting legislation, exercised within the framework of existing institutions and subject to judicial review in this regard. Legislation of extraordinary import, setting aside normal procedures and the rule of law, has been embodied in martial-law regulations and orders issued by or under the authority of the Chief Martial Law Administrator. Among these are, in addition to regulations of the nature of criminal law, regulations such as the West Pakistan Land Reforms Regulation of 1959 and those in 1969 concerning tax evasion, corruption, and illegal foreign exchange, which are not subject to judicial scrutiny except as provided by themselves. Legislation of constitutional import, affecting the administration of the affairs of the state, has been enacted by the President in the form of orders, such as the Laws (Continuance in Force) Order of October 10, 1958, and the Provisional Constitution Order of April 4, 1969, which are issued under the ultimate authority of martial law and determine the jurisdiction of the courts.

The pattern of executive-legislative relations in Pakistan has clearly been one in which the executive has retained the upper hand. Whether under parliamentary or presidential conditions, the legislature has never, since independence, been able to challenge the government successfully. The first Constituent Assembly claimed to be independent of the government but was actually manipulated by it, and on the only occasion that a confrontation occurred the Assembly was swept away by a resort to emergency power. The second Assembly was a vigorous forum of debate but was merely one of several arenas of struggle between rival political forces, both before and after the adoption of the Constitution of 1956, and became so irrelevant to the governmental process that in 1958 it in turn was swept away by martial law. The Constitution of 1962 recognized the need for a representative body but sought to keep it at arm's length from the levers of executive power in order to ensure both executive and legislative stability. Overwhelming government-party majorities, particularly after 1965, made it impossible for the Assembly to function adequately as a check on the executive, although bargaining was necessary for the passage of every major piece of legislation. Deeply engrained parliamentary traditions led members to compromise the constitutional independence of the Assembly and thus to contribute to the failure of the balance of power envisioned in the Constitution.

Provincial Autonomy

The definition of an appropriate relationship between the central government and the provinces has been a dominant theme in constitutional politics in the subcontinent for many years. Devolution of power to the provinces was a stage in the development of self-government during the British period, and a federal demarcation between central and provincial spheres was advanced as a means of minimizing the political consequences of distrust between Hindus and Muslims.

The Government of India Act of 1919 provided for the devolution of certain responsibilities to the provinces, while retaining overriding powers in the hands of the central government. The 1935 Act for the first time attempted to distinguish definite federal and provincial spheres, with a third area of concurrent jurisdiction. To provide for unforeseen contingencies in the transition from a centralized to a federal state, the federal government was empowered to issue directions to the provincial governments in regard to such matters as infectious diseases, the maintenance of strategic communications, and the prevention "of any grave menace to the peace or tranquillity or economic life" of the country, and during an emergency provincial autonomy could be completely suspended. The 1956 Constitution followed the example of the 1935 Act, with modifications in the details of the distribution of powers but the preservation in full of federal powers of direction and emergency control.

The substantive distribution of powers between the center and the provinces was a matter of intense controversy prior to the adoption of the Constitution of 1956. Under the 1935 Act only a few matters remained relatively free of federal legislative control, among them education, local government, land and land tenure, and agriculture. Practically all other matters could be affected by federal action in either the federal or concurrent lists of powers, leaving aside the overriding powers of the central government under the Indian Independence Act. Economic and social grievances in East Pakistan in the early 1950's generated extreme dissatisfaction with this state of affairs, and the Twenty-One Point Programme of the United Front in the provincial election of March 1954 included the demand for "complete regional autonomy according to the Lahore Resolution." In the second Constituent Assembly the Awami League emphasized the entirely different character of the two "countries" of which Pakistan was composed and for which autonomy was sought, and attempted unsuccessfully to limit federal powers to defense, foreign affairs, and currency.[3] The Constitution made some concessions to the autonomy demand by creating several special bodies to provide joint federal-provincial policy control in economic matters but otherwise followed remarkably closely the lists of the 1935 Act, partly to avoid the uncertainties of interpretation if federal powers were to be made in broad grants of defense and foreign affairs. Concurrent powers were extended, but the principal addition to exclusive provincial powers was the control of land and water surface transport, and even this was subject to federal direction in regard to strategic communications.

The 1962 Constitution set aside the problem of reconciling provincial autonomy with central controls by abandoning formal federalism. It provided one exclusive central list of powers, including in general: defense, external affairs, external commerce, planning, fiscal and insurance matters, air and sea navigation, posts and telecommunications, nuclear energy, gas and oil, elections, the Supreme Court and all-Pakistan services, and taxation. All other matters were normally left to the provinces, endowing them with a very large increase in practical autonomy. The center retained power to legislate concerning any matter whatever when the "national interest" so required in relation to "(a) the security of Pakistan, including the economic and financial stability of Pakistan; (b) planning or coordination; or (c) the achievement of uniformity in respect of any matter in different parts

[3] See, for example, the speech of Abul Mansur Ahmad in Constituent Assembly of Pakistan, *Debates*, I, No. 51 (January 16, 1956), p. 1825.

of Pakistan" (Article 131). The effect of this was to eliminate
the previous need for emergency powers to legislate in the
provincial sphere. In case of conflict central law prevailed,
although no law could be challenged as *ultra vires* of the legislature that adopted it.

Provincial executive authority under Pakistani constitutional law extends to all matters not covered by the exclusive
central list. Under the 1962 Constitution exceptions could
be specified by central law, a device analogous to the executive directions by the central government permissible under
laws in the concurrent lists of former constitutions. In 1962
institutions and programs no longer included in the central
sphere were transferred to the provinces, the most notable
being the railways and the bifurcated Pakistan Industrial
Development Corporation. Further executive responsibilities within the central sphere could be delegated to the provinces provided that the center paid the costs involved. The
1962 Constitution did not provide special powers to the central government to issue directions, since the governors were
subject at all times to the President's executive control.
These normal overriding powers ensured that if need be the
national government could step in without having to invoke
a state of emergency or a suspension of the Constitution in a
province, as had been so frequently the case before 1958
under Section 92A of the 1935 Act and Article 193 of the
1956 Constitution. After 1958, coordination between central
and provincial authorities was assured by the institution of
the governors' conference, a periodic meeting attended by
the President, governors, ministers, and senior officials, at
which high-level policy decisions were made. This body continued to function under martial law in 1969.

Adequate finance is essential for effective political autonomy, whatever the constitutional terms may be. The financial arrangements under the 1962 Constitution did not depart very far from the principles laid down in 1935 and 1956, but as implemented they provided greater financial resources for the provinces. The most important tax sources were assigned to the center: customs, excises (except alcohol and narcotics), corporation and income taxes, estate and succession duties, sales taxes, terminal and transit fees, taxes on oil, gas, and nuclear energy. The remaining tax sources were left to the provinces: land revenue, agricultural income tax, stamp duties, excises on alcohol and narcotics, and taxes on professions (subject to maxima set by central law); the provinces could not impose taxes restricting interprovincial trade. Because their independent tax sources were so inelastic, the provinces were constitutionally entitled to a share in certain central tax proceeds, on principles to be established periodically by a Finance Commission.

The National Finance Commission prescribed in the 1962 Constitution had its antecedents in the Constitution of 1956, the Indian Constitution of 1950, and the provisions of the 1935 Act regarding the allocation of resources. The Commission, to be constituted by the President at least fifteen months before the end of each five-year plan period, was to include the central and provincial finance ministers and such others—presumably on the basis of provincial parity—as the President might appoint after consulting the governors. Its primary function was to make recommendations for the distribution of shared taxes and to lay down principles governing the making of grants-in-aid by the center to the provinces and the exercise of borrowing powers by all three governments.

The allocation of shared taxes was prescribed originally in

Pakistan by an award by Sir Jeremy Raisman in 1952 (replacing the Niemeyer Award of 1936).[4] The Raisman terms slightly favored West Pakistan, and were superseded in 1962 by the recommendations of a commission appointed in December 1961. These provided that 50 per cent of income and corporation tax receipts and 60 per cent (previously 50 per cent) of sales taxes and excises on tea, betel, and tobacco constituted a pool to be divided between the provinces, while 100 per cent of the export duties on jute and cotton (previously 62.5 per cent of jute duties to East Pakistan alone) were assigned to the province of collection. The sales tax share was divided 70 per cent on the basis of population and 30 per cent on incidence, and the remainder of the pool on the basis of population (i.e., 54–46 in favor of East Pakistan). The result in the first year (1962–63) was the increase of East Pakistan's share from Rs 17.80 crores to Rs 36.06 crores, and West Pakistan's share from Rs 26.66 crores to Rs 34.76 crores. In 1964–65 the allocation was reviewed by the National Finance Commission and modified to provide a uniform provincial share of 65 per cent under all heads, the allocation between the provinces being made as before except that export duties were included in the 54–46 divisible pool. This seems to have been intended to increase the emphasis in the provincial share on the more elastic income and sales tax revenues, which are bound to increase rapidly as industrialization proceeds. These allocations should be reviewed again by a commission in 1969–70.

The Finance Commission's allocations were designed to transfer resources from West Pakistan to East Pakistan to compensate for the economic imbalance between the two

[4] Successive revenue awards are described in Ministry of Finance, *Economy of Pakistan 1948–68* (Islamabad, 1968), pp. 181–189.

zones, which has been the basis for demands for greater autonomy for East Pakistan. East Pakistan's relative poverty is indicated by the gap between her total revenues and those of West Pakistan, although proportionately the difference is not as great as it once was (see Table 5). Especially striking is the large proportion of East Pakistan's revenues contributed by her share of central taxes; the inelasticity of provincial tax sources generally is suggested by the gradual increase in the central contribution in both provinces. Central taxes are collected in overwhelming proportion in West Pakistan: according to a statement in the National Assembly in 1968, collections of central taxes in East Pakistan were only 15 per cent of the total in 1965–66, 17 per cent in 1966–67, and 18 per cent in 1967–68.[5] This is appropriate in terms of the differences in per capita income between the two zones and the higher cost of living in East Pakistan. In West Pakistan per capita income was Rs 366 in 1959–60, increasing to Rs 463 in 1966–67; the corresponding figures for East Pakistan were Rs 278 and Rs 313—an increase of some 26 per cent in West Pakistan and only slightly more than 12 per cent in East Pakistan.[6] The National Finance Commission was constitutionally obligated to report to the President six months before the end of each plan period on the progress—if any—made in removing disparities in per capita income, and to make recommendations concerning further measures to be taken under the next plan. The Commission's report and recommendations were supplied to the National Economic Council to aid it in the formulation of plans. The continued increase in disparities, despite constitutional obli-

[5] Khan Abdus Sobur Khan, minister of communications, in the National Assembly on June 21, 1968 (*Dawn,* June 22, 1968).

[6] *Dawn,* June 22, 1968.

gations and planning efforts, caused increased political resentment in East Pakistan, but it also underlined the need for continued and greater transfer of resources from West Pakistan. The contention that the adverse trend can be halted only through complete control by East Pakistan of its own economy, including trade policy and foreign exchange, seems ill-founded, particularly since East Pakistan's proportionate foreign-exchange earnings have now declined to less than half of Pakistan's total.

Table 5. Provincial revenues

Province	1950–51	1958–59	1962–63	1966–67
East Pakistan				
Total revenue *	18.20	52.28	74.52	124.70
Proportion from shared central revenues	36.7%	32.8%	49.5%	52.7%
West Pakistan				
Total revenue *	35.98	88.09	134.93	177.56
Proportion from shared central revenues	16.6%	22.1%	26.23%	35.75%

Source: Economic Adviser to the Government of Pakistan, *Pakistan Economic Survey, 1966–67* (Rawalpindi, Ministry of Finance, n.d.), Tables 44–47.

* In crores of rupees (one crore = 10,000,000).

THE PROVINCIAL EXECUTIVE

The role of the provincial governor, like that of the President, was transformed in 1958, in law if not in fact. Under the federal arrangements of the 1935 Act and the 1956 Constitution, the governor was a formal head of state and normally was expected to act on the advice of ministers responsible to the Provincial Assembly. If a situation arose in which normal procedures could not be followed, the central government retained powers under first Section 92A of the 1935 Act and later Article 193 of the 1956 Constitution to suspend parliamentary government in a province. On these occasions the governor acted as sole executive, subject to the direction of the center. In East Pakistan governor's rule was in effect from May 1954 to June 1955, for brief periods in May and August 1956 to surmount politically induced budget difficulties, and again for two months in the summer of 1958. In West Pakistan, governor's rule was in effect in Punjab from January 1949 to April 1951, in Sind from December 1951 to May 1953, and in the integrated province from March to July 1957. The North-West Frontier Province was the only province not to experience governor's rule at one time or another: even the princely state of Bahawalpur suffered the suspension of its constitution from November 1954 until the integration of West Pakistan.

The relations between the governor and his ministers during the parliamentary era were further complicated by central intervention in the cabinet-making process through both constitutional and party channels. The governor was appointed by the central government for an indefinite term and could be replaced at any time if he proved unwilling to comply with central directions, formal or informal. Between August 15, 1947, and the imposition of martial law on October 7, 1958, twenty different governors held office in the various western provinces, and eleven in East Pakistan. The extent of the manipulation of responsible government in West Pakistan prior to integration is indicated by the fact that on seven of the twelve occasions when a new premier took office in one of the provinces he was not at the time a member of the Provincial Assembly, and on only three occasions, at most, had the previous premier left office voluntarily. During the integration period (1954–55) the governors of each of the provinces in West Pakistan dismissed a premier at central direction. From 1955 to 1958 the balance of political forces in both East and West Pakistan was so close that the ruling central coalition of the day did not hesitate to attempt to use the governors in support of their provincial allies. The principle of ministerial responsibility was therefore seriously compromised in the provinces before it was terminated by martial law.

After 1958 the governor was constitutionally an independent executive, appointed by and responsible to the President alone and serving at his pleasure. Under the 1962 Constitution the governor was subject to the President's direction at all times, and accordingly there was no need for special powers of central intervention in provincial affairs analogous to Section 92A or Article 193. During the period when the executive power in the province was exercised under normal conditions by responsible ministers, it was possible and even appropriate for the governor to be a civil servant or other nonpolitical personality. Nevertheless fully half of the persons appointed to governorships before 1958 were politicians with continuing partisan loyalties. Under the 1962 Constitution it was appropriate that the governor share the political views of the President and be a person of political influence in his province. The latter consideration was emphasized in the resignation of Ghulam Faruque, a lifetime public servant, from the governorship of East Pakistan in October 1962 on the ground that he lacked the necessary skills to mobilize and maintain substantial political support for the government. Accordingly he was succeeded by an active politician, Abdul Monem Khan, a loyal and shrewd if unpopular political boss. In West Pakistan Nawab Amir Mohammad Khan of Kalabagh, an old-school Punjab landlord who served an unprecedented six years as governor, declared repeatedly that he was a government servant and hence obligated to steer clear of party controversies and to leave such matters to his ministers. In September 1966 he was replaced by Mohammed Musa, the retiring commander in chief of the army, in circumstances suggesting that the President had concluded that the Nawab was too autocratic and out of touch with political currents. In late March 1969, in connection with his concessions to the opposition in regard to constitutional change, President Ayub replaced Musa and Monem Khan with more politically acceptable figures (Yusuf Haroon, a Karachi businessman and politician, and Dr. M. N. Huda, an economics professor and until then East Pakistan's finance minister), but they had scarcely taken office when President Ayub's resignation and the imposition of martial law terminated their tenure.

In both provinces a primary consideration in the selection of ministers has always been the balancing of regions and interests. From 1955 to 1958 this was further complicated by party coalition factors. In West Pakistan there has usually been one woman minister, and in East Pakistan one non-Muslim (in recent years a Buddhist). Under the 1962 Constitution the rules concerning the qualifications and tenure of provincial ministers and parliamentary secretaries were the same, *mutatis mutandis,* as those applying to their counterparts at the center. In addition, because of the President's ultimate responsibility for provincial affairs, the governor was obliged to obtain his concurrence in the appointment and removal of ministers. Constitutionally, all ministers and parliamentary secretaries were to leave office with the governor who appointed them, to leave his successor free to construct a new team, but in fact cabinet changes ordinarily occurred after elections rather than at the time of a gubernatorial appointment.

After the proclamation of martial law, complete authority in the provinces was vested at first in Martial Law Administrators, the commanding generals in each zone. The governors and ministers ceased to hold office, and the Martial Law Administrators were directed to perform the functions and exercise the powers of the governors under the 1962 Constitution and any other laws. A distinct departure from the practice of 1958–1962, when there was always a separate governor and Martial Law Administrator in each province, this proved to be a transitional arrangement. On August 15, 1969, Air Marshal M. Nur Khan and Vice Admiral S. M. Ahsan, members of the President's council of administration, were appointed governors of West and East Pakistan. Subject to the direction of the President, the provincial government under martial law is carried out by the governor through the official secretaries to government, in cooperation with the Martial Law Administrator. The latter is empowered to legislate by means of martial-law regulations, but ordinary legislation is enacted by means of the governor's ordinance power. Under the 1962 Constitution (and previous constitutions) this was analogous in all respects to the ordinance power of the President, and with the dissolution of the Provincial Assembly it became the normal means of legislation, subject to no time limits.

THE PROVINCIAL LEGISLATURE

The legislatures of East Pakistan and West Pakistan were the heirs of the parliamentary tradition respectively of Calcutta and Lahore, dating from the introduction of ministerial government in 1921 if not from an earlier time. The Bengal legislature had been bicameral, but after independence the style in Pakistan, in the provinces as at the center, was a legislature consisting of one chamber and the head of state. Under successive constitutions the provisions in regard to Assembly meetings, organization, and function and the privileges of members have in the provinces been generally the same as those for the National Assembly. The Speaker and Deputy Speakers have had the same status and responsibilities, and Assembly procedure and practice in regard to official and private members' business, standing and select committees (including a Public Accounts Committee), Question Hour, and adjournment motions, has paralleled National Assembly practice, with minor exceptions for local tradition.

The size of the Provincial Assemblies has fluctuated, although under the parity agreement the 1956 and 1962 Constitutions provided that the National and Provincial Assemblies should all be of the same strength. After the provincial general election in 1954 the East Pakistan Assembly included 309 members, 12 of them women; 69 regular seats and 3 women's seats were filled by non-Muslim electorates. In early 1956 an Assembly was elected indirectly for the new united West Pakistan province by members of the legislatures of the integrating units and of other bodies. The total membership was 310, with the reservation of 10 seats for women and 10 for non-Muslims since separate electorates were not practicable. In order to weight the representation of the non-Punjabi areas, the representation of the former Punjab in the Provincial Assembly was limited to 40 per cent of the total until 1970. The Constitution of 1956 confirmed this limitation on Punjabi representation and prescribed a strength of 310, including 10 separately elected women, for all three Assemblies. These Assemblies were never elected, the East Pakistan Assembly of 1954 and the West Pakistan Assembly of 1956 continuing to function until dissolved under martial law in 1958. The 1962 Constitution reduced the prescribed strength of the Assemblies to 155, including 5 women elected by the regular members, and retained the limitation in West Pakistan on Punjabi representation. There were no reservations for non-Muslims, but a few were elected in East Pakistan. In 1967, in anticipation of the scheduled general election of 1970, the Constitution was amended to increase the strength of all three Assemblies to 200 regular members, 8 women and 10 "eminent persons." This made it possible to restore proportionate representation in the West Pakistan Assembly to the Punjabi area without reducing the number of members from the outlying regions.

The parliamentary collapse in the provinces between 1955 and 1958 was largely attributable to the cumulative effects of the manipulation of parliamentary government by the central authorities after independence. The governor and the premier were active rivals for political ascendancy, and very close political divisions encouraged a scramble for ministerial office among members of the Provincial Assemblies no different from that in the National Assembly. In general, parliamentary proceedings were more turbulent in the provinces than in the National Assembly. In both provinces the ministries evaded summoning the Assemblies for long periods while attempts were made to construct majorities, and in both the Speakers became embroiled in political controversy. In East Pakistan in September 1958 the Speaker was the focus of a conflict with the provincial cabinet over the disqualifications of members and was removed from the chair by dubious procedures, and the Deputy Speaker died after receiving an injury in a violent scene. It was this incident that seems to have precipitated the imposition of martial law in 1958.

Under the presidential Constitution the Provincial Assemblies were theoretically freed from executive control, but like the National Assembly they failed to organize successfully as independent bodies. In East Pakistan in August 1962 a session was summoned by the Speaker on the requisition of members and an abortive effort was made—in part building on the inappropriate attempts of the Speaker of 1955–1958—to assert the independent status of the Assembly under the 1962 Constitution. There was no parallel in West Pakistan. In both provinces the ministers, responsible to the governor and through him to the President, were permitted to assume leading roles during the year (1962–63) when most ministers were members of the Assemblies. The Assemblies functioned successfully and adequately, in the basic sense of legislating, questioning, and challenging the government, but did not depart from the pattern set by their predecessors. Legislative and financial procedures were the same as in the National Assembly, with provision for the referral to the President and National Assembly of conflicts over the refusal of the Assembly to pass or the refusal of the governor to assent to bills. Although conflict and disorder were not uncommon, large government majorities precluded the need for such a referral, which in any case was not very satisfactory from the point of view of provincial autonomy. Still, the final solution envisioned, if the National Assembly and the President were to back the governor in a dispute, was dissolution and referral to the electorate. If a new Assembly hostile to the governor and hence to the President were elected, the latter would have been obliged to change both governor and policy.

The extent of provincial autonomy has been consistently dependent more on policy than on formal constitutional prescriptions. Until the enforcement of the 1956 Constitution, the powers of the central government were unlimited, and even under that Constitution the formal central powers of supervision and direction, taken with the informal party interrelationships, rendered the federal distinctions practically meaningless. The 1962 Constitution was forthright in its recognition of overriding central powers, including the subordination of the governors to the President's policy, but through the device of the governors' conference that policy was framed in consultation with key members of the provincial executive. This cooperative pseudo federalism offered, institutionally at least, ample opportunity for provincial views to be expressed and evaluated and to influence national policy to recognize provincial needs. These needs, under the Constitution, should have been expressed by the Provincial Assembly as the sounding board of public opinion. To the degree that the Assembly, like its counterpart at the center, failed to do so effectively and to enforce a degree of sensitive responsibility on the part of the government, the fault lay in the realm of politics, or at most in the electoral system upon which public representation was based.

Elections

Aspects of the electoral system have been the subject of intense controversy throughout the independent existence of Pakistan. In any political system the nature of the electoral process determines the scope and meaning of participation by the public in their government. In Pakistan the main concerns have been the definition of the electorate and the extent of the legislative franchise. The former includes the question of separate electorates (discussed in Chapter 3), debate over which recurred periodically in connection with preparations for the first adult suffrage elections of Provincial Assemblies (Punjab and the Frontier in 1951, Sind in 1953, East Pakistan in 1954). Oddly enough, the question did not arise in regard to the indirect elections to the Constituent Assembly, in which separately elected Muslim and non-Muslim members of the Provincial Assemblies voted together, with reservation of seats for non-Muslim candidates instead of some form of separate election. The debate was renewed in late 1955 when the legislation establishing West Pakistan provided indirect elections for the new Provincial Assembly, utilizing electoral colleges consisting of members of the Assemblies of the integrating units grouped by district, and also provided common voting and reservation of seats for non-Muslims. The apparent abandonment of the principle of separation in a provincial election reopened the controversy, and it continued unabated under the 1956 Constitution until terminated by the imposition of martial law in 1958. Since that time the extent of the franchise has been the chief focus of attention, with the matter broadened to include presidential as well as legislative elections.

The adoption of universal adult suffrage after independence was considered symbolic of Pakistan's democratic aspirations. Previously the right to vote had been limited to persons with education, property, or other special qualifications. In keeping with democratic ideals, when new provincial elections fell due the franchise (formerly limited to about 14 per cent of the total population) was extended to all over the age of twenty-one. From 40 to 50 per cent of the electorate participated in these elections, which were conducted by election commissioners under the authority of the provincial governments. According to the Electoral Reforms Commission report of March 1956, extensive malpractices were common—faulty electoral rolls, "bogus" voters, stuffed or broken ballot boxes, intimidation of candidates and voters: "Threats, intimidation, terrorization and victimization of the most diverse kinds became operative." [7] Similar conditions prevailed in local government elections, which were described as "reprehensible election frauds, . . . enacted by the interplay of all the vicious, mean and abominable forces unscrupulous human ingenuity can muster up." [8] With some exceptions these abuses were not directly attributable to the election administration, since in terms of sheer mechanics the elections were conducted on the whole smoothly and fairly. The fault lay in the political context, the behavior of those seeking to manipulate a system based on an overwhelmingly illiterate and unsophisticated electorate in legislative constituencies including many tens of thousands of voters. Such an electorate was approachable only through the grossest oversimplification of issues, and given the mutual hostility of Pakistani parties and factions this meant emotional appeals most destructive of national unity and of notions of decency and fair play. The result by 1958 was an oppressive atmosphere of disillusion and frustration, of alienation rather than responsiveness between the elected and the electors.

[7] Ministry of Law, *Report of the Electoral Reforms Commission* (Karachi, 1956), para. 80.

[8] A. M. K. Leghari, CSP, *Report on the Sargodha District Board Elections 1952–53* (Lahore: Superintendent, Government Printing, Punjab, 1955), p. 55.

In justifying the imposition of martial law, General Ayub Khan promised to "restore democracy but of the type that people can understand and work." [9] This pledge was elaborated in the Basic Democracies system, which was founded on the presumption that the right to vote can be genuine and meaningful only when related to the problems and horizons of the voter. In this view, in the absence of universal education, adult suffrage was appropriate only for the election of local union councilors, since the mainly illiterate voters could then judge between candidates on the basis of personal knowledge and need not depend on party identification and slogans. The first such elections—on a common electoral roll—were held under martial law in December 1959 and January 1960, free from political parties and from party-inspired official pressures; 69 per cent of the electorate cast votes in contested constituencies for 144,284 candidates (17,394 were returned unopposed).[10] In February 1960 nearly 80,000 union councilors participated in a referendum in which 95.6 per cent of the votes cast endorsed President Ayub for a five-year term. This was recognized as an exercise in the secret ballot and not an election, and suggested the possibility that the councilors, by election the most responsible representatives of the people, might serve under the forthcoming constitution as the national electorate.

The Constitution of 1962 duly provided for the election of the President and of the Assemblies and the conduct of referenda through an electoral college chosen by adult suf-

[9] Address to the nation, October 8, 1958, in Field Marshal Mohammad Ayub Khan, *Speeches and Statements*, Vol. I, October 1958–June 1959 (Karachi, n.d.), p. 3.

[10] Shahid Javed Burki, "The System of Basic Democracies: Its Structure," *Pakistan Times*, May 7, 1967.

frage for a five-year term. A minimum of 40,000 electors was prescribed for each province; each elector was required to be at least twenty-five years of age and a resident of his electoral ward. It was an essential part of the system that the electors should become union councilors, and therefore would be chosen by the voters on the basis of their ability to act and hence to vote responsibly. The small wards for the electoral college and small electorates in the Assembly constituencies were intended to permit that close relationship between voter and candidate that President Ayub believed to be essential for the making of intelligent and independent choices. The system minimized the intermediary role of parties, reduced the cost to candidates and to the state, and eased the task of administering elections. It also had the merit of eliminating the separate-electorates controversy and ensured parity between the provinces in presidential elections. Initially the union councilors chosen in 1959–60 served as the electoral college, electing the National and Provincial Assemblies before the end of martial law in April and May 1962 and filling subsequent vacancies in by-elections. The first Electoral College Act was adopted in 1964, and under its terms the general elections of 1964–65 took place in primary wards of roughly 600–800 voters and National and Provincial Assembly constituencies of 533 and 267 electors respectively. The decision in 1967 to enlarge the three Assemblies for the 1969–70 general elections necessitated an expansion of the electoral college if legislative constituencies were not to become derisorily small. Population increase had inflated the basic elector-citizen ratio considerably beyond the rough 1:1,000 upon which the Basic Democracy structure was originally built, so expansion was justified both as a popularization of the structure to bring more people directly into the legislative and presidential election process and also as a means of reducing the size of the primary ward to its original dimensions. The Electoral College Act was amended to increase the college to 60,000 in each province for the election due in September 1969. With a national population of more than 120 million, each elector was to represent approximately 900 to 1,100 people and 450 to 550 voters, while the National and Provincial Assembly constituencies were to include respectively 600 and 300 electors.

Under the 1962 Constitution presidential elections were to be held normally before the end of the incumbent's five-year term, or in the case of a midterm election (consequent upon death, resignation, impeachment, or dissolution of the National Assembly), within ninety days of the vacancy. If "circumstances beyond the control" of the Election Commission—such as the death of a candidate just before the polling date—prevented the deadline from being met, it was to be extended for a maximum of four months. The Constitution was amended in 1964 to advance the end of President Ayub's first term from August 7 to March 22, 1965, making it possible for the new President to take office well before the end of the financial year and thus to take responsibility for the next year's budget.[11] The change was bitterly resisted by the opposition on the ground that the new schedule would permit the newly elected President to influence the subsequent election of the Assemblies. An individual who had been President for more than eight years was not to be eligible

[11] The "referendum" of February 14, 1960, was considered to have approved a five-year term for President Ayub. As promulgated, the Constitution of 1962 slightly extended this by providing (Article 226) that his term should end three years and sixty days from the Constitution Day (June 8, 1962).

for re-election unless his candidacy were approved by a joint sitting of the three Assemblies; this provision would have come into play had events permitted President Ayub to contest the 1970 election. If there were more than three candidates other than the incumbent, such a joint sitting was to select by secret ballot the three candidates entitled to contest. In 1964 the opposition expressed fears that this might be abused to eliminate the chief opposition candidate. These provisions were not to apply if one of the Provincial Assemblies were currently dissolved.

Assembly elections were to be held within four months before the expiry of the normal term. In case of dissolution, the National Assembly election was to occur "as soon as practicable" after the presidential election—in any case, soon enough that the new Assembly could meet within six months of the last meeting of the old. After a dissolution a Provincial Assembly was to be elected within three months. Ordinary members of the Assemblies were returned from single-member constituencies. For the election of women members the chief election commissioner divided each province into the appropriate number of provincial and national zones, and the regularly elected members of each Assembly then acted as electoral colleges to elect women from these zones. To qualify for election to an Assembly, an individual had to be a citizen, at least twenty-five years of age, on the electoral roll, and not bankrupt, in government service, or otherwise disqualified. Candidacy for more than one constituency was forbidden, nor could a candidate be at the time President, governor, minister, or member of another Assembly.

To ensure that the electoral machinery could not be manipulated on behalf of the party in power, the conduct of elections was the responsibility of an Election Commission under both the 1956 and 1962 Constitutions. The chief election commissioner, under the 1962 Constitution, was appointed by the President for a three-year term, with constitutionally protected tenure, and was not to hold any other official post for two years after leaving office. Before each election the President after consultation with the chief commissioner and the Chief Justices of the two High Courts appointed a judge from each province as member of the Commission. Election authorities in each province appointed by the chief commissioner were responsible for the preparation of electoral rolls, delimitation of wards, and other details in connection with the election of members of the electoral college. Other elections (and referenda) were conducted by the Commission itself.

It was the duty of the Election Commission under Article 153 of the 1962 Constitution "to ensure that the election is conducted honestly, justly, fairly and in accordance with the law and that corrupt practices are guarded against." Corruption and malpractices were possible under the indirect as well as the direct election system, the former being designed to secure a more informed electorate rather than necessarily to eliminate corruption. Candidates for the electoral college were required to provide their own ballot boxes (according to prescribed specifications), and the voter deposited his ballot in the appropriate box, identified by a symbol, in privacy. At legislative and presidential elections the electors marked their ballots in private and deposited them in one ballot box in view of the polling officer. Election laws and rules defined nomination and election procedures, corrupt and illegal practices; appeal procedures to decide disputes culminated in the Commission itself. Since there was a common electorate, the Electoral College Act (Section 61) declared it to be a corrupt practice to persuade "any person to vote, or refrain from voting, on the ground that he belongs to a particular religion, community, race, caste, sect or tribe." Further protection for the candidate for an Assembly seat or for the presidency was embodied in the unusual constitutional requirement that all candidates be ensured equal opportunity to address the voters, and the voters the opportunity to question each candidate "face to face." These "projection meetings" held under the auspices of the Election Commission were intended to protect the independent or small-party candidate from being overwhelmed and silenced by more powerful political interests.

The 1964–65 general election cycle provided the only full-scale testing of the two-tier Basic Democracy electoral system. Because of the key importance of the presidency, the presidential campaign began before the electoral college elections. Every effort was made by political parties to persuade voters to choose electors pledged to support one of the candidates, and public interest was very high. During late October and early November of 1964, 40,000 members of the electoral college were elected in each province, 77 per cent of the electorate in contested constituencies casting votes for 180,764 candidates (11,652 were returned unopposed).[12] Local considerations rather than presidential election pledges seem to have been decisive, although both the government party and the opposition alliance claimed that their supporters had won in a majority of wards. Intensive campaigning by and on behalf of Ayub Khan and Miss Fatima Jinnah for the opposition, including projection meetings to confront the electors, culminated in the presidential polling on Janu-

[12] Election Commission, *Report on General Elections in Pakistan 1964–65*, I (Karachi, 1967), 67.

ary 2, 1965. President Ayub won re-election with a majority in both provinces (63 per cent of the votes cast); only 300 of the 80,000 electors failed to vote.

The legislative elections, for the National Assembly on March 21 and for the Provincial Assemblies on May 16, aroused almost none of the popular interest evident earlier. In West Pakistan sixteen persons were returned unopposed to the National Assembly, and forty-seven to the Provincial Assembly, all of them Muslim League candidates or tribal "independents"; in East Pakistan only two unopposed candidates were returned to each Assembly, all of them members of the Muslim League. There was no lack of candidates in the remaining constituencies: 407 for 132 National Assembly seats, 345 for 103 West Pakistan Assembly seats, and 666 for 148 East Pakistan Assembly seats. Projection meetings organized by the regional election commissioners in consultation with district authorities were held in each constituency between four weeks and one week in advance of the polling day. Opposition disunity increased the substantial advantages of the Muslim League as the party in power. Although many independents were elected, particularly to the Provincial Assemblies, most aligned themselves with the League. As a result, League nominees were returned unopposed to the women's seats in the National and West Pakistan Assemblies, and in East Pakistan they were elected by margins of at least two to one. Only in East Pakistan did the size of the opposition—about forty—even approach the proportion of the electoral college vote won by Miss Jinnah (36 per cent); in the National Assembly the opposition held only seventeen seats, and in West Pakistan a tiny band of five faced a government party 150 strong.

The results of the elections confirmed the views of both

supporters and critics of the indirect election system. The distribution of the electoral wards throughout the remotest reaches of Pakisan forced political campaigners to seek out the citizenry in every village, including the entire adult population in a process of politicization. As intended, the members of the electoral college proved to be cushioned from popular pressures aroused in the campaign and, voting according to their own judgments (however formed), returned both President Ayub and majorities supporting him in all three Assemblies. According to the opposition, the system distorted and flouted public opinion, and its results were achieved by corruption and the powerful influence on the electors of governors, commissioners, and DC's. The opposition's sense of frustration and rejection of the constitutional order was increased by the experience of the election and by the consequent diminution of their voice in the National and West Pakistan Assemblies. In President Ayub's view the system proved its workability by permitting a vigorous expression of opposition sentiment while moderating the effect of public passions on political institutions. The Muslim League's electoral success was Pyrrhic, however, since it decreased the ability of the government to hear the voice of the opposition within the system and increased the determination of the opposition to repudiate and destroy the constitutional order.

The limitation of the legislative and presidential franchise to a predominantly rural electorate of local councilors was one of the most severely criticized features of the constitutional order devised by President Ayub Khan. Although the Basic Democracy electoral system was based on universal adult suffrage, denunciations of it with the cry for the "restoration of adult franchise" conveyed the impression that the people had been deprived of a right they previously enjoyed. The democratic credentials of the Assemblies themselves were challenged, further depreciating their status among those who already believed the legislatures to be "powerless." In fact the National Assemblies elected during the 1960's were based on a broader and more direct franchise than the two Constituent Assemblies. The 80,000 electors of 1962 and 1965 were easily accessible to their constituents, and in the latter year were elected with their electoral function a definite issue. In contrast, the few hundred provincial legislators of 1947 and 1955 were largely unknown and inaccessible to the populations of their constituencies, and their elections had not had the remotest reference to the election of a future national legislature. President Ayub's election after a nationwide campaign by an electorate including 80,000 voters made him far more representative than either his predecessor, elected almost casually by the eighty members of the National Assembly in 1956, or the prime ministers of former times. The single exercise of adult franchise in legislative elections of dubious propriety in each of the provinces during the 1950's could hardly have been a more significant experience to the illiterate rural voter than the two adult suffrage Basic Democracy elections of 1959 and 1964. On the contrary, the indirect election system freed the rural areas from urban political domination and forced rural interests to the fore. The attack on the indirect system stemmed primarily from the minority of literate voters who resented their inability to participate directly in legislative elections and lacked interest in local government. Their condemnations of the system gradually began to take root when the elitist pretentions of the union councilors had begun to antagonize the ordinary citizens whom they represented.

The alternative to the electoral college system was a return to direct elections, with either universal adult suffrage or a restricted franchise. Two successive independent bodies studied the franchise question, and although they agreed on important points their conclusions differed. The Constitution Commission of 1961 and the Franchise Commission appointed in 1962 agreed that the Assemblies and the President should be elected by the same electorate, and both were skeptical of the suitability of the Basic Democrats to serve as an electoral college on the ground that they would be no more intelligent or able than an adult suffrage electorate. The Constitution Commission therefore recommended that elections be direct but that the franchise be limited by literacy and property qualifications. The Franchise Commission's majority took an opposite approach and held that the trend since 1919 had been for direct elections and a wider franchise, and that in view of the psychological expectations thus created, direct elections by universal adult suffrage should be adopted. The assertions in their report concerning the meaning of the franchise and its implications in Pakistan were answered by counterassertions in a report by a special committee appointed by the law ministry. In the end, President Ayub felt secure enough to reject the recommendations of the second Commission as he had those of the first in favor of his own convictions. In doing so he underestimated the weight of the Franchise Commission's argument in regard to psychological expectations. Regardless of the social and political circumstances or the experience of the past, direct universal adult suffrage had become a value in itself and a symbol with which to conjure. In the hands of the opposition parties it became a fearsome weapon.

Under steady attack by its opponents, the constitutional

order of 1962 failed to preserve the stability it had been designed to make possible. Essentially it was a political rather than institutional failure, as indeed had been the case with the collapse of the parliamentary order of 1947–1958. Despite the carefully elaborated checks and balances between the executive and the Assemblies, at both central and provincial levels, a politically effective synthesis of the experience and experimentation of the past was not realized. The institutions themselves—executive, legislative, and electoral, central and provincial—were technically workable and adequate to Pakistan's needs, but the will to work them was absent. The manipulation and corruption of elections and legislatures under the parliamentary system had led to its collapse, and according to the opposition the same devices were used under the presidential Constitution. Neither the governing nor the opposition parties appreciated the need for independent legislative organization, and under parliamentary discipline the Assemblies could not perform their constitutional function of checking the executive. The opposition parties rejected the presidential system, and President Ayub failed to bring into being a vigorous party committed to its preservation. After more than two decades the wheel had gone full circle, and both politically and constitutionally Pakistan was as far from consensus in 1969 as she had been in 1947.

6. Parliamentary Politics: 1947-1958

Continuing political instability has been an inescapable result of the Pakistani search for agreed constitutional formulas. Lack of political consensus has prevented agreement on constitutional solutions, which in turn are expected to resolve contradictory claims and to compensate for political weaknesses. During the Pakistan movement the great majority of Indian Muslims were united by the Muslim League in the overriding determination to achieve a Muslim state. The peasant masses were aroused from their lethargy and mobilized for political action, while the traditional and modern elites submerged their differences in the revolutionary fervor of the struggle for independence. For the first year or two after partition the *élan* and dedication of the Pakistan movement imparted an impression of a greater degree of unity than actually existed. Gradually attentions returned to more mundane problems of existence, and considerations of social prestige, political or economic power, tribal or clan loyalties, sectarian or linguistic allegiances prevailed over any theoretical recognition of broader national interests. Diversity rather than unity proved to be the dominant characteristic of Pakistani politics.

The parliamentary system with which Pakistan began its independent career presupposed disciplined political parties based on shared values. The failure of the Muslim League to impose its own value system on the diverse components of the population during the first decade of independence reflected the lack of agreement on values and purposes within the party. Once Pakistan had been won the League's *raison d'être* disappeared, and before it could discover another Jinnah's death deprived it of his great moral authority. In the absence of agreed purpose or inspired leadership, the League disintegrated and was succeeded by a constellation of parties representing smaller societies, appealing to more limited and accordingly more homogeneous segments of the national community. Although there was general agreement among party leaders that a parliamentary form of government was desirable, their diverse political commitments precluded the consensus essential to its smooth working. The development of this fragmented political system must be traced to permit an understanding of the collapse of parliamentary government in 1958 and the resort to a presidential solution.

The Muslim League

In 1947 the Muslim League was the organ of the Pakistan movement and had no challengers for national leadership. It was faced nevertheless with the difficult task of transforming itself from a national movement into a political party competing with other parties. During the struggle for Pakistan the League had been overshadowed by Jinnah, its permanent president and leader, whose integrity and political ability made him a giant towering over his followers. Factions and interprovincial rivalries existed but were rendered harmless by the great moral authority of the Qaid-i-Azam and his dedication to the national cause. When at independence Jinnah became governor general and Liaqat Ali Khan (1896–

1951), the longtime general secretary of the League, became prime minister, the League became a distinctly secondary concern for them. Both men—Jinnah from Bombay, Liaqat from the old United Provinces—were above the provincial or factional identifications that became the basis of Pakistani politics.

In February 1948 the League Council resolved to bar members of the government from party office in order to clarify the distinction between the parliamentary and organizational leadership. The new leaders of the organization, many of them *émigrés* from India, lacked nationwide prestige and were unable to maintain control over the League. Resentment among the younger generation at the tendency of the old guard to entrench itself in office led to factional squabbles in the provinces and ultimately to desertions from the party. In 1950 the ban on ministers holding party office was rescinded, and Liaqat Ali Khan, who after Jinnah's death had become the unchallenged political leader of the nation, became League president. His example was followed in the provinces, and for the next six years the central and provincial party presidencies were in effect perquisites of the appropriate heads of government. Although this eliminated the evils of factional conflict between ministers and party officials, it reduced the League to the status of a tool of the government and blurred the distinction between state and party.

The decline of the League became evident after the assassination of Liaqat Ali Khan at Rawalpindi on October 16, 1951. Khwaja Nazimuddin (1894–1964), the next prime minister and president of the League, lacked sufficient force of character for his dual role. Confronted by mounting economic and social problems, he was unable to prevent the erosion of the League's popularity, particularly in his own province of East Pakistan. The nadir of the League's power was reached in 1953 when it was obliged to accept Mohammed Ali of Bogra (1909–1963) as its president when he was installed as prime minister by the governor general after the latter's dismissal of Nazimuddin. Mohammed Ali had been a junior member of the last pre-independence Muslim League government of Bengal, but had been abroad in the foreign service since 1948. The subsequent rout of the League in the East Bengal elections in March 1954 further discredited it and indicated Mohammed Ali's lack of political influence. The governor general took the initiative once more on October 24, 1954, with his dissolution of the League-dominated Constituent Assembly, and reconstituted Mohammed Ali's cabinet to include non-Leaguers for the first time. Other parties then began to assert themselves, and in consequence the League won only thirty-three seats in the new eighty-member Constituent Assembly in June 1955.

The end of the League's monopoly of power shocked the party into a reassertion of its independence. Demands for organizational reform began to be heard during the presidency of Mohammed Ali of Bogra in 1953–1955. The separation of party from governmental office was accomplished *de facto* in August 1955 when Chaudhri Muhammad Ali, the newly elected leader of the Muslim League Assembly party, succeeded in forming a coalition cabinet. Mohammed Ali of Bogra, the former prime minister, subsequently resigned from the League presidency, and the post was left unfilled until January 1956. In a constitutional revision, the League Council then reimposed the ban on ministers holding party office.

The new president, Sardar Abdur Rab Nishtar of Peshawar (1899–1958), moved to reassert the control of the party organization over League ministers and parliamentary parties. In East Pakistan this presented little difficulty since the League held only ten seats in the Provincial Assembly and had been in opposition since 1954. In West Pakistan the League continued to control all the provinces and states until the integration in October 1955. An interim ministry including League leaders from the former units was then formed under the nonparty leadership of Dr. Khan Sahib (1882–1958), the former Congress premier of the Frontier Province. After the indirect elections for the new West Pakistan Assembly in January 1956 had returned a League majority, Nishtar directed the Leaguers to form a parliamentary party and to elect a new leader if Dr. Khan Sahib refused to join. Since Prime Minister Chaudhri Muhammad Ali and other top Leaguers had promised that Dr. Khan Sahib's ministry would be supported on a nonpartisan basis, considerable dissension ensued within the League between the supporters of Nishtar and those who stood by the commitment to Dr. Khan Sahib. The result was the resignation of the former from the provincial ministry and the expulsion of the latter faction from the party. The League thereupon (in April 1956) found itself in opposition in both provinces and began to lose strength at the center.

During the last two years of the parliamentary era the League was in the political wilderness, in opposition—apart from the ephemeral Chundrigar coalition of October-December 1957—at the center as well as in the provinces. In early September 1956 tensions between Nishtar and Chaudhri Muhammad Ali led the Prime Minister to resign from office and from the party. The League was excluded from the new coalition cabinet, and therafter, anticipating elections under the Constitution of 1956, campaigned vigorously, unhampered by the responsibilities of power, to mobilize popular support. After Nishtar's sudden death the League Council in March 1958 elected Khan Abdul Qaiyum Khan (premier of the North-West Frontier Province from 1947 to 1953) to be its new president. Qaiyum, a bitter opponent of Dr. Khan Sahib and of President Iskander Mirza, sought to recreate the atmosphere of 1947 by renewing old cries on "Islamic" issues, equating opposition to the League or to separate electorates with opposition to Pakistan itself, and defending the "One Unit" policy. The bitterness of his denunciations of other parties—particularly the Republicans—in late summer of 1958 heightened tensions, and his threats of "bloody revolution" undoubtedly contributed to the decision of the generals to suspend the normal political process.

THE REPUBLICAN PARTY

The split in the West Pakistan Muslim League in spring 1956 resulted in the formation of the Republican party to support the provincial cabinet of Dr. Khan Sahib. To his banner rallied Leaguers who felt that the League had violated a pledge in opposing him, factions—especially in Sind and the Frontier—personally opposed to the current League leadership, and remnants of the old Punjab Unionist and Frontier Congress parties. With the patronage of office Dr. Khan Sahib was also able to lure to his side individuals who might otherwise have remained faithful to the League. Since most of the leading advocates of the integration of West Pakistan stayed with the Muslim League, the Republican party attracted many opponents of the "One Unit" policy despite the fact that Dr. Khan Sahib had been appointed premier particularly to consolidate the new province. By means of constitutional and political maneuvering, including the imposition of governor's rule under Article 193 from March until July 1957, the Republicans remained in power until the imposition of martial law by President Mirza, although it is doubtful whether they ever had significant popular support.

The increase in Republican strength in the National Assembly during 1956 and 1957 gave the new party a decisive voice in the formation of cabinets at the center. After the fall of Chaudhri Muhammad Ali's Muslim League coalition in September 1956, the Republicans joined in a coalition with the Awami League under H. S. Suhrawardy (1893–1963). When the latter publicly criticized the Republican leadership for being opportunist in their support of an anti–"One Unit" resolution in the Provincial Assembly, they withdrew from the coalition in pique, causing Suhrawardy's fall in October 1957. Reversing themselves immediately, the Republicans agreed to shelve the "One Unit" question until after the anticipated general election, and supported the short-lived Muslim League coalition led by I. I. Chundrigar (1897–1960). This anomalous alliance ended when the Republicans broke with the League over the electorates issue in December. By that time the Republicans, with twenty-one seats, were the largest party in the Assembly, and they formed a coalition under Malik Feroz Khan Noon (a pre-independence Unionist, and from 1953–1955 Muslim League premier of Punjab), which remained in power with Awami League support until unseated by the proclamation of martial law in October 1958.

The Awami League [1]

The East Pakistan Awami ("People's") Muslim League was founded in Dacca in June 1949, representing both genu-

[1] For information on the early years of the Awami League I am indebted to the following unpublished M.A. theses submitted in the

ine social protest and the political ambitions of frustrated Muslim Leaguers. H. S. Suhrawardy, the head of an ousted Bengal Muslim League faction,[2] and Maulana Abdul Hamid Khan Bhashani, demagogic leader of the old Assam Muslim League, brought together the principal groups of the organizationally dispossessed, and around them rallied the varied forces of discontent with the provincial Muslim League and ministry under Nurul Amin (premier of East Pakistan, 1948–1954). Suhrawardy assumed the national leadership and Bhashani was elected president of the party in East Pakistan. The Bengali language demand became the emotional rallying cry against the Muslim League, and was elevated to the level of a sacred cause when demonstrators were killed in police firing in Dacca in early 1952.

The formation of the All-Pakistan Jinnah-Awami Muslim League (JAML) at Lahore in December 1952 linked the East Pakistan party with opposition groups in West Pakistan. Under Suhrawardy's auspices dissident factions in the Frontier Province and Punjab joined forces to form the JAML, appealing to refugees and other discontented and dissatisfied

---

Department of Political Science, University of the Panjab, Lahore, in 1958: Mohammed Khurshid Alam, "The East Pakistan Awami League"; Mohammed Afzal Bajwa, "The National Awami Party"; Mohammed Aslam Noori, "The Organization and Working of a Political Party: The Awami League."

[2] Suhrawardy was premier of Bengal in 1946–47 but lost standing with the League by considering the idea of an independent united Bengal and therefore was excluded from power in the new province of East Bengal. He was elected to the Constituent Assembly but retained his residence in Calcutta after partition to work for communal peace. In 1948 he was unseated from the Assembly on the ground that he was not a resident of Pakistan. Accordingly when he moved permanently to Pakistan he became a natural focus for opposition to the Muslim League establishment.

elements in the community. Despite Suhrawardy's campaigning, the JAML won only 32 of 197 seats in the Punjab elections of March 1951, and only 4 of 97 seats in the Frontier election the succeeding November. In order to strengthen the party on a national basis, the Lahore convention brought into the alliance the East Pakistan Awami Muslim League and the Sind Awami Mahaz (which later managed to win 7 of the 111 seats in the Sind elections of April 1953). The convention adopted a manifesto pledging the party to democracy and "the eternal injunctions of Islam," outlining a hazy economic program, and denouncing the Muslim League's intolerance and proclivity to identify the state, party, and government; issues that might cause dissension were carefully avoided.

The high-sounding phrases of the manifesto did not bridge the gap between the various components of the party. Pressure from East Pakistan for declarations on language and provincial autonomy evoked resistance in West Pakistan, where the attitudes of Awami Muslim Leaguers did not differ significantly from those of the Muslim League. During 1953, friction between Suhrawardy and the party leader in Punjab led to the latter's return to the Muslim League and the consequent loss by the Awami Muslim League of most of its Punjabi strength. Thereafter the party tended to become the voice of non-Punjabi interests, and in 1955 Awami fragments in Sind and the Frontier continued to oppose the "One Unit" policy even after the national leadership had decided to accept the *fait accompli.* Another disruptive factor was the communal question, precipitated by the decision of the East Pakistan party in 1955 to open its membership to non-Muslims. This caused secessions in both parts of the country, and in West Pakistan efforts at reorganization were further delayed. A convention of those loyal to Suhrawardy and the noncommunal orientation of the party was held in Lahore in May 1958 and a constitution for the West Pakistan Awami League was adopted, but little could be done in terms of the construction of a party organization before martial law intervened.

When the manifesto adopted by the Lahore convention in December 1952 failed to deal with the language and other issues, the East Pakistan Awami Muslim League drafted its own manifesto for the coming provincial elections. Published in November 1953, it demanded, among other things, complete provincial autonomy, the recognition of Bengali as a state language, the nationalization of the jute industry, guarantees for civil and political liberties, and the abolition of landlordism. The following month this manifesto became the basis of the Twenty-One Point Programme adopted by a United Front linking the Awami Muslim League with other anti-Muslim League parties for the purpose of fighting the March 1954 elections.

THE KRISHAK SRAMIK PARTY (KSP)

The principal ally of the Awami Muslim League in the formation of the United Front was the Krishak Sramik ("Peasants and Workers") party of A. K. Fazlul Huq (1872–1962). Fazlul Huq, the first important political figure to emerge from the Muslim middle classes of eastern Bengal, built his entire career on his unmatched ability to appear as the champion of the exploited common man. Although he moved the Pakistan resolution in 1940, he revolted against League discipline in December 1941 and accordingly found himself isolated when the Pakistan movement swept toward victory. By the time of partition he had made peace with the

League and was elected to the Constituent Assembly, but he remained politically inactive while his old rival Nazimuddin served as premier of East Pakistan and then as governor general. In 1951 Nazimuddin's successor as premier in Dacca, Nurul Amin, sought to heal the breach with Fazlul Huq by appointing him advocate general. With the growth of popular discontent Fazlul Huq resigned office to offer himself again as a focus of opposition to the Muslim League, and in September 1953 he founded the KSP. In order to increase the likelihood of electoral success, he and Suhrawardy—longtime antagonists now linked by the common adversity of opposition—formed the United Front, combining the former's great popular appeal with the organization of the Awami Muslim League.

The United Front victory at the polls—it won 223 of 237 Muslim seats—was followed very soon by the disintegration of the alliance. The repudiation of the Muslim League by the East Pakistan electorate led the Front's leaders to demand the resignation of the Muslim League central government and the dissolution of the Constituent Assembly, so that a new Assembly and government responsive to the Twenty-One Point Programme might be chosen. Since Suhrawardy envisioned himself as the next prime minister, the task of forming a new ministry in Dacca was entrusted to Fazlul Huq. Disagreement between the Awami Muslim League and the KSP over the composition of the provincial cabinet was soon evident, and the continuing political uncertainty was accompanied by an apparent breakdown in law and order. When the central government under Mohammed Ali of Bogra intervened on May 30, dismissing the Fazlul Huq ministry and imposing governor's rule under Section 92A of the 1935 Act, the United Front forces were already in con-

siderable disarray. The political situation was further complicated in October by the governor general's dissolution of
the Constituent Assembly, which initially at least was welcomed by the United Front. Suhrawardy and his followers
saw in the situation the possibilities of a short cut to political
power and the speedy adoption of a constitution embodying
the East Pakistan demands. Accordingly in December 1954,
after some bargaining, he joined Mohammed Ali's new cabinet as law minister. When it became clear that Suhrawardy
had agreed to support a policy of unifying West Pakistan
and enacting by decree a new constitution based on parity
of East and West, the KSP-led United Front (in April 1955)
formally "disowned" him and suspended him and his principal Awami Muslim League lieutenants from the Front for
betraying the democratic principles underlying the Twenty-
One Point Programme. In the subsequent Constituent Assembly elections the United Front won sixteen seats and the
Awami League, by now a noncommunal party, won thirteen.

The political ferment in mid-1955 resulted in an alliance
between the KSP and the Muslim League, partially based on
both parties' dislike of the increasingly noncommunal orientation of the Awami League. Parliamentary government was
restored in Dacca in June with a KSP-led ministry, and in
August Fazlul Huq himself joined the new coalition under
Chaudhri Muhammad Ali in Karachi. Suhrawardy became
leader of the opposition, and Mohammed Ali of Bogra, who
fifteen months before had called Fazlul Huq a "traitor," once
again became ambassador in Washington. After successfully
delivering adequate Bengali support to pass the constitution
bill, Fazlul Huq went to East Pakistan in March 1956 as
governor in order to bolster the KSP position there. The
struggle to mobilize a legislative majority in East Pakistan

was fierce, and political and constitutional proprieties were not greatly respected. Finally the KSP premier (A. H. Sarkar, 1895–1969) resigned at the end of August 1956 rather than meet the Assembly as directed by the prime minister. Thereafter the KSP disintegrated into factions, each struggling for political preferment on its own, some quite successfully. Fazlul Huq himself was dismissed from the office of governor on April 1, 1958, for attempting to intervene on behalf of his party. He was then free to return to active politics, but the imposition of martial law forestalled any new plans he may have had and his subsequent death precluded any revival of his party.

THE EAST PAKISTAN AWAMI LEAGUE

The emergence of the East Pakistan Awami League as a national political force in its own right during 1955 occurred in a context of struggle for ascendancy with its erstwhile allies, particularly the KSP. Both parties' attempts to ensure majorities in the Provincial Assembly, in anticipation of an ultimate return to ministerial government, forced both to bid for the support of minor parties and most particularly of the seventy-two non-Muslim members. In April 1955, on the proposal of Maulana Bhashani, the East Pakistan Awami League opened its membership to non-Muslims. While this action won the party the favor of many non-Muslims, it alienated Muslims in East Pakistan who took seriously the original United Front dedication to the Islamic-state idea, and in effect destroyed the party in West Pakistan. The Awami League thus became a noncommunal Bengali party, pledged to joint electorates and representative democracy and opposed to any identification of Islam with the state.

In September 1956 the Awami League was called upon to

form ministries both in Karachi and in Dacca and was faced for the first time with the responsibilities of power. The parliamentary leaders (Suhrawardy and Ataur Rahman Khan) were obliged to modify Awami League dogma on matters such as the demand for provincial autonomy and an independent foreign policy, in order to conform to political realities and the views of their coalition partners. Prime Minister Suhrawardy was committed to the "One Unit" policy as the basis of constitutional equality between East and West, and contended that the Constitution secured "98 per cent" provincial autonomy. Serious conflict with the party militants, who regarded the Twenty-One Point Programme and the other party commitments as immutable pledges to the electorate, ended in a split between Suhrawardy and Bhashani on the foreign policy and autonomy issues. At the Kagmari Awami League conference in February 1957 Suhrawardy's foreign policy resolution endorsing the alliance system was approved, and in consequence Bhashani and the Left resigned from the party.

The prize for which the political battle raged in 1956–1958 was the possession of office during the anticipated general elections. National and provincial patronage was used to maintain the precarious majority of Ataur Rahman Khan's Awami League ministry in Dacca, for even after Suhrawardy's fall in October 1957 the dependence of the central government coalition on Awami support (apart from the brief Chundrigar interlude) ensured that central powers would be used where necessary to preserve the provincial ministry. The struggle became so bitter that in September 1958 the East Pakistan Assembly literally became a battleground, and the Deputy Speaker was fatally injured while in the chair. Although the tragedy marked the complete breakdown of the parliamentary system, the Republican-led central government was unable to intervene because of its dependence on the Awami League, which at that very time was negotiating to accept central ministerial office. The process of quarrelling over the allocation of portfolios continued through the end of September, culminating on October 7 in the announcement of the new distribution by Prime Minister Feroz Khan Noon. Later that same day the last act of the tragedy—or farce— was played when the new Awami League ministers resigned in dissatisfaction. A few hours later martial law was proclaimed.

The National Awami Party

The National Awami party (NAP) was founded at a convention in Dacca in July 1957. It was an alliance of leftist and provincialist groups from all parts of Pakistan, committed to complete provincial autonomy, the disintegration of West Pakistan, and an independent and nonaligned foreign policy. The principal organizers were Maulana Bhashani and his fellow seceders from the Awami League. They were joined by the Ganatantri Dal, the other major leftist component of the original United Front, a communist-influenced party founded by radical intellectuals and peasant leaders in December 1952.[3] These two groups provided the basis of the East Pakistan NAP, of which Bhashani became president and Mahmud Ali (of the Ganatantri Dal) general secretary. In keeping with the founders' concern for provincial rights, the constitution provided that the national organs of the party were to be established on the basis of East-West parity, with separate organizations in the former provinces of West

[3] Bajwa, *op. cit.*, p. 8. The thesis includes the NAP constitution and an appendix on the Redshirt movement.

Pakistan. The president and other officers and most of the working committee were to be elected by the national council, itself elected by the two regional councils. Pending party elections all powers were vested in an organizing committee with Bhashani as president.

In West Pakistan the NAP regional organization was based on six minor parties which had combined in December 1956 to form the Pakistan National party, with Khan Abdul Ghaffar Khan, the "Frontier Gandhi," as president. Ghaffar Khan had opposed the creation of Pakistan and in 1947 demanded instead an independent Pakhtun (Pathan) state; after independence he advocated a linguistically based autonomous Pakhtun province. Because his activities seemed to support the agitation sponsored by Afghanistan for the creation of a separate "Pakhtunistan," he was imprisoned from September 1948 until January 1954 despite the fact that he was a member of the Constituent Assembly. After his release he revived his old party, the Khudai Khidmatgars ("Servants of God") or Redshirts, and actively opposed the integration of West Pakistan. When the NAP was founded the Redshirts became its Frontier branch, with one of Ghaffar Khan's lieutenants as president. In neighboring Quetta division, Khan Abdus Samad Khan Achakzai, the local proponent of Pakhtunistan, transformed his Wrore Pashtoon into a NAP provincial branch, while the Baluchi nationalist Ustaman Gul led by Agha Abdul Karim Khan (a member of the ruling family of Kalat) became the Kalat NAP.

A genuinely leftist tone was evident in the Sindhi and Punjabi branches of the NAP. The Punjab organization was based on the Azad Pakistan party (APP) founded in 1952 by Mian Iftikharuddin (d. 1962), the wealthy publisher (until 1959) of the *Pakistan Times* of Lahore. Iftikharuddin was an intellectual socialist who left the Congress for the Muslim League in 1946, served briefly in the Punjab cabinet in 1947, then broke with the League in 1948 and sat as a radical independent in the Constituent Assembly until he organized his own party. The heyday of the APP was in its first year, when it boasted three members of the Constituent Assembly. By the end of 1953 two of them had returned to the Muslim League, and six months later the party split over the question of communist influence.[4] Although Iftikharuddin was active in the creation of the NAP, because of his ill health the leadership of the party in Punjab was assumed by Mahmud Ali Qasuri, a prominent Lahore lawyer who was also general secretary of the West Pakistan regional organization. The Sindhi NAP was built of the factions that had supported the Jinnah-Awami Muslim League in 1952–53: the Sind Hari Committee, a radical peasant movement, and the Sind Awami Mahaz led by G. M. Syed. Syed is a wealthy former Muslim Leaguer who lost out in the power struggle in 1946 and later moved into opposition to become the most vocal of Sindhi provincialists.

During 1957–58 the NAP was one of the most unstable elements on the political scene. Nationalization of industry, abolition of landlordism, and increased state social intervention were inconsistent with the goals of autonomy and decentralization cherished particularly by the wealthy provincialist leaders in West Pakistan. The various NAP components retained their own commitments and in some cases their separate organizations, and in West Pakistan their provincialist territorial aspirations were often in conflict. In both provinces, with the lines between opposing coalitions fairly evenly

[4] *Ibid.*, p. 10, and Dilshad Najmuddin, "Political Parties in Pakistan" (unpub. M.A. thesis, University of the Panjab, Lahore, 1955), p. 131.

drawn, the NAP was in a position of potentially great influence. In West Pakistan NAP groups were willing to support either the Muslim League or the Republicans provided they would agree to break up the integrated province, thus intensifying the struggle for majorities in the Provincial Assembly. In East Pakistan reversals of position by NAP members led in June 1958 to a political crisis in which the Awami League government was succeeded briefly by a KSP government and then by the imposition of governor's rule for two months before the Awami League returned to office. Their role in contributing to the breakdown of the national political order was presumably one of the reasons for the arrest of the principal NAP leaders—Bhashani, Ghaffar Khan, Achakzai, Abdul Karim, and G. M. Syed—as "antinational" elements immediately after the imposition of martial law.

The Nizam-i-Islam Party

The growing anti–Muslim League opinion in East Pakistan in the early 1950's had its conservative expression in the Nizam-i-Islam ("Rule of Islam") party (NIP). The failure of the ulama to secure government acceptance of their demand for action against the Ahmadi sect in 1953 and the consequent reassertion of modernist opinion in the Muslim League convinced some East Pakistan ulama that their religious organizations were insufficient to propagate their views. The most important of these was the Jamiat-ul-Ulama-i-Islam ("Society of Ulama of Islam"), the principal organ of the orthodox Deobandi school, founded in 1945 with the secession of pro–Muslim League ulama from the Congress-oriented Jamiat-ul-Ulama-i-Hind ("Society of Ulama of India"). The other major orthodox faction, the even more traditional Bareilly school, formed the Jamiat-ul-Ulama-i-Pakistan ("Society of Ulama of Pakistan") in 1948. Both were patronized by the Muslim League and the government because of their ability to command the respect of the common man, but the politicians had little sympathy with or understanding for their views. With the encouragement of the Jamiat-ul-Ulama-i-Islam, the Nizam-i-Islam party was formed to contest the 1954 provincial elections. Fazlul Huq made a ten-point agreement [5] with the NIP pledging the United Front to the two-nation theory, to an Islamic constitution based on the Holy Quran and Sunnah, to an acceptance of the authority of the Jamiat-ul-Ulama-i-Islam in the interpretation of the Shariah, and in general to the application of the spirit of these pledges in all the Front's activities. The NIP hoped by participating in the United Front to increase the political strength of the traditionalist Islamic-state demand. When the Awami League abandoned the agreement and became the champion of joint electorates and secularism, the NIP supported Chaudhri Muhammad Ali's Muslim League–KSP coalition with its three votes in order to secure the adoption of the "Islamic" Constitution of 1956.

The NIP commitment to the Islamic provisions of the 1956 Constitution was reinforced when Chaudhri Muhammad Ali, the Punjabi "father" of the Constitution, became leader of the party. Originally a career administrator, Muhammad Ali had been co-opted into the Muslim League leadership after the death of Liaqat Ali Khan. As prime minister he refused to be bound by the decisions of the League organization, in deference to his coalition and parliamentary re-

[5] Signed on December 28, 1953, according to a statement made in the Constituent Assembly by Mohammed Ali of Bogra, July 17, 1954. Constituent Assembly (Legislature) of Pakistan, *Debates,* Thirteenth Session, I, No. 26, p. 1501.

sponsibility. After resigning from the Muslim League in September 1956, Muhammad Ali gave more extreme expression to his religious and political views, and in December 1957 he founded his own party. In April 1958 he joined forces with the NIP, which by then had broken with the KSP over the electorates issues. The manifesto of the new NIP endorsed separate electorates, the unity of West Pakistan, agrarian reforms, and the achievement of a "progressive democratic welfare state" based on an Islamic social order as defined in the Holy Quran and Sunnah.

Jamaat-i-Islami Pakistan

The Nizam-i-Islam party was a religiously based political party pledged to implement a traditionalist view of the requirements of Islam through the secular political process; the Jamaat-i-Islami, on the other hand, was in origin a "movement" with the ultimate aim of replacing the political process with a divinely regulated Islamic order.[6] It was founded in 1941 by the self-educated but extremely able Maulana Abul Ala Maududi, aiming to "base and organize the entire human life in all its varied aspects . . . on the principle of submission and obedience to God Almighty and the guidance and instructions of His Apostles." This goal required the propagation of the reformed faith to nonbelievers in order to create a universal society based on the clear-cut injunctions of Maududi's fundamentalist interpretation of Islam. The Jamaat opposed the Pakistan movement on the ground that it was inherently incapable of producing an "Islamic state" since the leadership was in Maududi's terms immoral and unIslamic and since the creation of a separate nation-state would

[6] Mohammed Amin, "Jamaat-e-Islami Pakistan" (unpub. M.A. thesis, University of the Panjab, Lahore, 1958). See also Chapter 3, p. 94.

deny the universality of the Quranic message. After 1947 Maududi adapted his thinking to the changed circumstances, and the Jamaat began its work for the establishment in Pakistan of a constitutional order based on the Shariah.

The Jamaat's program for the creation of an Islamic order involved four tasks: the purification of Islam of its accretions; the search for righteous and honest people and their training; the reform of the society along Islamic lines; and the reform of the government and the national leadership through constitutional means. The first two of these were tackled directly by Maududi's exposition of the faith and the proselytizing activities of the Jamaat. The remaining two objectives required the Jamaat to engage in the political game, and so gradually to turn the course of events in the desired direction. Maududi was jailed in 1948–1950 on charges of "seditious" activities among the refugees, and again in 1953–54 in connection with the Jamaat's role in the West Pakistan anti-Ahmadi disturbances. These experiences made him a fervent advocate of democratic liberties and of an independent judiciary to enforce them. The Jamaat was less affected than other parties by the imposition of martial law in 1958, since its nonpolitical auxiliaries continued their activities and Maulana Maududi merely assumed the more conventional role of the religious scholar.

Non-Muslim Parties

Prior to 1958 several non-Muslim political parties were in the field. The Pakistan National Congress (PNC) was the rump in East Pakistan of the pre-independence Indian National Congress. Although it was the major parliamentary opposition in the first Constituent Assembly and in the East Pakistan Assembly until 1954, it could not escape the stigma of its former opposition to the Pakistan movement. The United Progressive party (UPP) appeared in 1955 with the disintegration of the United Front. Both of these parties were mainly supported by caste Hindus. In the competitive political situation in 1955–1958 the PNC and UPP, with initially four and two members respectively in the Constituent Assembly, were able to bargain with the major parties on behalf of non-Muslim interests and participated in successive central and provincial coalitions. The Scheduled Caste Federation functioned as a political party in East Pakistan until 1958, its members in the Assemblies frequently allied with the Muslim League. After 1955 non-Muslims were welcomed as full members by the Awami League and later by the NAP, and at least two non-Muslims in the central Assembly joined the Republican party. In West Pakistan, politically inclined non-Muslims usually found it wise to become associate members of the Muslim League. Other minority organizations generally functioned as pressure groups, although Christian organizations in West Pakistan supported candidates in provincial elections.

Politics Suspended

The bitter struggle between the political parties and the gradual collapse of parliamentary decencies produced a palpable atmosphere of political malaise in 1958. Every group had betrayed its professed principles at one time or another, and none could trust the *bona fides* of its opponents. The attempt of the Muslim League to use Islam as a unifying force without having any positive conception of its moral implications in the modern world proved to be divisive, provoking non-Muslims and Muslim factions alike into extreme statements of their own demands. The rise of parties appealing to ethnic rather than religious communities in turn provoked those who were committed, on secular or Islamic grounds, to the survival of Pakistan as a unified political community and state. The elections scheduled under the 1956 Constitution were awaited as a means of delivery from a most unsatisfactory situation, yet no party was willing to contemplate any other in the seat of power at election time. On October 7, 1958 the political tension was suddenly broken by the imposition of martial law and the abolition of all political parties.

President Iskander Mirza's martial-law proclamation was a vitriolic denunciation of Pakistani politicians. In it he alluded to his own role in the preceding years. Mirza has been much criticized and blamed for his alleged political manipulations and interventions. He made no secret of his scorn for politicians or of his skepticism concerning the workability of parliamentary democracy in Pakistan. He was enabled— or called upon—to play a political role by the very party weakness that caused him to doubt the suitability of the parliamentary system in Pakistan conditions. He was the scapegoat for party failings even before October 7, 1958, and has been since. Mirza expressed the view that a "vast majority" of the people had lost confidence in the existing system of government, and that they were "dangerously resentful" of their treatment by the political leaders. His evaluation of Pakistani parties was black, suggesting little hope for parliamentary democracy.

The mentality of the political parties has sunk so low that I am unable any longer to believe that elections will improve the present chaotic internal situation and enable us to form a strong and stable Government capable of dealing with the innumerable and complex problems facing us today. We cannot get men from the moon. The same group of people who have brought Pakistan on the verge of ruination will rig the elections for their own ends. They will come back more revengeful, because, I am sure, that the elections will be contested, mainly, on personal, regional and sectarian basis. When they return, they will use the same methods which have made a tragic farce of democracy and are the main causes of the present widespread frustration in the country. However much the administration may try, I am convinced, judging by shifting loyalties and the ceaseless and unscrupulous scramble for office, that election will neither be free nor fair. They will not solve our difficulties.[7]

Citing the danger of disintegration and his duty to preserve the integrity of Pakistan, President Mirza claimed to intervene on behalf of the "masses, finer men than whom it is difficult to imagine," against the "traitors and political adventurers." Ultimately a new constitution "more suitable to the genius of the Muslim people" would be devised. What future role he envisioned for political parties he did not say.

[7] Proclamation of the President dated October 7, 1958, and published in *Dawn* (Karachi), October 8, 1958.

7. Presidential Politics: 1958-1969

Pakistan inherited from the colonial era a dichotomy between "government" and "politics" that was reflected in the mutual dislike of the bureaucrat and the politician. Men of the latter sort achieved Pakistan through the mobilization of mass emotions and aspirations, but it was the dedication to duty of the former that enabled the new state to survive. When in the years after independence politicians seemed to lack the skills necessary to work the machinery of government, individuals from the ranks of the bureaucracy—Ghulam Mohammad, Iskander Mirza, Chaudhri Muhammad Ali—perforce assumed political leadership. While the Muslim League increasingly asserted its identity with Pakistan, and hence its right to control the government, its internal failings and lack of purpose caused it to lose the respect of and be manipulated by the public services. The military and civil services were further disenchanted by the unscrupulous struggle for office between the League and newer political groupings from 1955 to 1958, and ultimately they intervened to preserve the state by setting aside the conflicting political forces. Thereafter from 1958 to 1962 the services attempted under martial law to pursue the national interest without the overt conflicts of party politics. The wide acceptance in Pakistan of the belief that the government ought somehow to stand over and apart from the contending forces in society may stem from Islamic concepts of the unity of the community of the faithful under a rightly guided judge and interpreter of the divine Law. It was manifested before martial law in the assertion in some Muslim League circles that the League as the national movement and custodian of the "ideology of Pakistan" ought to have a permanent monopoly of office. Non-League elements naturally were hostile to this claim, as were almost all politicians to the martial-law arrangements that deprived them of a function in society.

The Constitution of 1962 attempted to compromise in returning to the normal bargaining process of democratic politics while keeping the executive independent of it as a sort of Gaullist arbiter. Some politicians accepted the new system, but others felt that it did not permit them full political self-expression. They remained unreconciled and alienated from the constitutional order, and directed an unrelenting attack on it. The political process from 1962 to 1969 accordingly functioned on two levels: one concerned with the pursuit of interests and the achievement of demands, the other with forcing changes in the system. By 1969 the attack on the system succeeded in preventing it from responding to political demands and brought about its collapse.

Revival of Political Parties

The 1962 Constitution was, according to President Ayub, designed to combine national unity with local autonomy in a system characterized by a free exchange of ideas without the "disruptive" presence of political parties. The citizen was to participate in the political process by the election of his local union councilor on the basis of merit and abilities; the 80,000 councilors in turn formed the electorate for the Assemblies and the President and were to choose on the basis of the ability and reputation of the candidates. Parties were forbidden to participate in the electoral process unless authorized by law. This system received a trial in the legislative elections of April-May 1962, but most of the members elected by it demanded a return to conventional politics and political parties. Accordingly, in mid-July a government-sponsored bill authorizing the formation of parties was passed by the new National Assembly.

In recognition of the disintegrative tendencies inherent in Pakistan's complex society, the Political Parties Act defined the limits within which parties could function legitimately.[1] Parties established "with the object of propagating any opinion, or acting in a manner, prejudicial to the Islamic ideology, integrity or security of Pakistan" and "foreign-aided" parties were prohibited. The Supreme Court, on a reference made by the central government, was to determine whether a party fell within one of these categories. Such a party was to be automatically dissolved and its officers disqualified from election to an Assembly for five years. With the hope of curtailing the scope for opportunism, the Parties Act provided that an individual elected to an Assembly as a party candidate was to forfeit his seat if he withdrew from that party. Further, in an effort to raise the standard of probity of party leaderships, the Act debarred persons who had betrayed the public trust in one form or another from serving as party members or officers. These included any person who (1) had been convicted of an offense and sentenced to at least two years' imprisonment, until five years after the expiry of his sentence; (2) had been removed from office as a minister or governor for

[1] Text reproduced in Muhammad Rafi Anwar, *Presidential Government in Pakistan* (Lahore, 1967), App. III, pp. 332–334.

misconduct under the Constitution, until the end of his period of disqualification for office; or (3) had been dismissed from the service of Pakistan, until five years had elapsed. A fourth provision debarred any person who had been disqualified from holding public office until December 31, 1966, under the Elective Bodies (Disqualification) Order, 1959 (EBDO). This last category was of great importance since it included about 100 former ministers and leading politicians (the EBDOnians) who either had been found guilty of gross misconduct in office by a tribunal or had "retired" from public life rather than face a tribunal.

Because the first six months of its life revealed the Parties Act to have a number of loopholes, it was amended in January 1963. The term "political party" was redefined to include a "group or combination of persons who are operating for the purpose of propagating any political opinion or indulging in any other political activity." Furthermore, persons disqualified under the Act were forbidden even to "associate" themselves with any party, and the central government was empowered to direct such persons to refrain from addressing meetings or issuing press statements for up to six months. These changes were introduced to bring the restrictions of the Act definitely to bear on a number of EBDOnians who refused to accept the intent of the disqualifications and engaged in political activity without formal membership in a "party" as originally defined.

After the adoption of the Political Parties Act, President Ayub hoped that political leaders would profit from the experience of the past and would seek to form new political organizations appropriate to the new circumstances. This implied acceptance of the changes since 1958 and the development of parties that looked forward rather than backward.

Ayub's reluctance to offer himself as a focus for a party to support his political ideas and program left a near-vacuum into which very many old politicians but very few new ideas rushed. The uncertainty of Ayub's supporters concerning the role he should play—whether "in" politics or "above" them —made it possible for the opponents of the new system to pose as champions of democracy against autocracy. Instead of new parties dealing with national problems, the EBDOnians and their allies attempted to prevent the establishment of any parties at all so long as any restrictions on political activity remained. When Ayub committed himself to the Muslim League as the vehicle of his philosophy this attempt to stifle the political process failed and other parties began gradually to resume activity. Their overriding goal was not to function within the new system but, singly and in successive alliances, to combat and destroy it.

THE MUSLIM LEAGUE

The interregnum of 1958–1962 eliminated the Republican party from the scene but also destroyed whatever unity the Muslim League had enjoyed just before martial law. Most of the front-rank leaders of the League—including its last president, Qaiyum—were disqualified under EBDO; of those who were not, some opposed the new constitutional order while others had accepted ministerial office. The issue was clear: was the Muslim League to become the party of the "revolution" of 1958, or was it to commit itself to a restoration of the parliamentary system? Since the EBDOnians and their allies controlled the old League organization, the ministers and others who accepted the new Constitution summoned a convention for a complete reconstruction of the party, in order to mobilize support for their political position. The convention, in Karachi in early September 1962, was attended by members of all factions, including some erstwhile Republicans, but its legitimacy was challenged by the EBDOnians who convened the old League Council (last elected in 1950) in Dacca in October. A third group of East Pakistan Leaguers opposed the revival of the party at all and backed the National Democratic Front when it appeared. A period of unedifying factional confusion followed, all too similar to pre-1958 politics, with each group claiming to represent genuine League opinion and seeking to lure support away from the others.

The Council Muslim League. For some months the major challenge to the reorganization of the Muslim League undertaken at the Karachi convention was offered by the EBDOnian former party oligarchs and their allies. In an effort to preserve their control over the party they resuscitated the former League Council and prevailed upon the venerable Khwaja Nazimuddin to emerge from retirement to become League president in succession to the EBDOnian Qaiyum. Thereafter the Council Muslim League (CML) did its utmost to gain support by attacking the "undemocratic" Constitution and the Political Parties Act. Its efforts to reorganize and recruit new members were hampered by its lack of any constructive policy and by the ineffective and factional character of its leadership. The transformation of the conventionist faction into a full-fledged governing party led increasing numbers of Council Leaguers to conclude that they had backed the wrong side, and in 1963–64 the party was repeatedly weakened by desertions. In anticipation of the 1964–65 elections the CML joined forces with the other opposition parties, but Nazimuddin's death in October 1964 left it leaderless at a crucial time. Renewed vigor was brought to the party after the expiry of the EBDO restrictions, in the person of Mian Mumtaz Muhammad Khan Daultana (premier of Punjab, 1951–1953), but his election as party president in early 1967 signalled a new outbreak of factional dissension. Under his leadership the CML joined with the other opposition parties in the anti-Ayub coalitions of 1967 and 1969.

Party Organization. A key factor in the calculations of the conventionists was the assumption that President Ayub, despite his oft-repeated distaste for political parties, would eventually join them. Ayub's opposition to parties stemmed from his conviction that they served only to undermine Pakistan's precarious national unity. He refused to offer himself as a focus for an "establishment" party or to involve himself in the political fray but indicated his willingness to cooperate with—and perhaps join—a "broad-based nationalistic political party" if one could be formed.[2] On May 21, 1963, presumably convinced that the Muslim League was undertaking a genuine reorganization and was attracting widespread popular support, Ayub joined the party in each province as an ordinary member, and on the following December 24 was elected League president by the newly constituted Council in Dacca. He urged that the Pakistan Muslim League (PML) organization be structured to parallel the Basic Democracy institutions, but in fact the "new" League of 1963 departed only in detail from the hierarchical pattern of the pre-1958 era. It was all too evident that the League "election" of 1963, which ended in the acclamation of Ayub

[2] *Pakistan Times,* July 21, 1962.

as party president, in fact reflected factional adjustments among rival bosses rather than open contests. Local leagues chosen on this basis lacked rapport with the local political situation, and in 1965 for the Assembly elections many such leagues secured the adoption as official party candidates of individuals who had little genuine constituency support. The defeat by independents—most of whom subsequently aligned themselves with the League—of over 100 League candidates for seats in the three Assemblies indicated serious inadequacies in the functioning of local party units and the need for further reorganization.

In April 1966, after a year's gestation, a new party constitution was promulgated by Ayub as president of the League.[3] It provided a unified structure for the party throughout Pakistan, based on the enrollment of primary members in Union Muslim Leagues in each union council area. (Non-Muslims could be enrolled as "associate members.") The membership fee was one rupee for five years, the term of all party bodies and officeholders, chosen to correspond with the term of the Basic Democracies and Assemblies under the 1962 Constitution. According to the party constitution, each Union Muslim League was to have an elected council, a small working committee, a chairman, and four officeholders. At higher levels there were Muslim League councils in the thanas, subdivisions, and districts in East Pakistan and in the tehsils, districts, and divisions in West Pakistan. The councils at the second and third tiers were made up of officeholders from the tier below, but the fourth-tier councils included in addition eleven elected representatives, ten persons co-opted to represent special interests (including associate members), and, ex

[3] Text in *Pakistan Times,* April 8 and 9, 1966.

officio, all elected Muslim League members of representative bodies at that level. Cities of over 200,000 were to have separate two-tier organizations based on union leagues and were represented directly in the Provincial Muslim League Council in East Pakistan and the appropriate Divisional Muslim League Council in West Pakistan. The provincial councils included the chairmen and secretaries from the tier below, 200 members elected from that tier, and thirty co-opted representatives of special interests. The Pakistan Muslim League Council included the presidents and secretaries of the two provincial Muslim Leagues and of the Islamabad Muslim League (which was independent of the West Pakistan organization), 200 elected members (100 from East Pakistan, 93 from West Pakistan, and 7 from Islamabad), and 25 per cent of the total number nominated by the president to represent special interests. Although provincial party presidents and other officeholders were elected by their councils, the provincial president appointed his working committee with the concurrence of the president of the Pakistan Muslim League, and the latter appointed all national officers as well as his thirty-member working committee. Holders of provincial and national offices and members of working committees were ex officio members of the appropriate council. Prior to the imposition of martial law in 1969 Muslim League governors, central and provincial ministers, and members of the National Assembly were ex officio members of both the national and their provincial councils, and members of Provincial Assemblies were ex officio members of the latter council. The first election under this constitution culminated in the re-election of Ayub as League president by the Pakistan Muslim League Council in Dacca in February 1969.

The party constitution had obvious parallels with both the

Basic Democracies and the 1962 Constitution of Pakistan, and was meant to mesh the political structure closely with national institutions. The president "shall exercise all the power inherent in his office"; his appointment power specifically secured his control over the national "high command," and he had a veto over the composition of the provincial executives. The decisions of the national and provincial League Councils and working committees were binding on all lower tiers. While Ayub was head of both the party and the government the ties between the two were close, and the disruptive conflict that plagued the League in 1956 was precluded. Until the imposition of martial law the highest officers in the national and provincial organizations were usually ministers, and the working committees were dominated by ministers and legislators. In each of the three Assemblies the leader of the League parliamentary party was a minister. Thus decisions reached at governmental level could be enforced—within the limits of the politically possible—both on the organization and on the parliamentary parties.

Central and provincial parliamentary boards were prescribed by the party constitution to deal with elections and the legislative side of party life. While the Assemblies existed, the provincial boards consisted of the president of the provincial League, twelve members chosen by him in consultation with the president of the national League, and the leader of the Assembly party. They were supervised by the central board, consisting of the president of the League, twelve others chosen by him, and the leader of the party in the National Assembly. The main functions of the boards were to choose party candidates for elections and to "exercise general control" over the appropriate Assembly party, with the central board serving as a court of appeal from the provincial boards. In February 1965 thirty-seven Leaguers were expelled from the party by the central board for filing nomination papers to oppose official party candidates in the National Assembly election, and many more were expelled for similar offenses in the provincial elections. Any lesson in party discipline was lost when expellees and others who had defeated the official candidates were permitted after the election to rejoin the party. Potentially, discipline over members elected as party candidates was strengthened by the provision in the Parties Act requiring such a member to forfeit his seat if he left his party, but this did not affect individuals elected as independents, who freely deserted the League in February and March of 1969. In February 1969 action was initiated against several Muslim League members who had crossed the floor in the National Assembly and West Pakistan Assembly, but the dissolution of the Assemblies occurred before their seats could be declared vacant.

Party Effectiveness. Under President Ayub's leadership the Muslim League once more claimed the mantle of the national movement. While he had earlier appealed for support on a nonparty basis, Ayub now appealed to all patriotic citizens to "unite, work and achieve" in the League. He identified the League with the people, with patriotism, and with Islam, but he also welcomed non-Muslims into the party and warned that if the League should lose contact with the people he would sever relations with it. By making the League all-inclusive he apparently hoped to eliminate the evils, as he saw them, of the party system and to reinforce national unity. Other parties he called parochial and regional, living on slogans and resolutions rather than realism and work. Criticizing the "negative" and "destructive" character of the opposition to his policies, Ayub said that the concept of an opposition was not reconcilable with Islamic politics, which envisioned a unified party of the faithful. However, since the conventional democratic notion of an opposition had been accepted in Pakistan, he said it had to be recognized as legitimate, although it should be "constructive." [4] Thus while Ayub did not deny his critics their right to organize, it is clear that he regarded them for the most part as "disruptionists" of whom the people should beware.

The Muslim League was committed to Ayub's philosophy of unity, stability, and hard work as exemplified in the policies of his government. The League manifesto published in March 1964 declared that the party "stands for a simple, austere and hard life." Ayub cautioned Leaguers to leave appeals "to the baser emotion of the people" to other parties and take up the more difficult task of appealing to their "cold logic and sound reason" in the task of national development.[5] The manifesto endorsed the presidential constitution, indirect elections, the system of Basic Democracies, and the preservation of the united province of West Pakistan, and outlined realistic objectives in the progress toward the development of a welfare state. Just before the presidential election on January 2, 1965, Ayub issued a personal manifesto outlining his beliefs and the objectives he would strive for in the next five years if elected.[6] In it he repeated his belief in democracy "based on pragmatism rather than dogmatism" and in a "Welfare State where basic necessities are available for

[4] Speech at Rawalpindi, March 13, 1964 (*Pakistan Times*, March 14, 1964).

[5] Speech at Rawalpindi, March 15, 1964 (*Pakistan Times*, March 16, 1964).

[6] *Pakistan News Digest* (Karachi), February 1, 1965.

all" with complete equality of opportunity. He maintained
the need for "self-reliance" and "practical realism" rather
than "doctrinaire" attitudes in dealing with national problems. He promised a variety of measures, to improve the economic condition of the ordinary citizen, to associate the
people further in the administration of their affairs, to
achieve parity and balanced growth throughout the country,
to encourage cultural integration, and "to provide full protection and safeguards to minorities in Pakistan and to ensure
for them equal opportunities, rights and privileges," among
other points. In closing he urged patience, faith, moderation
("Reform should be undertaken in a missionary and not in a
vainglorious spirit. The objective should be to produce a
better arrangement rather than to destroy an existing arrangement"), national outlook, and hard work ("Empty slogans
and fond hopes will get us nowhere"). This manifesto became
the basic political commitment of Ayub's government and of
his supporters in the Muslim League, and its principles were
reflected clearly in the "Aims and Objects" of the party constitution of 1966.

Despite the elaborate formal party structure and Ayub's
emphasis on the need for popular support, the Muslim
League failed to become a live and vigorous party. Ayub's
essential disbelief in parties led him to attempt to speak directly to the people—his presidential manifesto did not refer
to the party even once—and to deal with them through the
official channels of the administration. The Muslim League
became simply a device to maintain government control of
the Assemblies and to recognize and reward the government's supporters. According to an extremely frank report
by a West Pakistan Assembly party committee, the enrollment of members was largely bogus and based on money

rather than men, party elections were by compromise and arrangement and were not open contests, party discipline was flouted and loyalty ignored, and communications between the leadership and party workers, youth, and women were practically nonexistent.[7] Party members were not involved in the making of policies, which were formulated by official agencies without reference to party opinion. The important responsibility of any political party to serve as a means of communicating popular feelings, desires, and grievances to the leadership, especially if that leadership occupies government office, was almost completely neglected. The League's lack of genuine local strength and appeal thus made it impossible for Ayub and those who believed with him in the value of the presidential constitution to present any effective popular defense against the attacks of the opposition parties.

THE OPPOSITION

The National Democratic Front. Upon the withdrawal of martial law and the resumption of political activity, the ghost of the East Pakistan United Front walked again, arm-in-arm with its former enemy, Nurul Amin of the Muslim League. In a statement issued on June 24, 1962, the latter and eight leaders of the Awami League, the KSP, and other components of the erstwhile United Front proclaimed their opposition to the "undemocratic" Constitution, demanding another Constituent Assembly elected by adult franchise to adopt another constitution based on federal and parliamentary principles. The statement of the "Dacca Nine" became the basis for a campaign against the Constitution, political restric-

[7] *Pakistan Times,* February 6, 1969.

tions generally, and the Political Parties Act in particular. Since many of the leading figures were EBDOnians—including Suhrawardy, who joined them in August upon his release from detention—the alliance resolved not to re-establish political parties but to create a "people's front" to force President Ayub to yield to the "popular demand." By early October the National Democratic Front had emerged, under Suhrawardy's leadership, as a movement without formal organization and not, ostensibly, a party.

After initial successes in arousing public enthusiasm and interest, the NDF began to encounter difficulties and its internal incompatibilities asserted themselves. The decision of both the (conventionist) Muslim League and the CML to resume organized activity made leaders of other former parties extremely reluctant to submerge their identity in a heterogeneous alliance indefinitely and to lose contact with their own supporters. A severe blow was the amendment of the Parties Act to make it apply clearly to the NDF and to silence Suhrawardy and other EBDOnians. In late summer of 1963 there was an abortive attempt, largely inspired by Awami Leaguers, to merge the supporters of the former Awami League, National Awami party, and KSP into a National Democratic party to supersede the Front. The idea failed partly because of the insistence of some NDF stalwarts on keeping their policy against party revival but mainly because of differences between Suhrawardy and the NAP leadership.

The death of Suhrawardy in December 1963 left the rapidly disintegrating NDF without a leader of national stature. Thereafter, developments in the two provinces proceeded separately. In January 1964 the West Pakistan NDF was formally established, under a council representing three revived parties (Awami League, National Awami party, and CML) and members of the former Republican party and of the then banned Jamaat-i-Islami. The Front was described as a "democratic movement," not a "political party," with a program confined solely to constitutional reform.[8] Its component parties continued to function in the Assemblies and elsewhere on the basis of their differing policies, and within a year the NDF as such had disappeared. In East Pakistan an NDF committee was formed in early March 1964 under the chairmanship of Nurul Amin on the basis of the non-revival of parties. By this time the East Pakistan NDF had been "reduced to the dregs of all the original participants" and was described as the "Nothing Doing Front." [9]

The Awami League. When the attempt to create a National Democratic party collapsed, the demand for revival of the Awami League became irresistible. In both provinces the working committees announced the revival of their organizations during January 1964. In East Pakistan there was a split between the majority and a nonrevivalist faction led by the EBDOnian former premier, Ataur Rahman Khan, who remained loyal to Nurul Amin's NDF. The view that a working party organization was necessary for the effectual prosecution of a political program carried the day, and all local branches were directed to resume activity.

The major task of the Awami League was to re-establish its popular roots after an interval of more than five years. In West Pakistan there never had been a thorough enrollment of members and establishment of local committees. In East Pakistan in 1958 there were said to be 1.8 million

[8] *Pakistan Times,* January 22, 1964.
[9] *Pakistan Times,* March 5, 1964.

one-anna members and a province-wide hierarchy of local, city, and district committees, culminating in a provincial council which elected the president and party officers.[10] The council was usually dominated by the working committee of twelve officers and twenty-five others selected by the president. Since all these bodies and officers were elected for two-year terms, their replacement was long overdue. New officers were elected in both provinces in 1964, and the central leadership was reconstituted. A West Pakistani, Nawabzada Nasrullah Khan, was chosen president and head of the central organizing committee to emphasize the "national" character of the party despite its weakness in West Pakistan.

The platform of the East Pakistan Awami League led by Sheikh Mujibur Rehman was indicated in resolutions of its working committee in January 1964. These repeated the demands of 1954 for complete regional autonomy and full parity in terms of economic investment, distribution of government posts, and so on. Other resolutions opposed detention without trial, called for the elimination of all political restrictions, and demanded the dissolution of the province of West Pakistan. Finally, and most important, the working committee demanded "a full democratic Constitution recognizing the supremacy of the Parliament to which the representatives shall be elected directly by the people on the basis of adult franchise and wherein full autonomy of East and West Pakistan shall be guaranteed." [11]

[10] See Mohammed Aslam Noori, "The Organization and Working of a Political Party: The Awami League," and Mohammed Khurshid Alam, "The East Pakistan Awami League" (unpub. M.A. theses, Department of Political Science, University of the Panjab, Lahore, 1958).

[11] *Pakistan Times*, January 27, 1964.

The National Awami Party. Initially the NAP supported the alliance led by the "Dacca Nine" in demanding the removal of all political restrictions and the convening of another Constituent Assembly, in view of the continued detention of its major leaders and of many political workers in the Peshawar area who had been imprisoned in 1961 for violating the martial law ban on political activity. When Bhashani was released from restriction on November 3, 1962, after a brief hunger strike, the NAP began to move in the direction of revived party activity despite its professed support of NDF nonrevivalist slogans. At the end of December Bhashani revived his Krishak Samiti ("Peasants' Society"), an auxiliary of the NAP, as a means of launching an agitation for "the restoration of full democracy." Its demands included measures relating to rural economic grievances, an independent foreign policy, and withdrawal from the Central and Southeast Asia treaty organizations, in addition to the constitutional complaint. Although Bhashani and the West Pakistan leadership of the NAP felt that the prolonged adherence to the nonrevivalist position had damaged the opposition cause, a strong element in the East Pakistan NAP led by the general secretary (Mahmud Ali, one of the "Dacca Nine") insisted on loyalty to the NDF. The formal revival of the party on February 29, 1964, therefore, caused a break with the Mahmud Ali group.

The program of the revived NAP was outlined by the organizing committee at Dacca in September 1963. It hoped for cooperation with other parties on a Pakistan-wide basis for the achievement of a democratic constitution based on the sovereignty of the people and direct elections. As before 1958, this meant full provincial autonomy with a subfederation in West Pakistan, with only powers of defense, currency, and foreign affairs vested in the center. An "independent, nonaligned and neutral" foreign policy and the withdrawal of Pakistan from military pacts was demanded. Other points included guarantees for civil and political liberties, economic parity between the provinces, nationalization of key industries, and the elimination of local taxes. Party elections were held in July 1965 in both provinces. In Lahore Mahmud Ali Qasuri—who had been recently elected president of the West Pakistan High Court Bar Association—was chosen president by the West Pakistan general council, along with other officers, a twenty-member working committee, and delegates to the national council session in Dacca. In Dacca Maulana Bhashani was re-elected president of the East Pakistan NAP. The national council of the party then met for the first time since the founding session in 1957, and besides re-electing Bhashani as president, elected two vice-presidents (one from each province), other officers, and twenty members of the executive committee (the president appoints ten others).

After the end of martial law in 1962, communist influence in the NAP became increasingly evident. Communists had participated in the United Front in East Pakistan in 1954 both directly and through fronts such as the Ganatantri Dal, returning at least ten Communists and roughly fifty party-liners to the Provincial Assembly.[12] The communist threat was one justification given for central government intervention in East Pakistan in May 1954, and six weeks later the Communist party was banned throughout the country. With the subsequent disintegration of the United Front, communist elements supported Bhashani's Awami League and in due course assisted at the birth of the NAP. Communist in-

[12] Richard L. Park, "East Bengal: Pakistan's Troubled Province," *Far Eastern Survey*, XXIII, No. 5 (May 1954), p. 73.

fluence in West Pakistan was never very great, except in trade union circles immediately after independence. However, by mid-1954 the Azad Pakistan party, later to become one of the constituents of the NAP, was thoroughly infiltrated and thus rendered "anti-national, Communist and undemocratic." [13] Martial law imposed some limits on communist activities after 1958, but in 1961 it was reported that the Communist party of India was undertaking the revival of the party in East Pakistan, where there were said to be nearly 2,000 active Communists.[14]

In July 1965 the Dacca session of the national council of the NAP called for the withdrawal of the ban on the Communist party. By 1967 the NAP was divided into identifiable "pro-Moscow" and "pro-Peking" wings, the latter in the ascendancy. In repudiating the Pakistan Democratic Movement, the opposition alliance formed in May 1967, the working committees of the East Pakistan NAP and of the central NAP endorsed a united front "based on an anti-imperialist, anti-feudal and anti-capitalist struggle," but derived from the "unity of the people" as against "unity of parties and leaders," and declared that the "struggle for democratic rights and the struggle against imperialist domination are indivisible." [15] In other words, like the Communist party of India in the early 1950's, the NAP called for a Maoist alliance of all classes in opposition to the government, while supporting those aspects of its foreign policy which contributed to closer relations between Pakistan and the "Socialist countries." In 1968 the NAP split into rival parties, one

[13] Dilshad Najmuddin, "Political Parties in Pakistan" (unpub. M.A. thesis, University of the Panjab, Lahore, 1955), p. 131.

[14] *Pakistan Times,* April 24, 1961.

[15] *Pakistan Times,* May 19 and May 23, 1967.

("pro-Peking") led by Bhashani and the other ("pro-Moscow") led by Khan Abdul Wali Khan, son of Abdul Ghaffar Khan.

Nizam-i-Islam Party. Although extremely critical of the abrogation of the 1956 Constitution, the NIP adopted a relatively pragmatic approach to the post–martial law political situation. The party was revived with little delay, for in view of their experience with the United Front and their obvious policy differences with both the Awami League and the NAP, NIP leaders preferred to cooperate with other groups on a selective basis rather than submerge themselves in the nonrevivalist NDF. The party's demand for a more Islamic and democratic constitution was detailed at a convention in Dacca in January 1963. The NIP indicated willingness to accept the presidential system if the new Constitution were amended to provide direct elections on the basis of adult franchise for both the President and the Assemblies, increased financial powers for the latter, and justiciable fundamental rights. It also demanded the restoration of the Islamic provisions of the 1956 Constitution, and maintained its commitment to the unity of West Pakistan and to the development of an Islamic social order.

Jamaat-i-Islami Pakistan. When the Parties Act became law the Jamaat was summoned into open activity without delay or controversy and immediately joined the chorus of those demanding the "restoration of democracy." The purpose of this was to permit an appeal to a mass electorate, which Maududi was confident could be manipulated by means of religious slogans. Maududi did not support the demand for still another constitution, but instead recommended amendments to restore the Islamic provisions of 1956, provide for direct elections, and make the fundamental rights justiciable. He linked the "restoration of democracy" with the survival of Islam, criticizing martial law, the 1962 Constitution, and the Ayub government in terms which suggested that Ayub and his Constitution were at best indifferent to Islam. These attempts to place loyalty to Islam in contradistinction to loyalty to the existing constitutional order elicited from President Ayub a series of warnings to the public not to be misled by "those who exploit religion to seize political power." [16]

Maududi's religious absolutism poses a fundamental challenge to the sort of liberal social order to which most other politically significant elements in the society are professedly committed. The Jamaat is an elitist organization, its membership (in 1962 totaling 1,367) limited to Muslims who after probation and investigation have been found thoroughly committed and loyal.[17] These are the leaders, the hard-core activists who set the tone of the movement and in theory share in determining its policy. In a second category, under less severe discipline yet with definite obligations to fulfill, are the associates (30,337 in March 1958), of whom about 10,000 are active workers for the Jamaat. In a third category are the sympathizers, who support its activities financially and otherwise without formal affiliation with the Jamaat as such. Operating through medical and social welfare centers, educational and labor organizations, and the weekly open

[16] For example, in his November 1 address to the nation (*Pakistan Times,* November 2, 1963).

[17] Organizational details in these paragraphs are derived largely from Mohammed Amin, "Jamaat-e-Islami Pakistan" (unpub. M.A. thesis, University of the Panjab, Lahore, 1958).

meetings of local jamaats, the movement reaches many thousands of persons each year. The Jamaat's systematic dogmas have a considerable appeal to the urban lower middle class and to Urdu-educated students and professional men. Much of the Jamaat's recruitment is through its student auxiliary, the Jamiat-ul-Tulaba, which has been active in student agitations throughout the 1960's. It is patterned after the parent organization in terms of categories of membership, and has branches in colleges throughout the country. Reputedly more than 50 per cent of the Jamaat's members are "highly educated"—an extraordinary proportion indeed in a society such as that of Pakistan.

Maududi's supremacy in the movement is unchallengeable, since he is the source of the interpretation of Islam to which all members are by definition committed. He has been re-elected amir by the membership periodically since the organization was founded (in 1962 he received 99.7 per cent of the vote cast). The amir chooses a working committee of twelve and appoints other officers and the heads of the twelve territorial divisions (only one of them is in East Pakistan) of the Jamaat. The Majlis-i-Shura, the central council of fifty, is elected by the membership by proportional representation from each division. There are also district and local jamaats, each with its elected amir and council. Maududi's writings and statements are accepted by all as authoritative, and members and others influenced by the Jamaat try to guide their lives accordingly and to spread the message further.

Successive governments in Pakistan have regarded the Jamaat as a threat which cannot be adequately met by political means, in view of its authoritarian and allegedly conspiratorial organization and its reliance on divine sanctions to achieve its ends. In January 1964 the Ayub government followed precedent, and Maududi and the entire top leadership of the Jamaat were placed under preventive detention. The simultaneous attempt to ban the party as an "unlawful association" under the Criminal Law Amendment Act of 1908 was overturned by the Supreme Court in September 1964 as an unreasonable infringement of the freedom of association guaranteed by the Constitution. Shortly thereafter the West Pakistan High Court, on a habeas corpus petition, ordered the release of Maududi and his colleagues. With these decisions the Jamaat resumed its activities, since the government seemed unwilling to attempt to proceed against it by reference to the Supreme Court under the Political Parties Act on the grounds of its alleged disruptive and subversive activities.

The Combined Opposition Parties and the 1965 Elections

The Parties Act failed to prevent the reappearance of the pre-1958 political parties under the old leadership. Although the situation called for united opposition action, the first effort to join forces against the government—the National Democratic Front—collapsed in a welter of personal and policy disagreements. The separate parties then reappeared, but apart from the Jamaat (and possibly the East Pakistan Awami League) none of them made serious efforts to create or re-create a broadly based organization or to relate its activities to the actual needs and problems of the public it claimed to represent. Prior to 1958 the importance and power of political leaders was based precisely on the lack of any real links with the people which might have served to limit or restrict their freedom of action by imposing a degree of responsibility. Emotional appeals through slogans and public meetings provided the appearance of strength without the embarrassment of responsibility for programs or policies.

The only element in common among the diverse groups of the opposition prior to the 1965 elections was a sense of frustration born of their alienation from the existing constitutional order. They disagreed among themselves on the role of Islam in the state, the system of electorates, the unity of West Pakistan, economic policy, and foreign policy—in short, on every issue of importance. Their inability to compromise on a common and politically practicable program made it possible for Ayub's government to outmaneuver them repeatedly. By sponsoring the Parties Act and the addition of fundamental rights and Islamic provisions to the Constitution, Ayub's supporters pre-empted the role of liberalizers of the political system and deprived the opposition of their major grounds for joint action. Although the latter were able to force additional liberalization of successive government measures, their collective lack of political effectiveness was shown by their repeated defeats in by-elections during 1963–64. With the approach of the 1964–65 elections the need for a new basis of opposition cooperation against the League became manifest.

In July 1964 an alliance, soon to be designated the "Combined Opposition Parties" (COP), was formed by the Awami League, NAP, CML, NIP, and the Jamaat-i-Islami. Their program, in essence, was the "restoration of democracy" in the form of a return to the parliamentary system of government based on direct elections; other matters were covered by generalities and left to the future. Their standard-bearer to challenge Ayub for the presidency was Miss Fatima Jinnah (1893–1967), the sister of the Qaid-i-Azam, who in September 1964 agreed to emerge from retirement to stand as a nonpartisan candidate, pledged to resign after restoring the parliamentary constitution. Miss Jinnah, the "mother of the nation," was the only figure upon whom the essentially incompatible opposition parties could agree—and that because of her promise to hand over power to them if elected. The parties hoped that the magic of her name would sway the voters and that they would ride to power on her skirts, although some had serious reservations about the propriety of a woman candidate for head of state.

Even during the presidential election campaign the various parties barely preserved the pretense of alliance. Struggles for position, apparent prior to the electoral college election in October–November 1964, continued. The result was that the rival claims of popular support persuaded both the COP and President Ayub himself that Miss Jinnah's strength was greater than in fact it was. After the shock of defeat in the presidential election, the COP was torn by conflicting counsels in regard to the Assembly elections. The decision to contest precipitated new battles over strategy and candidates. In East Pakistan the NAP split with the COP and put up its own candidates for the National Assembly, while the NDF, which stood for partyless unity, allied itself with the COP. In the Provincial Assembly election the position was reversed: the NAP again formed part of the COP list of candidates, while the NDF contested separately. In West Pakistan (where the NDF had ceased to exist) the COP rather petulantly withdrew from the Provincial Assembly contest, excusing its failure in the National Assembly election by accusing the government of twisting the voters with "terror and temptation."

The results of the elections confirmed the hopes of President Ayub and the fears of the opposition. The mass enthusiasm with which Miss Jinnah was received on her campaign tours was translated into only 46 per cent of the votes in

East Pakistan and a meager 26 per cent in West Pakistan. It is an arguable question how much of this enthusiasm and support was attributable to her—or her brother's—name and how much to conscious support for her political views. In any case her popularity was not transferable, and the electors made their own decisions in the Assembly elections despite party pressures, although in some instances these decisions may have been secured by corruption or official influences. The internal divisions among the opposition groups provoked the contempt of the electors and by presenting a multitude of candidates permitted the return of Muslim League candidates in some constituencies on a minority poll. Finally, the COP-NDF record of denunciation and denigration of the Basic Democracy system had placed them in an impossible position when they were obliged to appeal to the newly elected Basic Democrats for their votes.

The actual postelection strength of the opposition parties remained unclear until the Assemblies had met and the allegiance of the independents was determined. Three of the sixteen National Assembly independents joined the fourteen COP members in opposition. The United Parliamentary party led by Nurul Amin (NDF), official leader of the opposition, included four other members of the NDF, five from the Awami League, and four from the CML; the three NAP members remained separate. In West Pakistan only one COP candidate was elected, from the CML; he was joined in opposition by four of the fifty independents. In East Pakistan eleven Awami Leaguers, four members of the NAP, three from the NDF, three from the CML, one from the Jamaat-i-Islami, and one from the NIP comprised the core of the opposition; they were joined by roughly twenty of the sixty independents.

The Pakistan Democratic Movement (PDM)

Following their electoral failure in 1965 the opposition parties were once more in disarray. The international tensions climaxing in the September War with India caused all Pakistanis to forget their differences for a time, but the "morning after" brought renewed disagreements. In West Pakistan, opposition parties sought to make political capital out of the widespread and violently expressed popular disappointment with the Tashkent Agreement, while in East Pakistan—where there was some retrospective horror at the dangers to which the province had been exposed because of Kashmir—the opposition generally welcomed it. The isolation and apparent defenselessness of East Pakistan during the conflict had its aftereffects, and dissatisfaction was expressed over the state of defense preparedness in the province. In February 1966 Sheikh Mujibur Rehman, president of the East Pakistan Awami League, put forward a "Six-Point Demand" calling for a federal form of government "on the basis of the Lahore Resolution of 1940," with the federal government deprived of taxing powers and limited to responsibility for foreign affairs and defense, and separate fiscal and monetary policies, external trade accounts, and territorial forces for each federating state. President Ayub reacted strongly, warning in speeches during March that the "evil designs" of "certain individuals" would be "nipped in the bud," and (speaking in East Pakistan) that if necessary Pakistan would face a civil war to preserve its unity.[18] Ayub's tactless threat of force and the arrest of Mujibur Rehman

[18] See Ayub's address to the nation on March 1, 1966 (*Pakistan Times,* March 2, 1966) and speeches in East Pakistan reported in the issues of March 20 and March 21, 1966.

under the Defence of Pakistan Rules did not deter the East Pakistan Awami League from adopting the six points as its program in June. Other opposition parties were critical of Mujibur Rehman's demands, but the end result was the resumption of the opposition debate on the bases of joint action.

An opposition conference in Dacca in April 1967 concluded with the formation of the Pakistan Democratic Movement. East Pakistan Awami League representatives accepted an expansion of the six points to eight, which leaders of the NDF, CML, NIP, Jamaat-i-Islami, and West Pakistan Awami League agreed to endorse. The "Eight Point Programme" [19] called for: (1) a parliamentary federal form of government with direct elections by adult franchise, fundamental rights, free press, and an independent judiciary on the basis of the 1956 Constitution; (2) federal powers limited to defense, foreign affairs, currency and federal finance, and interprovincial communications and trade; (3) full regional autonomy with residuary powers vested "in Governments as established by the Constitution in the two Wings"; (4) removal of economic disparity within ten years, with foreign exchange at the disposal of the province earning it; (5) currency, banking, foreign exchange, foreign trade and interwing trade and communications to be managed by a board elected on the basis of parity by members of the National Assembly from the two wings; (6) parity in all central services, including autonomous bodies and the Supreme Court, within ten years; (7) parity in defense fighting and fire power in the two wings, transfer of naval headquarters to East Pakistan, and constitution of a defense council on the basis of

[19] Reported in the *Pakistan Times,* May 3, 1967.

parity; and (8) points 2 through 7 to be incorporated into the 1956 Constitution by the parliamentary National Assembly as a first order of business after its election. By confining their manifesto to constitutional and parity questions—and by using sufficiently cryptic language—the drafters hoped to satisfy the whole political spectrum from the provincialist Left of the East Pakistan Awami League to the centralist and right-wing elements in the CML, NIP, and Jamaat, including both the advocates of the disintegration of West Pakistan and the proponents of its unity, and the supporters and opponents of the 1956 Constitution. Economic matters and foreign policy were mentioned only in vague and innocuous terms in the accompanying press communiqué in order not to cause divisions over nationalization and the military pacts.

Although intended to provide a unifying common platform for opposition groups in both provinces, the creation of the PDM resulted in further splits in both the Awami League and the NAP. Despite the selection of Awami League chief Nasrullah Khan to be PDM president, the militant wing of the East Pakistan Awami League regarded the PDM program to be a negation of the original six points and refused to participate. By a process of expulsion and counter-expulsion in August 1967, the Awami League divided into the anti-PDM "Six Point" Awami League headed by Mujibur Rehman and the pro-PDM "Nasrullah group" Awami League, both claiming to be all-Pakistan organizations. The NAP had been excluded from the PDM conference, reflecting both the increased rightist influence in the other parties, particularly in West Pakistan, and the further leftward drift of the NAP under Bhashani's leadership. Immediately after the PDM was formed, the NAP condemned it for sidestepping the major issues of the day—foreign affairs (the demand for a nonaligned foreign policy and withdrawal from military pacts), economic affairs (nationalization of industry, banks, and foreign trade), national unity (regional autonomy, the dissolution of West Pakistan, and the achievement of the people's "real demands"), and civil liberties (ending the emergency and all "repressive" laws)—and for defending the "semifeudal, semicolonial socioeconomic order now existing in Pakistan." [20] Bhashani rebuffed pressures from the "right-wing leftists" for an accommodation at least with the Six Point Awami League, apparently because the latter gave insufficient recognition to national unity. Tensions continued, and in early 1968 the NAP split in both provinces; the leftist wing under Bhashani became dominant in East Pakistan, and the rightist wing under Wali Khan and Mahmud Ali Qasuri dominated in West Pakistan.

During 1968 several factors combined to transform the political situation for the divided and faction-ridden opposition. In January 1968 the government announced the discovery of a conspiracy to bring about the secession of East Pakistan with Indian aid. A total of thirty-five accused persons—including Sheikh Mujibur Rehman, three CSP officers, and several middle-ranking naval and army officers—were implicated in the "Agartala conspiracy case," which went to trial in Dacca in June before a special tribunal presided over by S. A. Rahman, former Chief Justice of Pakistan. Whatever the truth of the charges, their triviality and the incompetence of the alleged conspirators as revealed in the prosecution brief made the trial seem unnecessary; certainly it was a grave political blunder.[21] To the public it

[20] Reported in the *Pakistan Times,* May 23, 1967.

[21] The prosecution brief and the names of the accused were published in *Dawn,* June 20 and 21, 1968.

took on the aura of a persecution, made a martyr of Mujibur Rehman, and provided a dramatic focus in Dacca for the autonomy demand of the Six Point Awami League. Shortly after the discovery of the "conspiracy" President Ayub fell seriously ill, but although he was incapacitated for several weeks the constitutional provisions providing that his functions should be assumed by the Speaker as Acting President were ignored. Pakistan was in effect without a chief executive for more than two months, revealing the dependence of the presidential Constitution on the person of President Ayub and causing open speculation on the stability of the system.

A further stimulus to the opposition was provided by the juxtaposition of the continuing state of emergency and the year-long celebrations (October 1967 to October 1968) of the accomplishments of the Ayub administration in its ten years in office. The retention by the government as election year approached of extraordinary powers enabling it to impose restrictions on political activity did not harmonize well with the constant stream of official praise for the effectiveness of the Basic Democracies and the stability of the presidential system. Throughout the year the public heard much of economic achievements during the "Decade of Development," while the personal economic lot of many was far from happy. The claims of political and economic progress advanced in the torrent of speeches, statements, and occasions generated an air of apparent official complacency that increasingly angered citizens who could see around them the shortcomings of the administration. The ineffectiveness of the Muslim League as a channel of communication left the government isolated and, relying ever more heavily on official rather than political structures, apparently unaware of increasing public disquiet.

Democratic Action Committee (DAC)

Symptomatic of the changing political climate was the appearance of new political figures in the opposition. Foremost among these was Zulfikar Ali Bhutto, the wealthy Sindhi aristocrat who had served in Ayub's cabinet from October 1958 until June 1966, for the last three and a half years in charge of the foreign ministry. Bhutto had been the architect of the confrontation with India that culminated in the September War of 1965 and, disapproving strongly of the Tashkent Agreement which restored the earlier status quo in Kashmir, was forced to leave the government in June 1966. Having broken with Ayub on this issue, Bhutto proceeded to discover that the government he had served for more than seven years was based on coercion, oppression, and misrule.[22] In mid-1967 he assumed the mantle of a prophet of democracy and began to denounce the system that he had defended stoutly until immediately before his departure from office. His attacks on the Tashkent settlement and hints of betrayal and secret agreements both elicited a wide response in West Pakistan and alarmed Ayub and his colleagues, who preferred that book to remain closed. In November 1967, instead of aligning himself with one of the existing opposition parties, Bhutto founded the Pakistan People's party (PPP), professedly both Islamic and socialist.

[22] Bhutto himself makes it quite clear, in his affidavit before the High Court in Lahore in connection with a habeas corpus petition against his detention, that his disagreement with Ayub came solely over the issue of the conduct of the September War and the subsequent Tashkent Agreement, not over the domestic policies or behavior of the government or its constitutional base (text in *Pakistan Times,* February 6, 1969).

Bhutto had the peculiar authority of one so recently a member of the governing establishment, and he carefully cultivated the student community, to whom—bored with or indifferent to the existing political spectrum—his party had the attraction of novelty. The PDM and other opposition parties were skeptical and suspicious, although during 1968 Bhutto and his supporters were subjected to increasing official and Muslim League harassment.

The sudden outbreak of violence involving students in West Pakistan in early November 1968 marked a new phase in the opposition campaign. The perpetual student unrest, perhaps fanned by the events earlier in the year in Berlin and Paris, intersected with Bhutto's campaign to rally support in anticipation of the 1969 presidential elections. Equivocal and rhetorical allusions to violence and bloodshed in Bhutto's attacks on the government, which might have been commonplace and ignored if uttered by a less prominent personality, contributed to the students' sense of alienation from authority. On November 7 student protest in Rawalpindi at the confiscation by the police a few days earlier of goods purchased by students at the smugglers' bazaar in Landikotal in the Khyber Pass coincided with Bhutto's arrival in the city. Clashes with the police escalated, until firing occurred in which a student was killed. In the next few days protest demonstrations and processions occurred throughout West Pakistan, resulting inevitably in further violence, and on November 10 at a Muslim League mass meeting in Peshawar a youth attempted to assassinate President Ayub. This was the logical result of the overidentification of the system with Ayub, which had been emphasized during his illness in the previous spring. The government's response was the arrest under the Defence of Pakistan Rules of the "preachers of violence"—Bhutto, Wali Khan of the NAP, and leading members of their respective parties. Assurances were promptly given that student grievances would be met, and on December 1 Ayub announced concessions in regard to examinations, degree standards, eligibility for admission, and elimination of the much disliked provision in the University Ordinances for the forfeiture of degrees as a punishment for certain offenses. Nevertheless, activist students in both provinces continued to organize and present further demands for educational and political concessions.

The arrests and violence of November threw the students into the antigovernment campaign, the leadership of which became ever more diverse. On November 17 Air Marshal Asghar Khan, who had retired as commander in chief of the air force in summer 1965, announced his entry into politics, denouncing the government for suppressing democratic values and liberties, particularly by the maintenance of the emergency. Asghar Khan's unimpeachable integrity and military background made him a formidable addition to the opposition. S. M. Murshed, former Chief Justice of East Pakistan, stepped onto the political stage a few days later, envisioning himself as a possible presidential candidate. In early December they were joined by the retired Lt. General Azam Khan, a former colleague of Ayub who had gained great popularity as governor of East Pakistan in 1960–1962. The independents attracted public enthusiasm and were welcomed by the more conservative parties, especially in West Pakistan, but because of their lack of specific policy commitments they were regarded with suspicion by the two NAP's and the Six Point Awami League. Their role, therefore, became yet another matter of disagreement hampering the effort to forge a larger alliance against the government.

In early January 1969 the opposition forces once more undertook the task of devising a basis of agreement among all parties for the ensuing election year. Since 1967 the hostility between the PDM, committed to the restoration of the 1956 Constitution as a first step, and the Six Point Awami League, pledged in effect to the creation of a confederal Pakistan, had been confirmed on the issue of the unity both of West Pakistan and of the country as a whole. The split in the NAP had somewhat clarified the alignment of the Left, bringing under Bhashani's banner the revolutionary socialist elements aiming at nationalization and social revolution throughout Pakistan, while the Wali Khan party brought together the ethnically defined provincialist groups, both social democratic and traditional—not to say feudal. Unlike the former, the latter NAP was inclined to affiliate with the PDM, but the issue of the compatibility of Wali Khan's commitment to "Pakhtunistan" with national territorial integrity prevented agreement. The PPP added a complication to the political equation in that its "Islamic socialist" professions antagonized the PDM, particularly the Jamaat, and were only slowly and with skepticism accepted by Bhashani's NAP. Broadly, there was appearing a distinction—not yet a polarization—between the Islamic Right and a socialist or "Islamic socialist" Left, with the Six Point Awami League more or less at the center. From the Right, the remainder of the spectrum covered the PDM (the Jamaat, NIP, CML, NDF, and the Nasrullah Awami League), and the independents; proceeding toward the Left were the Wali Khan NAP, the PPP, and the Bhashani NAP. On the autonomy issue the Six Point Awami League and the Wali Khan NAP took the most extreme anticentrist positions. Only the Bhashani NAP clearly advocated boycott of the elections and a mass movement to bring about a complete social, economic, and political change in the country. To the "leader-studded" PDM and the Wali Khan NAP an election boycott was a means of constitutional bargaining, adopted primarily because of the impossibility of agreement on an opposition presidential candidate. Despite his revolutionary rhetoric, PPP chief Bhutto showed himself to be essentially a constitutionalist and was willing to challenge Ayub on his own ground by contesting the presidential election, in unilateral defiance of the opposition consensus.

After lengthy and delicate negotiations in Dacca the birth of the Democratic Action Committee was announced on January 8, 1969. The participating organizations were the Jamaat, NIP, CML, NDF, Nasrullah Awami League, Wali Khan NAP, Six Point Awami League, and the orthodox Jamiat-ul-Ulama-i-Islam. The participation of this last body, a principal sponsor of the NIP at its founding, indicated the political reactivization of Muslim religious organizations for the first time since 1953. Asghar Khan and other independents supported the DAC without formally participating in it. In an extravagantly phrased manifesto, the DAC denounced the "autocratic and oppressive one-man dictatorship" which "maintains its oppressive power and operates on the basis of widespread detention of political leaders, on a totally unjustified continuation of a state of emergency and on a monstrous and ever-increasing imposition of arbitrary laws taking away basic rights and civil liberties," and called for a boycott of the scheduled elections at all stages. To bring about the establishment of "full and complete democracy in Pakistan and to restore complete political power to the people," the DAC set out eight points: (1) a federal parliamentary system of government, (2) direct elections by adult franchise, (3) an end to the state of emergency, (4) the repeal of "black laws" including detention laws, (5) release of political prisoners including Mujibur Rehman and Bhutto, (6) the withdrawal of preventive orders under Section 144 of the Criminal Procedure Code, (7) the restoration to labor of the right to strike, and (8) the withdrawal of all press restrictions and the return of Progressive Papers, Limited (the *Pakistan Times*), to its original owners.[23] This compromise formulation omitted reference to the contentious questions of the 1956 Constitution, regional autonomy, and "One Unit" and avoided all social and economic matters. Because of the latter omission, Bhashani's NAP (which had not participated in the negotiations) did not join, although Bhashani approved the DAC boycott decision. The PPP, with Bhutto still in detention, remained committed to his presidential candidacy and independent political action. The DAC manifesto ended with a pledge to launch "a relentless non-violent, organized and disciplined mass movement for the early, speedy and complete realisation" of its objectives.

The mass upsurge sparked by the DAC in mid-January was neither nonviolent nor disciplined and soon generated its own momentum based on pent-up social and economic grievances. A DAC protest day on January 17 began a chain of events that led to police firing in Dacca and the death of a student on January 20, and thereafter to steadily escalating violence throughout Pakistan. Student-called protest hartals (strikes) on January 24 resulted in more violence and the use of the army in support of the police in Dacca and, during the ensuing week, in Karachi, Lahore, and other cities, with

[23] Text of the manifesto, from which the quotations in this paragraph are taken, in *Pakistan Times,* January 9, 1969. See page 295 in regard to Progressive Papers, Limited.

further casualties and destruction of public and private property. Student grievances concerning fees, examinations, and
restrictions on student political activity under the University
Ordinances were supplemented by demands for investigation
of police conduct, compensation for victims of firing, and
release of the arrested. These were fully endorsed by the
legal profession, long the mainstay of the opposition, through
bar association resolutions and processions. Beginning on
January 18 with a province-wide demonstration in West
Pakistan by doctors, other groups—engineers, journalists,
postmen, clerks—began increasingly to take to the streets
with economic demands. The ulama, who became involved
after a procession at the end of Ramzan, the Muslim fasting
month, on December 20 was roughly handled by the police,
were represented in the DAC by the Jamiat-ul-Ulama-i-
Islam. After police pursued rioters into a Karachi mosque
on January 24, denunciations of the "un-Islamic" policies of
the government, including the provincial *auqaf* departments
and the family laws legislation, became more widespread. At
the same time, tensions between the Islamic Right and the
socialist Left became more evident.

President Ayub's announcement on February 1 of his willingness to meet opposition leaders to discuss constitutional
changes "in the larger interest of the people" was greeted
with relief by DAC leaders. It signified the beginning of the
end for the Ayub system, but the situation was already passing beyond the control of the party leaders, whose behavior
was increasingly influenced by mob pressures. Amid continuing conflict between urban mobs and the police and army,
a growing number of resignations by Basic Democrats, and
more and more statements by Muslim Leaguers favoring the
opposition's constitutional demands, the President made suc-

cessive concessions in an effort to get the conference started. Bhutto and other prisoners under the Defence of Pakistan Regulations were released on February 14, the emergency was ended effective February 17, and invitations to the conference were sent to all leaders, including Bhutto, Bhashani, Asghar, and other independents. On February 21 Ayub announced his "final and irrevocable" decision not to be a candidate at the presidential election, in an effort to prove his sincerity and break the deadlock. The next day the Agartala conspiracy case was withdrawn, and Mujibur Rehman and other accused were released.

The primary constitutional objectives of the opposition—a return to parliamentary federalism and direct adult franchise—having been implicitly conceded in the President's statement of February 21, the various parties and leaders fell out once more. Bhashani consistently maintained his opposition to a leaders' conference on the valid ground that bargaining among politicians could only effect a redistribution of power and office among the elite and would not solve the genuine social and economic problems of ordinary peasants and workers, which had given the mass impetus to the agitation. Bhutto seemed to agree and, expressing suspicion of the motives of the DAC leaders, advocated the resignation of Ayub and his governors and the election of a new Assembly to deal with contentious issues. The DAC and independent leaders were eager to settle by negotiation as many of the outstanding issues as possible and to secure a smooth transfer of power to a new representative system, but their differences proved too great. The PDM parties generally favored the restoration of the 1956 Constitution, which presupposed the West Pakistan unit and East-West parity. Mujibur Rehman, supported by his Awami League, opposed the 1956

Constitution and, in effect resuming his party's constitutional demands of 1955, dropped a bombshell by repudiating parliamentary parity, until then unchallenged in the demands of the various parties.[24] The demand for the dissolution of "One Unit," previously voiced primarily by the East Pakistan parties and Wali Khan's NAP, was taken up by a multitude of voices in West Pakistan, with unrestrained and conflicting territorial claims for separate provinces and states. Even in East Pakistan demands were advanced for a separate province for relatively neglected north Bengal. The extent of federal powers, and hence of provincial (or regional) autonomy, was another area of disagreement between the Awami League and the PDM parties. Ayub shared the view that the conference (March 10–12) had no mandate to resolve these questions, and on March 13 he announced that the Constitution would be amended to restore a parliamentary federal system based on direct elections and that all other issues would be left to a newly elected National Assembly. This announcement was hailed as a success for the DAC, which was thereupon dissolved by Nasrullah Khan.

The disintegration of both political and public authority during February and March was not halted by the results of the conference. By early February student organizations—particularly the East Pakistan Students' All-Party Committee of Action—had seized the initiative, opposing negotiation between the opposition and the government. Both Bhashani and, after his release, Mujibur Rehman added to their own party demands the eleven educational, political, and economic demands of the East Pakistan students, the acceptance of which was advanced (by the students and Bhashani) as a

[24] Speaking in Dacca on February 23, shortly after his release (*Pakistan Times,* February 24, 1969).

prerequisite for a round-table conference.[25] While Mujibur Rehman agreed to participate in the conference, both Bhutto and Bhashani inveighed against negotiation and warned against efforts to frustrate the "people's demands." Amid constant demonstrations and a growing plague of strikes and *gherao*s ("lock-ins"), Bhashani's advocacy of fundamental economic and social changes based on "Islamic socialism" was expressed in provocative terms. He denied preaching violence and blamed the government for any that occurred, but he said that those who opposed the "people" would "not be spared" and would be "wiped out," and on one occasion even warned industrialists that the people would "slit their throats and eat them up." [26] Bhutto echoed Bhashani's call for Islamic socialism in somewhat more guarded terms, and in the prevailing highly charged emotional atmosphere both PPP and NAP supporters were involved in street fights with

[25] The so-called eleven points of the East Pakistan Students' All-Party Committee of Action were: (1) fourteen demands relating to education; (2) parliamentary democracy on the basis of universal adult franchise; (3) a: federal form of government and sovereign legislature; b: federal powers to be confined to defense, foreign policy, and currency; (4) sub-federation of Baluchistan, N.-W.F.P., and Sind with regional autonomy for each unit; (5) nationalization of banks, insurance companies, and all big industries; (6) reduction in rates of taxes on peasants; (7) fair wages and bonus for workers; (8) flood-control measures for East Pakistan; (9) withdrawal of all emergency laws, security acts, and other prohibitive orders; (10) withdrawal from SEATO, CENTO, and Pakistan-U.S. military pacts; and (11) release of all political prisoners including those under the Agartala conspiracy case. These demands and those of the PDM, DAC, Six Point Awami League, PPP, NAP (Bhashani), and NAP (Wali Khan) were conveniently published together in the *Pakistan Times*, February 25, 1969.

[26] Speaking on arrival at Lahore, March 8, 1969 (*Pakistan Times*, March 9, 1969; also reported in *The Times* [London], March 10, 1969).

followers of Maududi's antisocialist Jamaat. Nor were political leaders spared, for Bhashani himself was attacked in a train in West Pakistan, apparently by young supporters of Maududi,[27] and in Dacca the general secretary of the PDM, Mahmud Ali, was kidnapped and forced to withdraw remarks critical of Mujibur Rehman.[28] By mid-March violence against non-Sindhis had broken out in Sind, and in East Pakistan a *jacquerie* of murder and burning began to sweep across north Bengal. The local administration, weak at best, lost its will to function when Ayub abdicated, and its functionaries were terrified and helpless before the mob frenzy. These developments, together with the burning of the houses of ministers during February, gave grim meaning to the East Pakistan students' earlier ultimatum to Basic Democrats and members of the Assemblies to resign by May 3.[29] Bhashani's repudiation of the results of the conference, and the Six Point Awami League's determination to continue a "relentless struggle" for its goals fed the unrest. Alarm over the breakdown of law and order was expressed both by government and opposition, each blaming the other for the deteriorating situation. It was in this context, with PDM leaders accusing Bhutto and Bhashani of inciting the young and leading the country into anarchy,[30] that President Ayub concluded that it would be impossible for the Assembly to meet and for a constitutional transition to take place. He therefore resigned and handed the country over to the army.

[27] *Pakistan Times,* March 15 and 16, 1969.

[28] *Pakistan Times,* March 25, 1969.

[29] *Pakistan Times,* March 1, 1969.

[30] In a public meeting at Lahore, March 23, 1969 (*Pakistan Times,* March 25, 1969).

Martial Law and the Future of the Parties

Political parties were not abolished by the proclamation of martial law of March 25, 1969, nor by the subsequent martial-law regulations.[31] Meetings and processions were forbidden except by permission of martial law authorities (MLR 21), and strikes, lock-outs, and agitations in industries or educational institutions were prohibited (MLR 18). Spoken or written criticism of the imposition or operation of martial law (MLR 6), and the dissemination of "reports on provincial, sectarian and linguistic basis calculated towards territorial or administrative dismemberment of Pakistan" (MLR 19) were punishable by ten and fourteen years imprisonment. Subject to these restrictions, which were justified as necessary to permit a period of quiet in which passions could cool, parties continued to function. Unlike Mirza and Ayub in 1958, Yahya Khan made no blanket condemnation of parties or politicians nor did he claim to have a solution to the constitutional problem. His responsibility, he said, was to tackle immediate economic and administrative problems and help to create an atmosphere of mutual trust and good will.

Such an atmosphere will help in producing national consensus on the basis of which a system should be established to satisfy all sections of the people and at the same time safeguard the integrity of the country. We as soldiers have assumed the responsibility of creating such an atmosphere. That is the maximum that we can hope to achieve. The responsibility of reconstructing healthy political life in the country must be assumed

[31] Texts of the proclamation and of the martial law regulations (MLR), in *Pakistan Times,* March 26, 1969.

and honourably discharged by the people themselves. The community cannot and must not evade this responsibility.[32]

According to Yahya it was essential for the parties to work out a consensus on political conduct and behavior before full political activity could be resumed, and to reach general agreement on the basis of a new constitutional system, but he could not tell them what to do.[33] He also let it be known that a reduction in the number of parties would facilitate a return to normalcy.

The imposition of martial law brought great relief to the ordinary population, surfeited with five months of disruption of daily life, violence, intimidation, and terror, but it could not have been welcomed across the entire political spectrum. On the left, Bhutto and Bhashani had warned on the eve of martial law that attempts to "betray" the people and to "subvert" their cause would not be allowed to succeed.[34] They must have regarded the imposition of martial law as such an attempt, although they had been demanding Ayub's resignation and the establishment of an interim government. Cooperation between their two parties had been pledged in an all but meaningless pact signed in mid-March, of which only the last of the three points had any substance. The points called "for the establishment of democracy of the people on the basis of the recognized demands of the people," "for the establishment of socialism in conformity with the ideology of Pakistan," and for the elimination of foreign influence and withdrawal from military pacts.[35] The octogenarian

[32] Statement to the press, April 10, 1969 (*Pakistan Times,* April 11, 1969).

[33] *Pakistan Times,* April 30, 1969.

[34] *Pakistan Times,* March 25, 1969.

[35] *Pakistan Times,* March 11, 1969.

Bhashani was a genuine man of the people with widespread support, particularly in north Bengal, and was a fervent Muslim with a socialism derived from Quranic egalitarianism. His demagogy was an emotional utopianism for the masses, an anticonstitutionalist appeal for the solution of the problems of the down-trodden by an immediate transformation of society through nationalization and expropriation. Experience had shown him that elections changed nothing, and he both demanded a boycott and threatened that if anyone attempted to participate in elections "we will burn his house and crush him." [36] Bhashani's Islamic utopianism had mass appeal in West Pakistan but his supporters there mainly derived their socialism from Marx rather than Muhammad. Bhutto, the elegant product of Berkeley and Oxford, derived his socialism and his demagogy from a careful sensing of the political winds, having discovered the appeal of a complex of socialism, Islam, and nationalism to the students of West Pakistan. He had little following in East Pakistan. Throughout his career as an opposition politician he was carefully equivocal in his language, refraining from overcommitment, and unlike Bhashani was by inclination a constitutionalist, convinced of the utility of elections whether direct or indirect. His statements in the summer of 1969 showed a return to more thoughtful and pragmatic analysis, and he went so far as to praise the martial-law authorities for laying down the condition that parties must work for the integrity of Pakistan and the glory of Islam.[37] A leftist alliance between

[36] Speaking to workers at Landhi, Karachi, on March 17, 1969 (*Pakistan Times*, March 18, 1969). Subsequently, after the imposition of martial law, Bhashani seemed to be willing to participate in elections if held.

[37] *Pakistan Times*, June 11, 1969.

Bhutto and Bhashani can only be tactical, to disintegrate when it becomes necessary to pass from generalities to particular problems.

Sheikh Mujibur Rehman's Awami League found its hopes for the realization of its constitutional demands postponed indefinitely by the return to military rule. As had been the case when the Awami League first appeared on the national scene after the election of 1954, its leaders publicly insisted that their party pledges were immutable: "We are fighting for the people's rights. We cannot sacrifice them." [38] Hence after the round-table conference of March 10–12, 1969, Mujibur Rehman insisted that the party would continue a "relentless struggle" to achieve its goals. In fact the six points of 1966 were modified by Mujibur Rehman's endorsement of the students' eleven points, and on March 24 the official Awami League proposals showed some flexibility.[39] These called for: a federation of two states of East and West Pakistan, the latter being organized as a subfederation of four provinces, with each province and state and the federation to have a parliamentary responsible government; all legislatures to be elected directly on the basis of population except the West Pakistan Assembly, which would be elected by the four provincial legislatures of the subfederation; federal powers to be limited to defense, foreign affairs (including citizenship, aliens, and so on), currency, public debt and property of the federation, and salaries of federal officials; a National Finance Commission of six from each state to make levies for federal purposes on the two state governments; seat of the federal government and Supreme Court to be in

[38] Sheikh Mujibur Rehman, at Lahore, February 24, 1969 (*Pakistan Times,* February 25, 1969).

[39] *Pakistan Times,* March 25, 1969.

Dacca, and of the legislature at Islamabad; procedures of the Political Parties Act in regard to crossing the floor to be incorporated in the constitution, with further provision that expulsion from or failure to vote with his party shall deprive a member of his seat; preventive detention to be prohibited; and a State Bank consisting of two separate regional banks with responsibility for foreign exchange and movement of capital. A hint of further negotiation was contained in the report that the questions of the location of the federal capital, federal taxation power, and separate foreign exchange and trade dealings were adjustable. No reference was made to the role of Islam. The Awami League contended that by accepting this constitutional framework the aspirations and needs of all parts of Pakistan would be met, and the country would be unified and strengthened rather than weakened. On the basis of this program the Awami League can probably maintain its strength in East Pakistan and build alliances with elements at least of the Wali Khan NAP and of the former Nasrullah Awami League faction in West Pakistan.

The strongest expressions of approval of martial law came from the Muslim League segment of the political spectrum, which was glad to have the demagogy of Bhutto and Bhashani stopped.[40] Ayub continued to be president of the PML, although the legality of his election to that post was challenged by an East Pakistan faction. On May 14 a new working committee and slate of party officers was announced, on the basis of parity between East and West Pakistan. These included two vice-presidents from each wing, but both the

[40] See statements by, among others, Abul Quasem, general secretary of the CML, and Syed Hassan Mahmud of the PML, in *Pakistan Times,* March 27, 1969.

secretary-general and the treasurer were from West Pakistan. Leaders of the CML faction, dissident members of the PML, and Khan Abdul Qaiyum Khan, who in March had announced the formation of the Qaid-i-Azam Muslim League, were involved in tentative political discussions during the summer of 1969. A reunification of the trifurcated Muslim League may eventuate, providing Qaiyum's demand for the abandonment of "One Unit" and parity and the CML commitment to the 1956 Constitution can be reconciled with the views of Ayub's supporters. Such a Muslim League, backed by the full party treasury acquired under Ayub and a more authentic enrollment of members than had yet been attempted, could become once more a significant political force.

The more conservative minor parties of the DAC were the first to act seriously on the problem of reducing the number of political parties. On March 13 Asghar Khan had announced the formation of the Justice party, dedicated to unity, Islamic values, and the "basic human needs of the poor masses." Organizational activity was forestalled by the imposition of martial law, which Asghar could not have approved in view of his strong statements against the possibility in the preceding weeks.[41] After lengthy negotiations and consultations, on June 24, 1969, the Pakistan Democratic party (PDP), rich in leaders but short on followers, was founded in Dacca with the encouragement of Maududi.[42] It united the NDF, the Nasrullah Awami League, the NIP, and the Justice party, all of which were dissolved in the none too confident hope that their memberships would accept merger into the new party. Nurul Amin was elected convenor, with a

41 For example, on March 10, 1969 (*Pakistan Times,* March 11, 1969).

42 *Pakistan Times,* June 25, 1969.

sixteen-member committee. The party's general objectives were to ensure the integrity of the country and the political and economic rights of the people of all parts of Pakistan, and to uphold democratic and traditional Islamic values of life. In regard to provincial autonomy, the party was committed to the terms of the PDM program; the "One Unit" question was to be decided in consultation with the people of the smaller regions of West Pakistan. For the restoration of normalcy, the PDP advocated a return to the 1956 Constitution. A convention to organize the party and approve a manifesto was held in August 1969 in Dacca.

During the anti-Ayub agitation the Jamaat-i-Islami's national political influence became once more a source of controversy. The Jamaat's organization and dedicated workers made it the most important component of the PDM, and through the Jamiat-ul-Tulaba it was actively involved in the organization of student protest. The Jamaat aroused some criticism by its opposition to Chinese communism, unpopular in the pro-China climate in Pakistan during the 1960's, and was accused of being pro-American. The Jamaat was the source of an antisocialist campaign that resulted, at the height of the agitation against the Ayub government, in violent confrontations between partisans of the Jamaat and of the PPP and NAP. Despite the Jamaat's attacks on socialism, its economic reform program of 1969 called for nationalization of "basic and key industries" with worker ownership, a minimum wage of Rs 150 per month, the acquisition of landholdings above 200 acres with fair compensation and the sale of the acquired land to the cultivators, and the abolition of interest and speculation to "cut away the root of capitalism." [43] This was necessary, according to the Jamaat, to make

[43] *Pakistan Times,* March 23, 1969.

possible a free economy and the growth of democracy. Out-
lines of reforms in other aspects of national life in conformity
with Islam were promised in an all-inclusive manifesto.

The meaning of democracy to the Jamaat was questioned
after Maududi issued in June 1969 a draft code of ethics for
political behavior.[44] He proposed, in general, courtesy and
mutual respect for each other's activities among parties, each
pledging not to abuse the opportunities of office for party
purposes if elected. The code sought to forbid resort to "undemocratic and revolutionary" methods, particularly—in
clear reference to Bhashani—forcibly preventing people
from participating in the election process. More arguable
and controversial, it declared that "nobody is entitled to do
or say anything repugnant to the ideology of Pakistan i.e.
Islamic democratic order of life and the solidarity of Pakistan" and stipulated that "no party which does not believe
in the Islamic basis or oneness and solidarity of Pakistan, or
wants to establish any other system against the democratic
will of our people, should be allowed to take part in the elections." In view of the Jamaat's elitist political theory and its
conception of an Islamic state in which non-Muslims would
have a special status, there is reason to question the implications of the terms "Islamic democratic order" and "democratic will of our people" when used by the Jamaat.[45]

The process of constructing a political consensus based on
the "integrity of Pakistan and the glory of Islam" revealed
continuing disagreement on basic issues. The restoration in
some manner of the 1956 Constitution was advocated by

[44] *Pakistan Times,* June 15, 1969.
[45] See letter to the editor, *Pakistan Times,* June 20, 1969, from Malik
Mohammed Jafar: "Does the Maulana really believe in democracy, in
any known or conceivable sense of the word?"

many political leaders but rejected by Bhashani and Mujibur Rehman, among others. Even its supporters had reservations and expected that it would be immediately altered by a new National Assembly. The basic and always interlinked issues of parity and "One Unit" and the controversy over the distribution of powers between the federal and provincial governments would therefore dominate in any general election. Some opinion favored the imposition of a constitutional framework by President Yahya Khan, who hinted at the possibility in emphasizing that these constitutional disputes could not be allowed to become points of electoral conflict. In late July 1969 political restrictions were relaxed to permit party meetings and conventions (but not public meetings or processions), so that the search for political accommodation could proceed.[46] The popular strength of the differing viewpoints remained uncertain, with at least nine parties remaining in the field: the Jamaat, PDP, three Muslim Leagues, the Awami League, the PPP, and two NAP's. The Jamaat and Bhashani's NAP, in their very different ways, were alike in showing primary concern for social and economic issues and the reconstruction of society on the basis of Islam, although only the former offered a genuine program. The other parties, from Bhutto and Wali Khan on the Left to the PDP on the Right were primarily concerned with the manipulation of political institutions and only secondarily with their differing socioeconomic programs and interpretations of Islam.

[46] Address to the nation by President Yahya Khan, July 28, 1969 (*Pakistan Times,* July 29, 1969; see also the *New York Times* of the same date).

8. Political Forces
and National Problems

Along with the continued constitutional controversy and institutional instability, a political process that must now be regarded as normal has developed in Pakistan. In somewhat oversimplified terms, three major features in this process stand out. First, political parties have concentrated their attention on ideology and constitutional formulas to the practical exclusion of all else. Second, the parties have concerned themselves with substantive social and economic issues and have made policy commitments only when resisting or exploiting the pressures which aggrieved interests have directed against those in office. Third, the day-to-day resolution of the conflicting demands advanced by interest groups has been left to the bureaucracy. The distinction traditionally made in the subcontinent between government and politics, between the realm of rules, regulations, and decisions affecting the ordinary lives of the people and the realm of debate about form and procedure, has been confirmed. The latter is deemed the proper concern of parties and the former the responsibility of professional administrators, subject to more or less random "political" intervention by ministers acting to modify established procedures in response to particularistic pressures. There has been an evident tendency to enlarge the sphere of the administrator by the creation of autonomous bureaucracies—the WAPDA's, PIDC's, and the like—in order to remove additional matters from immediate "party-political" influence. On the whole the system has worked well enough, but it has broken down when the accumulation of conflicting demands upon which the party in power has been unwilling or unable to commit itself has overtaxed the ability of the bureaucracy to find solutions.

A breakdown of the political system resulting in the displacement of "politics" by "government" has occurred on three occasions in Pakistan's first twenty-two years, each time under circumstances more grave than the last. On each occasion a nonpolitical (or at least nonparty) leadership based on the permanent public services, military and civil, has made the necessary policy and structural changes to enable the bureaucracy to deal with the most pressing demands on the system and to facilitate a return to party politics. The first such breakdown, following the economic crisis of 1953–54, did not lead to a constitutional collapse because Pakistan's dominion constitution was sufficiently flexible to absorb the consequences of the governor general's proclamation of emergency and dismissal of both ministers and Assembly. Political life was not suspended, and under the compulsion of the Federal Court a new Constituent Assembly was elected which with little delay produced the 1956 Constitution, cutting the link with the British Crown but retaining the federal parliamentary pattern. In 1958 the recurrence of political blockages in the parliamentary system led to a second breakdown, but in the changed context it was necessary for President Mirza to invoke martial law and to abrogate the Constitution in order to displace the cabinet and parliament. After ousting Mirza, Ayub attempted to use martial law to lay the groundwork for a new pattern of institutions. The 1962 Constitution sought to provide a workable alternative to the parliamentary system, bypassing the parties and linking the presidential executive directly with the people. With the resumption of party politics, the new institutions, like the old, proved unable to provide effective channels between the political leadership and social and economic interests. Like its predecessors, Ayub's government lost its ability to assess the political significance of interest group demands and to respond appropriately.[1] Political and constitutional disintegration was halted by the second imposition of martial law and the abrogation of Pakistan's third Constitution.

The resort to martial law to surmount political and constitutional crises has come as a natural extension of the earlier use of proclamations of emergency for that purpose. Martial law in 1958 and again in 1969 was said to provide "cover" for the administration, a pseudo-constitutional authority both for normal legislation and for fundamental changes in the constitutional order. Martial-law regulations have aimed at preventing any challenge to the regime and have also been used to enact ex post facto legislation for the most part relating to matters such as corruption and smuggling. The jurisdiction of the courts has been altered only to the extent inherent in the abrogation of the former basic

[1] Cf. Gabriel Almond's comment in his foreword to Myron Weiner's *The Politics of Scarcity* (Chicago: University of Chicago Press, 1962), p. x: ". . . governmental and bureaucratic elites, overwhelmed by the problems of economic development and the scarcity of resources available to them, inevitably acquire a technocratic and antipolitical frame of mind. Particularistic demands of whatever kind are denied legitimacy. As a consequence, interest groups either become captives of the government and bureaucracy and lose much of their followings or are alienated from the political system."

law and the creation of a separate system of military courts and review procedures to deal with most offenses against martial-law regulations. The differences between the two martial-law regimes arise from the changed circumstances. In the political collapse of 1958 the "One Unit" and electorates questions were the only constitutional issues directly involved, and army intervention was genuinely welcomed. In 1969 so grave was the political and constitutional breakdown that all constitutional issues were open, and army intervention was regarded in some quarters as the last act of vested interests to forestall the revolution. The 1969 regime had the advantage of the precedents of 1958–1962 in formulating its measures, but it also had the disadvantage of a population experienced in living with martial law and hence not as awed as in 1958. Accordingly it was obliged to be more severe in its enforcement of martial-law regulations than its predecessor had been [2] and was less tolerant of judicial challenge or review of the actions of martial-law authorities or tribunals.

Despite the unpleasant connotations of the term "martial law," the principal significance of its imposition, both in

[2] The punishments prescribed for offenses under martial-law regulations both in 1958 and 1969 included death, imprisonment up to fourteen years, whipping, fine, and/or forfeiture of property. To the best of my knowledge the death penalty was invoked only against persons convicted of crimes such as kidnaping and rape, which were punishable under martial-law regulations. One close observer of the Ayub martial-law regime was of the opinion that its lack of severity and readiness to pardon persons convicted of martial-law offenses was a major failing. See Herbert Feldman, *Revolution in Pakistan: A Study of the Martial Law Administration* (London, 1967). In 1969 relatively long prison sentences, heavy fines, and forfeiture of property were frequently reported in the press.

1958 and in 1969, was the replacement of a party leadership with one stemming initially from the military services. In each instance the original proclamation and a subsequent presidential order were recognized by the courts as interim constitutional instruments, confirming or altering the powers and functions of public authorities. In no real sense was there direct rule by the army, although for the first four months of the Yahya Khan regime there were no civilian ministers or governors. Under the watchful guidance of the military policy makers, the bureaucracy continued in both periods to receive and respond to the demands and pressures of social and economic interests, drawing on traditions formed long before the arrival of politicians in the seats of power. Structurally the martial-law regimes have been revivals from a viceregal past, without even the feeble legislatures of the nineteenth century. Ayub's presidential Constitution was in spirit a return to the 1919 Act, beginning a new process of political education while retaining a fairly free hand for the administration to deal with the conflicting demands on the system, unhampered by "politics." Its failure poses for Yahya Khan the same problem of reforging a link between the politician's world of form and procedure and that of the administrator responding to the daily needs of the increasingly vocal and demanding interests that make up the society.

Interest Groups

The distinction between political parties and interest groups is sometimes difficult to make in Pakistan. Long before independence, organizations of all sorts had adopted the practice of expressing their views on the political and social issues of the day, and because of the system of representing interests (labor, landlords, commerce) in the legislatures some of these organizations put up candidates in elections. It is still the case that most of the myriad economic, social, cultural, and religious organizations in the country would feel their annual (or more frequent) conferences to be incomplete without the usual barrage of political resolutions in addition to those dealing with their more particular grievances. These conferences would also be incomplete without the presence of a high official on the platform to respond to the views put forward by the organization. Some interest groups have no identifiable partisan leanings or affiliations, some have links with political parties, and still others occasionally function as parties. The method of action varies, from the submission of a memorandum or the organization of a deputation, through the public meeting, to the street procession and demonstration, to the riot. At this stage, especially when the issue is an emotional or religious one such as the Bengali language movement or the anti-Ahmadi agitation, political parties are often involved in the formation of "action committees" or "fronts" to keep up the pressure on the authority concerned. All of these techniques, combining interest-group and party action, were utilized in the anti-Ayub agitation of November 1968 to March 1969. Interest groups were subjected to the same restrictions as political parties under martial law in 1969, with the general curtailment of freedom of expression.

Although it is fairly easy to distinguish the major power structures and pressure groups, it is rather more difficult to evaluate their influence and effectiveness in achieving their demands. Broadly, groups seeking to influence policy may be categorized as "modern" or "traditional" with reference to the manner in which their constituencies are defined. The civil and military services, the legal profession, the student community, and urban economic interests—both labor and management—may be described as modern forces in that participation in them is largely voluntary. Religious, ethnic, and landlord groupings are traditional in the sense that membership in them is usually a matter of birth rather than choice. Forces in the former category tend to be highly institutionalized while the latter groups rely to a greater extent on more casual and unstructured patterns of action. The line cannot be drawn with precision, for there are one or two quite sophisticated religious organizations, while student activities, for example, are relatively anarchic. Political parties normally seek to enlist the support of as many of these groups as possible and in turn are subject to pressures by them.

In Pakistan the public services constitute political interests of unique importance. As a body the Civil Service of Pakistan, acting through the CSP Association, is the most powerful, as the struggle over the Cornelius Report has shown. Other professional organizations of civil servants made themselves felt in the agitation of early 1969 in public attacks on CSP dominance. Not only are officials key channels through which outside interests apply pressures to the appropriate decision makers, but through the exercise of their official responsibility committed officers can legitimately advance particular policies or programs. From this derives the great importance of equitable regional representation in the central superior services. The economic needs of East Pakistan have been vigorously argued by the growing number of East Pakistani officials and technical specialists in the Planning Commission and elsewhere with considerably more success than by politicians in Assemblies and party meetings. The great public corporations—the PIDC's, WAPDA's, ADC's, and so on—are powerful forces linked closely to the administrative bureaucracy but with independent identities and interests akin to those of the rising industrial families. Retiring members of the public services often move into management positions in private industry. The concern of corporate enterprise, both public and private, for stability and ordered progress aligns it further in sympathy with the administrative elite.

Economic interests of the private sector are represented in one all-Pakistan association, the Federation of Chambers of Commerce and Industry (FCCI), organized by direction of the Ayub martial-law government to consolidate a multitude of earlier bodies. In 1961 it included eight regional chambers of commerce and forty-one specialized, nationally organized trade and industrial associations, established under statutory provisions to ensure that each is representative of its industry and responsibly run and to prevent fragmentation by factionalism. The FCCI is the principal channel of communication between business and government. It nominates management representatives on industrial courts and labor advisory bodies, and on the central and provincial governments' advisory councils for commerce, labor, and natural resources. These councils associate private enterprise with representatives of public corporations and the bureaucracy in formulating policy, drafting legislation, and evaluating current arrangements.

Industrial labor is organizationally weak despite government encouragement of the All-Pakistan Confederation of Labour (APCOL), consisting of the East Pakistan and West Pakistan Federations of Labour. Only a small proportion of the work force belongs to unions, factional strife and schism is common, and many "national" unions are not affiliated with

APCOL. The lack of unity arises from the poverty, illiteracy, and lack of sophistication of the workers, the hostility of many employers, and the ineffectiveness in the past of government machinery intended to safeguard workers' interests. Until 1969 industrial courts for the settlement of registration and recognition disputes or labor-management disputes after the failure of compulsory arbitration were so dilatory as practically to eliminate the right to strike, leaving the workers to the mercy of management with no alternative but illegal strikes and political protests. Although the unions have generally remained free of specific party alignments, political exploitation has been common because many labor leaders are primarily politicians, usually middle-class lawyers, holding office in a multiplicity of tiny unions. Among political parties the NAP's and the Jamaat-i-Islami have been the most active in the labor field, the latter linking religious with economic grievances. Government efforts to limit the proportion of outsiders among union officers have been criticized as restrictions on the freedom of association recognized in ILO conventions. Trade union views are expressed to government and management in the central government's labor standing committee and the Tripartite Labour Conference, and in the provincial governments' labor advisory boards.

The legal profession has always played a leading role in the politics of the subcontinent. Its members have imbibed through their training a thoroughly Western and individualist political and social philosophy, and a predisposition to challenge the claims of constituted authority. In general they are committed to the principles of British parliamentary constitutionalism, supported the Constituent Assembly's claim to supremacy in 1954–55, and opposed the overthrow of the 1956 Constitution by Mirza. Ayub tended to blame lawyers

for many of the difficulties of the country, and sought to reduce their influence by increasing the use of special tribunals
from which lawyers were barred and by eliminating justiciable fundamental rights. In return, most lawyers were hostile
to the 1962 Constitution and predisposed to support opposition views. An increasing tendency for bar associations to
adopt political resolutions in 1968 carried with it the danger
that the bar as such—and, indirectly, the courts—would be
identified with a particular political viewpoint, with far-
reaching implications for the coherence and integrity of the
profession. A related problem was noted by the retiring and
incoming Chief Justices of Pakistan in November 1968,
namely the tendency of judges to make speeches "on every
conceivable occasion" and so to obtain undesirable notoriety,
detracting from their neutrality and possibly compromising
them in regard to subsequently justiciable social or political
issues.[3]

The student community has had a tradition of activism
extending from the Khilafat and noncooperation movements of the 1920's through the Pakistan movement of the
1940's. By definition literate, young, and vigorous, students
are keenly aware of the rights that citizens in a democracy
should enjoy, and of the limitations of the society around
them. In addition, overcrowding in the colleges and universities, stereotyped teaching, language problems, lack of library and study facilities, and the expense of books and fees,
have been major and constant difficulties contributing to
student discontent. Concentrated in major cities, often bored

[3] The quoted phrase is from the retirement address of Chief Justice
Fazle Akbar, reported in the *Pakistan Times,* November 16, 1968; related comments by Chief Justice Hamoodur Rahman were reported
in an interview, *Pakistan Times,* November 17, 1968.

and eager for extracurricular diversions, students provide ready material for demonstrations and protests. Some of these are spontaneous expressions of feeling on political issues, some arise out of valid academic grievances, and most are exploited for political purposes. The leading student role in the agitation of 1968–69 was the result of an explosive combination of all three factors.

A major shortcoming of the political system is the lack of regular and established channels through which students can express their views directly to the provincial and central governments. Occasionally a minister or a senior official will address a student conference and will hear opinions and complaints on diverse subjects. Rather than making a serious assessment of their problems, the normal government response to student unrest is to advise them to concentrate on study and not to be "led astray." This attitude is made the easier because student organizations, like organizations in other segments of the society, are usually weak and faction-ridden and hence unable to speak persuasively in a united voice in the interest of the student community. The Muslim League's failure to establish healthy links with the student community during the 1960's allowed the government's case to go undefended and left the field open for dedicated opposition groups such as the Jamiat-ul-Tulaba. Once student unrest had moved into the streets, the authorities were compelled to stand firm for "law and order," with disastrous results when police firing and loss of life occurred. As had been the case in the anti–Muslim League movement in East Pakistan in the early 1950's, the government was made to appear oppressive and tyrannical and the entire student community was mobilized in a campaign for "democracy." Whatever the political result of such agitations, the academic interests of the students suffer when academic institutions are closed and irretrievable time is lost.

Closely allied to the student and legal communities is the press, which shares their commitment to the ideals of democracy with an added professional concern for freedom of speech and expression. The press has had to contend with a number of handicaps, including poor communications and newsgathering facilities, scarcity and high cost of newsprint, and poor wages and working conditions for journalists. Wage boards established under 1960 legislation have improved the newspaperman's lot, but in doing so have added to the economic burdens of the newspaper managements. The economic weakness of many papers has made them unduly subject to pressures from private backers or, more commonly, from governments by their granting or withdrawal of advertising. In 1959 Progressive Papers, Limited, publishers of the *Pakistan Times* and other periodicals, was expropriated by the martial-law regime under the Security of Pakistan Act, on the ground of its subordination to foreign (Soviet) interests, and sold at auction.[4] After the termination of martial law a National Press Trust (NPT) was established in 1964 by a group of businessmen with implicit central government support, to provide a sound economic basis for the publication of newspapers devoted to "national progress and solidarity." The NPT was much criticized by the opposition, and its acquisition of, among others, the *Morning News* of

[4] Progressive Papers, Limited, was owned by Mian Iftikharuddin, a wealthy member of a well-connected Punjabi political family, who died in 1962, and his son Arif Iftikhar. Both father and son were prominent in the NAP, which was deprived of a powerful organ by the enforced sale. A useful review of the press in Pakistan during and after the Ayub martial law is contained in Feldman, *op. cit.*, App. VI, pp. 226–230.

Dacca and Karachi and Progressive Papers was regarded as a front for government control.

In fact the press in Pakistan is not government-controlled, if that is taken to mean that the papers are sycophantic and publish only what the government wants them to publish. Government control over the publication of books and papers in the subcontinent has always been concerned with the problem of the impact of misleading or distorted reporting in a largely illiterate society which highly esteems the written word. The registration of presses has been prescribed for many years, with provision for security deposits to ensure financial responsibility and to prevent scurrility. Various other restrictions are possible under the Criminal Procedure Code and the preventive laws dealing with public order, and these restrictions are subject to challenge in the courts. When the Press and Publications Ordinances were promulgated in 1963 a principal reason for the nationwide protest organized by the Council of Pakistan Newspaper Editors and the Pakistan Federal Union of Journalists was a clause providing that appeals against restrictive action by the government should be heard by a special tribunal rather than by the regular courts. The government was forced to yield to the extent of providing opportunity for a hearing before action could be taken. Restrictive powers can be used to intimidate and have been invoked by past governments to silence particular papers, but to do so on a large scale is self-defeating and merely provokes opposition. Prior to 1969 the only period of substantive restrictions on reporting of matters of political interest was under martial law from 1958 to 1962, and at least during the first years the press fully supported the regime. Actions against certain papers during the emergency of 1965–1969 did not intimidate the press at large, and the

Pakistan Observer of Dacca continued a vehement opposition to the Ayub government throughout the post-1962
period.

Politically inspired official action against the press is not
the only important threat to press freedom. The law of contempt of court is very strict and imposes severe limitations
on reporting and comment. Legislatures have been extremely
sensitive to press criticism, on the ground that the representatives of the people should be above challenge. The 1963
ordinances were in part elicited by the government's desire
to prevent partial and misleading reports of legislative and
court proceedings and other official materials by requiring
publication in full. This formidable requirement was later
relaxed to require merely that reporting be "fair and reason-
ably correct." Since 1963 the press has policed itself through
a "court of honor" which hears complaints of unethical conduct brought against papers by government or offended individuals or interests. A grave menace to freedom has been
mob intimidation, particularly by students displeased with
newspaper policies. Recent examples were the burning of
NPT newspaper premises in Dacca on January 24 and of a
Lahore paper on January 27, 1969. Party-inspired campaigns
of intimidation against individual journalists have also occurred.[5] Despite these difficulties, the Pakistani press, on its
own initiative or inspired by an indignant letter to the editor,
can be both enterprising and muckraking. At its best, in
Dawn, the *Pakistan Times,* and the Urdu *Nawa-i-Waqt,* it
can be very good indeed and at its worst no worse than
scandal sheets known elsewhere in the world.

In a sense the military—as in Western countries, an ex-

[5] See resolution of the Pakistan Federal Union of Journalists, reported in *Pakistan Times,* July 5, 1969.

tremely powerful interest in itself—provides a link between the modernizing and traditional forces in the society. Army recruitment patterns in West Pakistan have developed intimate links over generations with the rural areas and with particular clans and families. The army (and to a different extent the other services) is a socializing and modernizing force, providing basic literacy and technical and leadership training to the men and maintaining contact with them after retirement through regimental reunions and ex-servicemen's economic development schemes. Land allotments to retired commissioned and noncommissioned officers are intended to provide energetic and stable leadership in newly colonized barrage areas.

In West Pakistan the traditional authority structure has been a network of landlords, clan and tribal chiefs, and religious leaders—the pirs and custodians of shrines. Often these categories overlapped. The Punjab Unionist party was built on an alliance of rural potentates against the urban middle class, while politics in Sind could be described as a struggle between rival "feudal" factions, in several important instances led by religious figures. In the Frontier, politics was essentially a struggle between greater and lesser khans, with the non-Muslim urban interest thrown into the balance prior to independence. After partition and the influx of refugees from India the situation began to change in Punjab and Sind because of the new urban concentrations without loyalties to the established territorial magnates. Muslim League politics—and Republican, in due course—were still built on alliances and rivalries of Legharis, Daultanas, Qizilbashes, Langarials, Tiwanas, and other families and tribes in Punjab, of Talpurs and Khosos, pirs and makhdums in Sind, of Mazaris, Bugtis, and Maris in Baluchistan, and the delicate balancing of tribal interrelationships in the Frontier. These groups dominated the legislatures prior to 1958, in the style of eighteenth-century England. Socioeconomic developments over the succeeding decade brought about important changes in the context of politics, with a rapid increase in industrialization and urbanization, the land reform of 1959 and the subsequent agricultural revolution, and the politicization of the villages through the Basic Democracy system. The great families remain influential, but future trends will be toward the decline in effectiveness of the old ties of blood and economic obligation and their replacement by more personal and local alliances such as have long existed in East Pakistan.

East Pakistan has never in modern times had a social structure like West Pakistan's, and with the elimination of the zamindari system the dominant rural class disappeared. Bengali politics has been in overwhelming degree the preserve of urban lawyers and teachers from "respectable" middle-class families, connected by marriage, college ties, and local patriotism based on their home district or even subdivision. Locally influential peasant families with ties to members of the political class link the latter with factions in the rural areas. The Basic Democracy system and rural economic change is altering the relationships between the rural petty notables, who dominate the unions, and the urban political class, themselves now challenged by the town proletariat. It may well be that as West Pakistan moves from a feudal to a more personal style of localized political relationships, East Pakistan will move from the latter to something akin to a bargaining system between different classes.

A further dimension of political action is the appeal based on ethnic identity. This underlay the Bengali-language movement and also the East Pakistan autonomy drive, with the latter's stated and unstated antipathies to non-Bengalis in the administration and in the business world. In times of political stress non-Bengalis, especially the Urdu-speaking Bihari immigrant laboring class, have been a vulnerable scapegoat for popular frustrations. In West Pakistan the anti–"One Unit" agitation in the non-Punjabi areas is essentially based on ethnic exclusivity. In Sind in 1969 it took the form of vigilante action to drive out non-Sindhi settlers in the barrage areas, particularly Pathans and Punjabis, who were considered to have deprived the Sindhi landless of their birthright. A more constructive use of the ethnic appeal is seen in the societies founded to foster regional languages and literature, dance, and music, which act as pressure groups in educational and cultural matters and which sometimes come into conflict with orthodox Islamic groups.

Finally, religious interests must be reckoned with politically. Christian, Hindu, and Buddhist organizations are now primarily concerned with educational and cultural matters, and with the defense of community interests against Islamic extremists. Apart from the Jamaat-i-Islami, Muslim religious organizations have not been politically prominent since the failure of the anti-Ahmadi movement in 1953 deprived them of credibility and respectability. The two principal organizations of ulama, the Jamiat-ul-Ulama-i-Islam and the Jamiat-ul-Ulama-i-Pakistan, retained influence in the rural areas, which continue to be intensely conservative and strongly influenced by local saints and mosque functionaries. By their participation in the anti-Ayub agitation of 1969 the Jamiats regained a measure of political prestige among the urban and more educated population. Other Islamic societies, for example the Anjuman-i-Himayyat-i-Islam and the Ahmadi,

Shia, and Ismaili community organizations, are concerned more directly with social welfare and education but could under appropriate circumstances become politically involved. The debate concerning the compatibility of socialism and Islam that developed in 1969 foreshadows a new controversy on the meaning of the Islamic state, one that could violently disrupt the community and force a general taking of sides.

The Political Process: From Martial Law to Martial Law

In the interplay of parties and social and economic forces in the Pakistani political process, ideological and personal threads are closely interwoven. As yet party politics concerns only a fairly small although growing proportion of the population. The great majority are concerned with the conditions of their livelihood and with securing justice from the local administration, and have little interest in or comprehension of the form and policies of governments. Political ideologies influence an elite, but personal ties extend throughout the society, affecting every interest group, and the ideologies are important insofar as they are reinforced by personal relationships. Because ideologies are seldom consistent and Pakistani leaders seldom rigid in their adherence to them, alliances of expediency including both parties and organized interests occur from time to time when leaders believe circumstances to be sufficiently compelling. Pakistani parties have typically been limited to a class of self-designated "leaders" and "political workers" whose alliances in power or in opposition have little relevance to the actual interests of the ordinary citizens who are recruited to serve, as in a stage army, in the processions and meetings that constitute the political struggle. Much the same can be said for many formal interest-group organizations, with all-Pakistan pretensions and a handful of members. Genuine mass support is won by the ability of a Jinnah or an Ayub to inspire public confidence—and the latter did do so in his early years in office—or by the ability of a Fazlul Huq or a Bhashani to exploit popular grievances against authority. The mobilization of interests and the construction of personal alliances, not large-scale ideological conversion, is the key to effective political action.

The upheaval that overthrew the Ayub system was a manifestation of dissatisfaction among a wide variety of interests and only in part the result of the political leadership of the opposition parties. Despite their continuous agitation since 1962 over the issues of parliamentary government, adult franchise, and provincial autonomy, the politicians had little impact until social and economic grievances produced a general atmosphere of discontent. Even so, only when the grievances of the offended interests began to be expressed independently in the streets did the agitation take on real substance. The government's loss of touch with popular feeling resulted in part from the hierarchical nature of the system, which imprisoned Ayub within the bureaucracy, in part from the failings of the Muslim League, which deprived him of alternative channels of information, and in part from his estrangement from the political opposition, which prevented his heeding and evaluating their criticisms correctly. In these circumstances, the centralization of powers and independence of the executive under the 1962 Constitution, designed to avoid the confusion and delay of the parliamentary system, made it both unresponsive and inflexible.

The inflexibility of the presidential system was paradoxical, considering Ayub's explicit recognition that constitutions must be subject to change and his repeated modification of his views in accordance with political realities. His dependence on official and sychophantic information prevented him from appreciating the changes that had followed upon the reforms enacted between 1958 and 1962. Taking advantage of the immobilization of vested interests, the Ayub martial-law regime had appointed a series of investigating commissions to study obvious national problems. A greater or lesser degree of reform had followed in many spheres: agriculture, land tenure, public administration and finance, education and labor relations. This dose of very moderate revolution facilitated the rapid economic development of the 1960's, in consequence of which new stresses and strains appeared. New vested interests developed, and the Ayub government, having given high priority to economic growth, tended to regard demands for further change as "disruptionist," to be disregarded or, if possible, suppressed. Thus, for example, labor and university legislation was utilized to restrict the activities of workers and students rather than to serve their interests.

By 1969 the Pakistan that in 1958 had welcomed the end of party politics and the advent of a forceful government had undergone many changes. The relative stagnation of the 1950's was followed by rapid economic growth, but the distribution of the rewards of greater national wealth was far from even. The distance between poor and rich became more evident, with a larger, more affluent upper middle class and increasing concentration of wealth and economic power in relatively few hands—the "twenty families" so often attacked from political platforms. The interprovincial disparities disclosed in economic statistics were obvious to the casual observer moving from Karachi or Lahore to Dacca. Within East Pakistan far-reaching improvements in administration and communications laid the groundwork for growth, but devastating floods and cyclones year after year had disastrous effects on the province's economy and on the lives of millions of Bengali cultivators. The resulting sense of despair and frustration in East Pakistan at the inability of government to "do something" was paralleled in both provinces by mounting dissatisfaction in the new industrial cities among workers caught between the pressures of low wages for long hours and rising prices for poor goods. The Basic Democracy councils proved inadequate to mediate these pressures to the administration, since in urban areas the union committees were rootless and ineffective and in the rural areas they tended to be dominated by the more prosperous villagers. However, the very existence of the 1962 constitutional order brought about changes in the political context. The Basic Democracy and presidential elections contributed to the politicization of the country, as did, in an unanticipated way, the sustained and vocal opposition to the presidential system maintained by persons of prestige and stature.

Despite the abuse and rhetoric of the opposition, the Gaullist presidential system under Ayub was not a dictatorship in any but a pejorative sense. The freedom with which the opposition attacked the government, both verbally and physically, was refutation in itself of such charges. The emergency of 1965–1969, with the vast powers it gave the executive, was unable to prevent the agitation that ultimately caused Ayub to resign. Even apart from the question of justiciable fundamental rights, the Constitution (specifically Article 98) was interpreted by the High Courts and Supreme Court to permit closer judicial scrutiny of official action than had been possible ever before, and this jurisdiction was exercised by the courts throughout the emergency. The use of restrictive laws by the government was, in a political sense, ineffective and merely antagonized further segments of the population. As a result, demands for the elimination of preventive detention and other restrictive laws were prominent in the agitation for constitutional change.

One remarkable aspect of the attack on the presidential system in the anti-Ayub campaign was the great value attached to the principles of parliamentary democracy. Agitations elsewhere in the developing world, and youth movements in the parliamentary democracies of the West, are contemptuous of parliament and seek its overthrow. In Pakistan the entire spectrum of opposition parties, with the possible exception of the Jamaat-i-Islami on the right and Bhashani's NAP on the left, seem committed in principle to representative parliamentary democracy. Despite Ayub's plea for a pattern of institutions based on indigenous circumstances and needs, the educated elite seems to regard British parliamentary democracy as an ideal from which any departure is to be regretted. The experience of 1947–1958 shows that unmodified British parliamentarism does not correspond with political and social reality in Pakistan; the experience of 1962–1969 suggests that a presidential system does not permit an adequate sense of political participation and tends to isolate the President. Some compromise arrangements, profiting from the lessons of both periods on these and other constitutional issues, would seem to be in order.

The lack of constitutional consensus in March 1969 was Ayub's justification for inviting the army to assume power. The administrative collapse brought on by the avalanche of demands for wage increases and structural changes in many economic and social institutions could not be dealt with unless the constitutional controversy were ended. This Yahya

Khan accomplished, by imposing martial law to freeze the constitutional situation while immediate problems were resolved. As had been the case in 1958, measures to deal with corruption and tax evasion and to screen government servants for improperly acquired wealth were among the first martial-law regulations and orders. Some senior officials were retired, and committees were appointed to study administrative matters such as financial procedures, the decentralization of West Pakistan, and the organization of the police. The first major full-scale policy statement was that on educaional reform and reorganization (see Chapter 2), issued on July 3, 1969, along with draft legislation. By dealing comprehensively with the educational system the regime intended to bring it into line with the egalitarian social principles of Islam and at the same time to eliminate the major causes of student discontent and thus to detach them from the forces of unrest.

Responding to the evident social and political strains caused by the rapid economic growth of the preceding years, the martial-law regime also introduced measures to increase the emphasis on the equitable distribution of wealth. According to one source, in 1959—at the start of the era of expansion under Ayub—thirty families controlled industry contributing 3 per cent of the gross domestic product; fifteen families owned three-quarters of the shares in all banks and insurance companies.[6] Free rein to these tendencies had been

[6] Gustav F. Papanek, *Pakistan's Development: Social Goals and Private Incentives* (Cambridge, Mass., 1967), pp. 67–72. According to a report in the *Pakistan Times,* June 21, 1969, alluding to statements by Dr. Mahbubul Huq of the Planning Commission, the "twenty families" owned 60 per cent of all major manufacturing industry and controlled an even larger proportion of other sectors of the economy.

given by the economic policies of the Ayub government, resulting in an increasing identification of the government with big business. In a direct attack on this pattern, the new government published draft legislation providing for the regulation of the securities market and for the creation of a Monopoly Control Authority to prevent "concentration of economic power, growth of monopolies and unfair trade practices." [7] The immediate interests of the working class were dealt with in a new labor policy, formulated after tripartite discussions with labor and management representatives and published on July 5, 1969.[8] The new policy, which recognized that "the worker has not had a fair deal in the past," set minimum monthly wages for unskilled labor at Rs 115 to Rs 140 (an increase of about 30 per cent), guaranteed the right of workers—including government employees—to join unions and reduced the number of essential services in which strikes were forbidden, provided a new conciliation and arbitration procedure, and established a labor welfare fund supported by government and private employers to finance housing and other services. Finally, the central and provincial budgets for 1969–70 increased social-sector expenditures and introduced tax changes benefiting consumers and encouraging investment in East Pakistan, which was allotted 53 per cent of all development expenditures. Whether the martial-law authorities would also undertake further land reform measures in West Pakistan, for example by lowering the maximum holding to 250 acres, remained to be seen.

The Yahya Khan martial-law regime of 1969 was professedly more temporary and less interested in new political or constitutional directions than the Ayub regime of 1958.

[7] Texts in *Pakistan Times,* July 1, 1969.
[8] *Pakistan Times,* July 6, 1969.

Its principal concern was the solution of immediate social and economic problems in such a way as to defuse them politically and permit an approach to constitutional issues in a calmer atmosphere. The nature of the problem facing the country was stated as follows:

No basic constitutional changes could however be enforced by decree. While electoral preparations go on, the political parties, instead of hurling vituperatives at one another, should be persuaded to get together to reach consensus on a fresh or amended Constitution answering the requirements of party discipline, governmental stability and social justice. A durable constitution is not imposed by one region upon another or by one faction upon the entire country; it must embody the largest measure of agreement among people's chosen representatives on a system of government emerging from the national background and reflecting national priorities. The task should brook no further delay. There can be no illusion about where this country can be landed by party strife, political vacuum, perpetual framing and abrogation of Constitutions, and the establishment of Martial Law as the normal pattern of administration.[9]

The Constitutional Future: Is Martial Law Normal?

The quest for constitutional consensus in Pakistan is severely handicapped by the desire for instant solutions, for panaceas—a favorite political term—for the ills of society. Alone among political leaders of the post-Jinnah era, Ayub Khan refused to deal in absolute answers and infallible institutions, insisting that problem solving requires time, patience, and the adjustment of theories to social and political realities, and appealing to reason rather than emotion. Others

[9] Abdul Majid, "The Test of the Merger Pudding," *Pakistan Times,* July 3, 1969.

have insisted on perfection in terms of a party ideology, and the result has been continual agitation and institutional uncertainty. Many groups cherish the conviction that once enlightened by the appropriate ideology the entire population will rally together, leaving only the "enemies of Islam," "disruptionists," or "anti-people" elements beyond the pale. This tendency may be derived in part from the Islamic ideal of unity of belief and action, translated into the political sphere and accepted even by those who are only nominally Muslims. It has been true of the Muslim League and of groups as diverse as the Jamaat-i-Islami and the Communists, while every successive opposition formation has arrogated to itself the sole right to speak for "the people." Far from uniting the various political forces, this one-party ideal divides them further, for each envisions a different constitutional order based on its own ideology. Parties not in power seek not to advance alternative policies but to alter the constitutional framework to their own advantage. Those in power regard their critics with suspicion and refuse to credit them with either honesty or sincerity. Since each group believes itself to have a monopoly of virtue, cooperation is almost as difficult between groups in the opposition as between the opposition and the party in power.

Despite the apparent emphasis on ideological commitment—or perhaps because of it—Pakistani parties are extremely dependent on personal allegiances. Even the Jamaat, with its rigid ideological base, would collapse without Maududi. The Muslim League was strong and factionalism suppressed under Jinnah, less so under Liaqat, and then disintegrated under his successors. The United Front of East Pakistan was the creation of Fazlul Huq, Suhrawardy, and Bhashani and fell apart when they disagreed. The NDF,

COP, PDM, and DAC have all been alliances based on momentarily compatible personalities and their individual followings. The Awami League and the NAP have always claimed to be popular parties, but personal rivalries more than doctrinal differences have caused successive schisms. The post-1962 Muslim League was transformed from a collection of factions into a united party by the leadership of Ayub, and began to disintegrate when he lost his grip on power. The CML was from the start a monument to the personal interests of its leaders, and like it the PDP was the creation of leaders who were unable even to command the loyalty of all factions of their former parties. In short, personality clashes compound the ideological fragmentation of the political community.

The basic weakness in Pakistan has been the lack of a firm set of shared values in the society. Democracy is a system under which the members of a society have freedom of choice: freedom to choose between alternative courses of action or solutions to problems, and accordingly freedom of discussion upon which to base the choice. In turn, free discussion implies agreement on the legitimacy of differing viewpoints, and agreement by the minority to accept the decisions of the majority as their own and to attempt to change them only through further discussion. All this presupposes common values, a framework of things that are "done" and things that are "not done" which will restrain persons from abusing their power—be it economic, social, or political—to curtail freedom of discussion and choice or to set aside the decisions of the society. The impact of modern education has created a ruling elite with at least an academic familiarity with and commitment to the moral values of liberal democracy, but the mass of the people adhere to the traditional mores of Indo-Islamic society in their particular Bengali, Sindhi, Punjabi, or Pathan manifestations. Between the dominant elite and the traditional mass is the indefinite but large and growing bloc of those who, under the influence of the Western impact, have been shaken away from the traditional system and are no longer subject to its sanctions, but who still cannot be said either to share the values of Western democracy or to have agreed upon an effective Islamic value structure. None of these various elements in the society can fully understand what motivates the others, nor can the moral sanctions of one control the conduct of members of another in the social or in the political sphere. The preservation of formal democratic institutions therefore rests on a very precarious base.

The importance of the Islamic issue in the political and constitutional debate is that it seeks to come to grips with the basic problem of consensus. Unfortunately Islam has proved to be a divisive rather than an integrating force, in that various schools of thought have been advanced in ways that have led to further alienation and antagonism between groups. The recently awakened controversy concerning Islam and socialism is an example, although the debate could prove to be healthy and constructive if it were possible to keep it within reasonable bounds. The educational policy of the martial-law regime in 1969, in putting renewed emphasis on Islam as a vehicle of national integration and in moving to diminish the hitherto powerful influence of foreign Christian institutions, recognizes the critical importance of the schools in closing the gaps in a society in which 45 per cent of the population is below fifteen years of age.

The lack of consensus is revealed most graphically in the federal issue. Demands for separate provincial entities in

West Pakistan and for virtually unlimited autonomy for East Pakistan reveal a deep sense of mutual distrust, which is particularly evident in the inflexible stand of the Awami League since 1954 on the question of limiting federal powers to defense, foreign affairs, and currency. East Pakistani fears and demands have been dogmatized with an ideological justification by reference to the Lahore Resolution of 1940, although it seems clear that the latter was superseded by the reference in the Delhi Resolution of 1946 to one united Pakistan. Awami League demands for the elimination of federal taxation powers do not seem consistent with the League's declared objective of a strong and united Pakistan. The repudiation of parity by East Pakistanis and their insistence on the dissolution of West Pakistan are further indications of distrust, which seem sure to be countered by a renewal of the electorates controversy and the argument over the merits of a bicameral legislature to guard against a regionally biased parliamentary majority.

The insistence of Pakistani politicians on the restoration of a parliamentary system poses grave problems for the society, since agreement among political leaders goes no further. The system of parliamentary democracy developed in England works on the basis of conventions and understandings, the agreement of gentlemen that public business will be conducted in a particular way and that gentlemen may disagree yet still work in the public interest. Such agreement has not existed in Pakistan; in the past the conventions imported from Britain have been overthrown and the morality of gentlemen abandoned, and disagreement has been regarded as sedition or worse. Prior to independence Muslim leaders were skeptical about the suitability of parliamentary democracy in the subcontinent, and Jinnah's apparent presumption that a system he regarded as unworkable by Hindus and Muslims together would be workable by Muslims alone has not received much substantiation in the Pakistani experience. Parliamentary government permits a broader sense of participation than is possible in a single-executive presidential system, but only if there is sufficient party stability to maintain an effective cabinet in office for significant periods. Unless a remarkable conversion to pragmatism occurs, it does not seem that there will be a political consensus upon which a stable party system can be built or an effective representative government can function.

In the absence of agreement, the only alternative is the imposition of a political consensus. In principle the agency for such an imposition could be a powerful party or political movement, a foreign power by means of conquest, or an internal force of some kind. The lack of the first up until the present time has already been made clear, and the second is by definition beyond the limits of domestic politics. The third of these possibilities has become a reality in Pakistan. Preventive and restrictive powers are essentially instruments for the imposition of limits—a legally defined consensus— on the behavior of individuals or groups within the society who do not accept or recognize the established legal norms. Emergency powers apply the same principle to situations in which the political and institutional norms embodied in the Constitution are threatened. Pakistan's political system has in effect recognized martial law as an acceptable, if not yet normal, extension of emergency powers for the purpose of overcoming constitutional deadlocks in the transition from one stage of development to the next. By an implicit negative consensus, most elements in the society appear to rely upon the professional and nonpolitical services to follow the traditions of their colonial predecessors and to enforce the broad limits within which political controversy, consistent with the integrity of the state, may proceed. Ayub imposed such a consensus under a very mild martial-law regime and introduced a Constitution intended to embrace both unity and diversity, hoping it would provide stability and permit a broad agreement to evolve through the Basic Democracies. The circumstances of the collapse of the presidential system indicated that in 1969 the society was still not sufficiently coherent to be able to work out its problems within a given constitutional order. Yahya Khan cannot avoid the obligation of laying down ground rules for the future, although the difficulties of imposing constitutional solutions on an awakening populace are mounting.

Glossary

anna: one-sixteenth of a rupee.

barrage: a structure that obstructs river flow to divert water for irrigation purposes, differing from a dam in not creating a reservoir.

bhakti: worship, adoration; devotionalism.

bigha: an East Pakistan land measure; one-third of an acre.

crore: ten million.

Hadith: an anecdote or tradition concerning the Prophet or his Companions; also, the body of such anecdotes or traditions.

imam: one who leads the prayer.

jihad: holy war; to exert one's self "in the path of Allah."

khilafat: caliphate; rule by a caliph (khalifa).

makhdum: a holy man (see pir).

mujahid: one who participates in jihad.

pir: a holy man or saint, usually a Sufi.

polder: a tract of submerged land reclaimed by the use of dikes and dams.

qadi: a Muslim judge.

Quran: God's revelation to the Prophet Muhammad; the Koran.

raj: rule or government.

Shariah: the law of Islam.

Shia: the smaller of the two major sects of Islam; originally, the followers of Ali, the Prophet's cousin and son-in-law.

Sufi: a follower of one of the mystic schools of thought within Sunni Islam.

Sunnah: exemplary or normative tradition and practice of the Prophet and the orthodox community.

Sunni: orthodox Islam; the larger of the two major sects.

tehsil: a revenue jurisdiction; in West Pakistan, the principal administrative unit below the district.

thana: a police jurisdiction; in East Pakistan, the lowest general territorial administrative unit.

ulama: those who are learned in the law of Islam; singular, *alim.*

waqf: a charitable trust established under Islamic law; plural, *auqaf.*

zamindar: in East Pakistan prior to the enactment of State Acquisition legislation in 1951, one of a class of landholders responsible for the collection of land revenue and its payment directly to the state; in West Pakistan, a peasant proprietor.

Selected Bibliography

Indian Islam and the Pakistan Movement

Abbott, Freeland. *Islam and Pakistan.* Ithaca: Cornell University Press, 1968. A survey of intellectual trends and reform movements in British India and modern Pakistan.

Afzal, M. Rafique, ed. *Selected Speeches and Statements of the Quaid-i-Azam Mohammad Ali Jinnah (1911–34 and 1947–48).* Lahore: Research Society of Pakistan, University of the Punjab, 1966. Includes materials not contained in Jamil-ud-Din Ahmad's collection.

Aga Khan, His Highness the. *The Memoirs of Aga Khan: World Enough and Time.* London: Cassell, 1954. The autobiography of one of the founders of the Muslim League.

Ahmad, Aziz. *Studies in Islamic Culture in the Indian Environment.* Oxford: Clarendon Press, 1964. An indispensable study of the cultural interaction between Islam and Hinduism.

———. *Islamic Modernism in India and Pakistan, 1857–1964.* London: Oxford University Press, 1967. A technical analysis of trends in Islam since 1857, a good complement to Abbott's study.

Ahmad, Jamil-ud-Din, ed. *Some Recent Speeches and Writings of Mr. Jinnah.* Lahore: Shaikh Muhammad Ashraf. Vol. I, 5th ed., 1952. Vol. II, 1947.

Albiruni, A. H. *Makers of Pakistan and Modern Muslim India.* Lahore: Shaikh Muhammad Ashraf, 1950. Short biographical sketches of Muslim leaders from Sir Syed Ahmad Khan to Liaqat Ali Khan.

Ali, Chaudhri Muhammad. *The Emergence of Pakistan.* New York and London: Columbia University Press, 1967. An authoritative account of the circumstances of partition by the senior Muslim official involved, who was later secretary-general of the government of Pakistan and (1955–56) prime minister.

Allana, G., ed. *Pakistan Movement: Historic Documents.* Karachi: Department of International Relations, University of Karachi, 1967. Includes letters, statements, and documents from 1882 to 1947.

———. *Quaid-e-Azam Jinnah: The Story of a Nation.* Lahore: Ferozsons, 1967. Includes much hitherto unpublished information, especially on Jinnah's early life and family background.

Ambedkar, B. R. *Pakistan; or, The Partition of India.* 3d ed. Bombay: Thacker, 1946. The demand for Pakistan as seen by the leader of India's untouchables.

Ameer Ali, Syed. *The Spirit of Islam.* London: Christophers, 1922. The classic modernist statement of Islam as a liberal and progressive faith.

Ashraf, Muhammad, comp. *Cabinet Mission and After.* Lahore: Shaikh Muhammad Ashraf, 1946. Letters and documents covering negotiations leading up to the formation of the interim government by Congress in 1946, from the Pakistani viewpoint.

Aziz, K. K. *Britain and Muslim India.* London: Heinemann, 1963. Traces factors and agencies involved in the formation of public opinion in Britain on Muslim India and the Pakistan movement.

Baljon, J. M. S. *The Reforms and Religious Ideas of Sir Sayyid Ahmad Khan.* 2d ed. Lahore: Orientalia, 1958. A short but thorough study of the life and contributions of the father of the Aligarh movement and the Muslim revival.

Birdwood, Christopher Bromhead, Baron. *A Continent Experiments.* London: Skeffington, 1946. A British officer's sympathetic and understanding picture of the political situation in India at the close of the second world war.

Bolitho, Hector. *Jinnah: Creator of Pakistan.* London: John

Murray, 1954. A readable but superficial biography of Pakistan's founder.

Campbell-Johnson, Alan. *Mission with Mountbatten.* London: Robert Hale, 1951. A day-by-day record by Mountbatten's press attaché critical of the part played by the Muslim League.

Coupland, Sir Reginald. *The Indian Problem.* New York: Oxford University Press, 1944. Published originally in England in three volumes: I, *The Indian Problem, 1833–1935* (1942); II, *Indian Politics, 1936–1942* (1943); III, *The Future of India* (1943). An indispensable survey of Indian political history, especially valuable for the period 1936–1943.

——. *India: A Re-statement.* London: Oxford University Press, 1945. A summary of the preceding work, brought up to the end of the war.

Dar, Bashir Ahmad. *Religious Thought of Sayyid Ahmad Khan.* Lahore: Institute of Islamic Culture, 1957. A Pakistani study of the life and work of Sir Syed Ahmad Khan.

De Bary, William T., ed. *Sources of Indian Tradition.* New York: Columbia University Press, 1958. Especially relevant are sections by P. Hardy, "Islam in Medieval India," and Dr. I. H. Qureshi, "The Muslim Revival."

Faruqi, Ziya-ul-Hasan. *The Deoband School and the Demand for Pakistan.* London: Asia Publishing House, 1963. A careful analysis of those strands of Indian Muslim opinion which opposed the creation of Pakistan.

Gibb, Sir Hamilton. *Mohammedanism: An Historical Survey.* New York: New American Library, 1955. A brief study of the meaning of Islam by a leading authority.

Gopal, Ram. *Indian Muslims: A Political History (1858–1947).* London: Asia Publishing House, 1959. A Hindu account of the Muslim separatist movement, including much valuable information.

Hasan, K. Sarwar, ed. *The Transfer of Power.* Documents on the Foreign Relations of Pakistan. Karachi: Pakistan Institute of International Affairs, 1966.

Hobson, H. V. *The Great Divide: Britain-India-Pakistan.* London: Hutchinson, 1969. An admirable account, by a former constitutional adviser to Viceroy Lord Linlithgow, of the political and constitutional developments culminating in the partition of the Indian Empire, using the Mountbatten papers.

Hollister, John. *The Shi'a of India.* London: Luzac, 1953. Although written before independence, this work contains much information of value concerning Shia groups of great importance in Pakistan.

Hunter, Sir William W. *The Indian Musalmans.* Reprinted from 3d ed., 1876. Calcutta: Comrade Publishers, 1945. A classic work, essential for the understanding of the growth of Muslim separatist sentiment.

Iqbal, Sir Muhammad. *The Reconstruction of Religious Thought in Islam.* Lahore: Shaikh Muhammad Ashraf, 1954. A reprint of lectures delivered in 1926 by one who is now considered the philosopher of the Pakistan movement.

Ispahani, M. A. H. *Qaid-e-Azam Jinnah as I Knew Him.* Karachi: Forward Publications, 1966. Essentially an account of Jinnah's leadership after 1937, with particular reference to the interrelationships between all-India and Bengal politics.

Khaliquzzaman, Choudhry. *Pathway to Pakistan.* Lahore: Longmans, Pakistan Branch, 1961. The memoirs of the former leader of the Muslim League in the United Provinces, giving an inside view of the Pakistan movement.

Lumby, E. W. R. *The Transfer of Power in India.* London: Allen and Unwin, 1954. A British scholar's analysis of the events leading up to 1947, somewhat shorter in length than V. P. Menon's account.

Malik, Hafeez. *Moslem Nationalism in India and Pakistan.* Washington: Public Affairs Press, 1963. A useful, although not profound, history of the Indian Muslim community from the beginnings.

Menon, V. P. *The Transfer of Power in India.* Princeton: Princeton University Press, 1957. A detailed record from 1939 to 1947 by a senior Indian civil servant who was close to the center of power.

Moon, Sir Penderel. *Strangers in India.* London: Faber and Faber, 1944. An excellent little book reviewing the problems of India through the eyes of a young civil servant and commended by former President Ayub Khan for its insights.

——. *Divide and Quit.* London: Chatto and Windus, 1961. An account of the genesis of Pakistan and its consequences in the partition disturbances in Bahawalpur state in 1947.

Mosley, Leonard. *The Last Days of the British Raj.* London: Weidenfeld and Nicholson, 1961. A critique of the transfer of power in which Mountbatten loses some luster—a good antidote for Alan Campbell-Johnson's adulation.

Pirzada, Syed Sharifuddin. *Evolution of Pakistan.* Lahore: All-Pakistan Legal Decisions, 1963. A historical survey of Muslim separatism by a former attorney general and foreign minister, with extensive quotations from documents and letters.

——. *Quaid-e-Azam Jinnah's Correspondence.* 2d ed. Karachi: Guild Publishing House, 1966. Letters to and from various British and Indo-Pakistani public figures from 1918 to 1948.

Qureshi, I. H. *The Muslim Community in the Indo-Pakistan Subcontinent, 610–1947: A Brief Historical Analysis.* The Hague: Mouton, 1962. A landmark work, which should be read as background for the following book.

——. *The Struggle for Pakistan.* Karachi: University of Karachi Press, 1965. A recapitulation by a scholar involved in the growth of Muslim separatism during the twentieth century, relying on published sources and on his own knowledge.

Rajput, A. B. *Muslim League, Yesterday and Today.* Lahore: Shaikh Muhammad Ashraf, 1948. A rather poor account of the Muslim League from 1906, with emphasis on the Cabinet Mission period.

Ravoof, A. A. *Meet Mr. Jinnah.* 3d ed. Lahore: Shaikh Muhammad Ashraf, 1955. Jinnah's career up to 1946, as written by a disciple.

Saiyid, Matlubul Hasan. *Mohammad Ali Jinnah.* 2d ed. Lahore: Shaikh Muhammad Ashraf, 1953. A political biography of the Qaid-i-Azam, much the best available.

Sayeed, Khalid Bin. *Pakistan: The Formative Phase, 1857–1948.* 2d ed. London: Oxford University Press, 1968. An excellent study by a Canadian political scientist, emphasizing the Pakistan movement from 1940 until Jinnah's death.

Sen, Sachin. *The Birth of Pakistan.* Calcutta: General Printers and Publishers, 1955. The origins of Muslim separatism and the development of the Pakistan movement.

Smith, W. Cantwell. *Modern Islam in India.* London: Gollancz, 1946. An excellent analysis of Muslim social and political thought written when the author held Marxist views.

Stephens, Ian. *Pakistan.* New York: Praeger, 1963. A valuable survey and evaluation of the events of 1946–1948, including the Punjab slaughter and the Kashmir conflict, by one sympathetic to the Pakistani view.

Symonds, Richard. *The Making of Pakistan.* London: Faber and Faber, 1950. A good introduction to modern Pakistan.

Titus, Murray. *Indian Islam.* London: Oxford University Press, 1930. A survey of intellectual and religious movements in Indian Islam.

Tuker, Sir Francis. *While Memory Serves.* London: Cassell, 1950. The Calcutta riots and communal troubles in eastern India as seen by the last British General Officer Commanding-in-Chief, Eastern Command.

Waheed-uz-Zaman. *Towards Pakistan.* Lahore: Publishers United, 1964. A scholarly study of the years 1928–1940.

Wasti, S. R. *Lord Minto and the Indian Nationalist Movement.* Oxford: Clarendon Press, 1964. A thorough and objective study of a critical period for Indian Muslims, including the founding of the Muslim League.

Politics and Constitution-Making

Adams, Charles J. "The Ideology of Mawlana Mawdudi." In D. E. Smith, ed., *South Asian Politics and Religion.* Princeton:

Princeton University Press, 1966. An excellent short analysis of the views of the founder of the Jamaat-i-Islami Pakistan.

Ahmad, Mohammad. *My Chief*. Lahore: Longmans, Green, Pakistan Branch, 1960. A short biography of President Ayub Khan by his former private secretary, recounting General Ayub's relations with Governor General Ghulam Mohammad.

Ahmad, Munir. *Legislatures in Pakistan, 1947–58*. Lahore: Department of Political Science, University of the Panjab, 1960. A thorough analysis by a Pakistani student of the inner workings of the national and provincial legislatures.

Ahmad, Mushtaq. *Government and Politics in Pakistan*. 2d ed. Karachi: Pakistan Publishing House, 1963. An excellent survey of Pakistan politics both before and after martial law, including tabular appendixes on the various legislatures.

Anwar, Muhammad Rafi. *Presidential Government in Pakistan*. Lahore: Caravan Book House, 1967. A textbook study of the 1962 constitutional order.

Binder, Leonard. *Religion and Politics in Pakistan*. Berkeley and Los Angeles: University of California Press, 1961. A detailed study of the religious factor in the working of the first Constituent Assembly, including the role of Maududi and the Jamaat-i-Islami.

Calder, Grace. "Constitutional Debates in Pakistan," *Muslim World*, XLVI (January, April, and July, 1956). An easily accessible summary of the activities of the second Constituent Assembly.

Callard, Keith. *Pakistan: A Political Study*. New York: Macmillan, 1958. This is still the best over-all study of Pakistan politics during the first decade easily available in the United States.

Choudhury, G. W. *Constitutional Development in Pakistan*. Lahore: Longmans, Pakistan Branch, 1959. An analysis of the constitutional issues as dealt with by the Constituent Assemblies and embodied in the 1956 Constitution.

——. *Democracy in Pakistan*. Dacca: Green Book House, 1964. A survey of the trials and tribulations of democratic institutions in Pakistan by a leading political scientist at Dacca University.

Feldman, Herbert. *A Constitution for Pakistan*. Karachi: Oxford University Press, 1956. An account of the political crises of 1953–1955.

——. *Revolution in Pakistan: A Study of the Martial Law Administration*. London: Oxford University Press, 1967. A careful and occasionally witty account of the martial law period, 1958–1962.

Gledhill, Alan. *Pakistan: The Development of Its Laws and Constitution*. 2d ed. London: Stevens, 1967. An exhaustive legal study.

Jennings, Sir Ivor. *Constitutional Problems in Pakistan*. Cambridge, England: The University Press, 1957. The texts of the Federal Court's constitutional decisions of 1955, with an explanatory essay.

Jinnah, M. A. *Quaid-i-Azam Mahomed Ali Jinnah: Speeches as Governor-General of Pakistan, 1947–48*. Karachi: Pakistan Publishers, n.d.

Kayani, M. R. *Not the Whole Truth*. Lahore: Pakistan Writers' Cooperative Society, 1963. This is a partial collection of the witty and provocative speeches of the late Chief Justice of the West Pakistan High Court, exploring the problems of liberty and authority under martial law.

——. *Half Truths*. Lahore: Pakistan Writers' Cooperative Society, 1968. Addresses to the West Pakistan CSP Association.

Khan, Major General Fazal Muqeem. *The Story of the Pakistan Army*. 2d ed. Lahore: Oxford University Press, 1964. An excellent account of the civil and military role of the army, reporting in detail the events of October, 1958.

Khan, Field Marshal Mohammad Ayub. *Speeches and Statements*. Annual volumes from June 1959. Karachi: Pakistan Publications.

——. *Friends Not Masters*. London: Oxford University Press, 1967. A political autobiography indispensable for anyone who wants to understand Pakistan and its domestic and foreign policies under President Ayub Khan.

Maududi, Syed Abul Ala. *Islamic Law and Constitution*. Karachi: Jamaat-e-Islami Publications, 1955. This and the following item are pamphlets giving the fundamentalist ideology of the Jamaat-i-Islami.

——. *Political Theory of Islam*. Lahore: Markazi Maktaba Jamaat-i-Islami Pakistan, n.d.

Misra, K. P., M. V. Lakhi, and V. Narain. *Pakistan's Search for Constitutional Consensus*. New Delhi: Impex India, 1967. A study of the 1964–65 elections, based on a careful reading of the Pakistani press; includes various party manifestoes as appendixes.

Pakistan, Cabinet Secretariat. *Report of the Constitution Commission, Pakistan 1961*. Karachi: Manager of Publications, 1962.

Pakistan, Election Commission. *Pakistan General Elections, 1962*. Karachi: Manager of Publications, 1963.

——. *Report on General Elections in Pakistan 1964–65*. Karachi: Manager of Publications. Vol. I (Report), 1967. Vol. II (Appendixes), 1968.

Pakistan, Ministry of Law. *The Constitution of the Islamic Republic of Pakistan*. Karachi: Manager of Publications, 1956.

——. *Report of the Electoral Reforms Commission*. Karachi: Manager of Publications, 1956.

——. *The Constitution of the Republic of Pakistan*. Karachi: Manager of Publications, 1962.

——. *Report of the Franchise Commission*. Karachi: Manager of Publications, 1963.

——. *An Analysis of the Report of the Franchise Commission*. Karachi: Department of Films and Publications, 1964.

Pirzada, Syed Sharifuddin. *Fundamental Rights and Constitutional Remedies in Pakistan*. Lahore: All-Pakistan Legal Decisions, 1966. An analysis of the provisions of the 1962 Constitution relating to fundamental rights with relevant judicial precedents.

Punjab, Province of the. *Report of the Court of Inquiry Consti-*

tuted under Punjab Act II of 1954 to Enquire into the Punjab Disturbances of 1953. Lahore: Superintendent, Government Printing, 1954. Known as the Munir Report, this document provides invaluable insights into the relationships between politics and the maintenance of order in Pakistan.

Qureshi, I. H. *Pakistan: An Islamic Democracy.* Lahore: Institute of Islamic Culture, n.d. An essay on the meaning of the Islamic state by one of Pakistan's leading modernist scholars.

Sayeed, Khalid Bin. "The Jamaat-i-Islami Movement in Pakistan." *Pacific Affairs,* XXX (March 1957).

———. *Pakistan: The Formative Phase.* Karachi: Pakistan Publishing House, 1960. A solid study of Pakistani politics under Liaqat Ali Khan, with reference to the background of the Pakistan movement and to the subsequent political breakdown. Not to be confused with the second edition (listed in the first section of this bibliography), which concludes in 1948.

———. *The Political System of Pakistan.* Boston: Houghton Mifflin, 1967. The latest general survey of Pakistan politics, a worthy successor to Callard's study.

Schuler, E. A. and K. R. *Public Opinion and Constitution Making in Pakistan, 1958–1962.* East Lansing: Michigan State University Press, 1967. A survey, based on press reports primarily from *Dawn* (Karachi) and the *Pakistan Observer* (Dacca), of the muted constitutional debate under martial law.

Sharma, M. S. M. *Peeps into Pakistan.* Patna: Pustak Bhandar, 1954. An *émigré* Hindu writes with bitterness of politics in Karachi.

Smith, W. Cantwell. *Islam in Modern History.* Princeton: Princeton University Press, 1957. See especially chapter 5, "Pakistan: Islamic State."

Suleri, Z. A. *Politicians and Ayub.* Lahore: Lion Art Press, 1964. A review of the disintegration and reconstruction of Pakistani politics under Ayub by a leading Pakistani journalist sympathetic to the presidential system.

Wilcox, Wayne. *Pakistan: The Integration of a Nation.* New

York: Columbia University Press, 1963. An account of the integration of the princely states in West Pakistan.

Williams, L. F. R. *The State of Pakistan*. Rev. ed. London: Faber and Faber, 1966. A sympathetic survey of Pakistani problems, especially valuable for the martial-law period and the inauguration of the Basic Democracies.

Public Administration, Development, and Planning

Ahmad, Munir. *The Civil Servant in Pakistan*. Karachi, Lahore, and Dacca: Oxford University Press, 1964. An attitudinal and behavioral survey of public servants in the Lahore area.

Ahmad, Nafis. *An Economic Geography of East Pakistan*. 2d ed. London: Oxford University Press, 1968. A valuable study of the economic and social setting of East Pakistan.

Andrus, J. Russell, and A. F. Mohammed. *Trade, Finance, and Development in Pakistan*. London: Oxford University Press, 1966.

Braibanti, Ralph. *Research on the Bureaucracy of Pakistan*. Durham: Duke University Press, 1966. Indispensable for the student of Pakistan's higher bureaucracy and public services.

Bureau of National Reconstruction and Pakistan Academy for Rural Development. *An Analysis of the Working of Basic Democracy Institutions in East Pakistan*. Comilla: Pakistan Academy for Rural Development, 1963. Investigates the workings of union, thana, and district councils during the first two years.

Choudhuri, M. A. *The Civil Service in Pakistan*. Dacca: National Institute of Public Administration, 1963. An exhaustive study of the organization and training of the Civil Service of Pakistan.

Davis, Kingsley. *The Population of India and Pakistan*. Princeton: Princeton University Press, 1951. A demographic study based on the 1941 census.

Huq, Mahbub ul. *The Strategy of Economic Planning: A Case Study of Pakistan*. Karachi, Lahore, and Dacca: Oxford University Press, 1963. An outstandingly readable study by the chief of the perspective planning division of the Planning Commission.

Inayatullah. *Basic Democracy, District Administration, and Development.* Peshawar: Pakistan Academy for Rural Development, n.d. A study of local councils in West Pakistan based on survey interviews with elected members and officials.

——. *Bureaucracy and Development in Pakistan.* Peshawar: Pakistan Academy for Rural Development, 1963. A collection of papers dealing with various aspects of administration in Pakistan, including important studies of the CSP by Ralph Braibanti and M. A. Choudhuri.

Karim, Nazmul. *Changing Society in India and Pakistan.* Dacca: Oxford University Press, 1956. A sociological study of Bengali society.

Mahmood, Afzal. *Law and Principles of Local Government in Pakistan: Basic Democracies.* Separate West Pakistan and East Pakistan editions. Lahore: All-Pakistan Legal Decisions, 1964. Annotated editions of Basic Democracy legislation, including rules and standing orders.

Maron, Stanley, ed. *Pakistan: Society and Culture.* New Haven: Human Relations Area Files, 1957. A collection of essays concerning various social groups.

Michel, Aloys A. *The Indus Rivers: A Study of the Effects of Partition.* New Haven and London: Yale University Press, 1967. An extremely thorough study of the development problems of the Indus basin.

Pakistan Academy for Rural Development publications:

A New Rural Cooperative System for Comilla Thana. Annual reports since 1961.

The Comilla Rural Administration Experiment. Annual Reports since 1962–63.

The Comilla District Development Project. 1964.

The Works Programme in Comilla: A Case Study. 1966.

An Evaluation Report on the Progress of the Seven Thana

Projects under the Comilla District Integrated Rural Development Programme (September 1967). 1967.

Pakistan, Ministry of Finance. *Economy of Pakistan 1948–68.* Islamabad: Department of Films and Publications, 1968.

Pakistan, National Planning Board. *The First Five Year Plan, 1955–60.* Karachi: Manager of Publications, 1958.

Pakistan, Pay and Services Commission. *Report, 1959–1962.* Karachi: Manager of Publications, 1969. Known as the Cornelius Report, the Commission's controversial recommendations for administrative reform became an important public issue in connection with the overthrow of President Ayub Khan.

Pakistan, Planning Commission. *The Second Five Year Plan (1960–65).* Karachi: Manager of Publications, 1960.

——. *The Third Five Year Plan (1965–70).* Karachi: Manager of Publications, 1965; rev. ed., 1967.

Papanek, Gustav F. *Pakistan's Development: Social Goals and Private Incentives.* Cambridge, Mass.: Harvard University Press, 1967. A study of the role of private enterprise generally and of particular entrepreneurial groups in the rapid growth since the 1950's.

Qureshi, I. H. *The Pakistani Way of Life.* London: Heinemann, 1956. An introduction to the history and culture of Pakistan.

Rahim, S. A. *Communications and Personal Influence in an East Pakistan Village.* Comilla: Pakistan Academy for Rural Development, 1965. An excellent brief analysis showing the interlinkages between traditional and modern influence roles.

Rahman, A. T. R. *Basic Democracies at the Grass Roots.* Comilla: Pakistan Academy for Rural Development, 1962. A first-rate study of three union councils in the Comilla area.

Rashid, Haroun Er. *East Pakistan: A Systematic Regional Geography and Its Development Planning Aspects.* Lahore: Sh. Ghulam Ali and Sons, 1965. An excellent study by a young CSP officer, quite different from Nafis Ahmad's economic geography.

Tayyeb, A. *Pakistan: A Political Geography*. London: Oxford University Press, 1966. A review of national problems, including the East Pakistan demand for autonomy, from the point of view of Pakistan's geographic situation.

Tepper, Eliot. *Changing Patterns of Administration in Rural East Pakistan*. Asian Studies Center Occasional Paper No. 5. East Lansing: Asian Studies Center, Michigan State University, 1966. A thorough survey of the evolution of departmental administration and local government institutions since the mid-nineteenth century.

Waterston, A. *Planning in Pakistan*. Baltimore: Economic Planning Institute, International Bank for Reconstruction and Development, 1963. A study of the evolution of the Pakistani planning structure.

West Pakistan, Land Reforms Commission. *Report*. Lahore: Superintendent, Government Printing, 1959.

Wheeler, Richard S. *Divisional Councils in East Pakistan, 1960–1965: An Evaluation*. South Asia Monograph Series, no. 4. Durham: Duke University, 1967. An analysis of the working of the highest Basic Democracy tier in East Pakistan.

Index

The Politics of Pakistan

A Constitutional Quest

Designed by R. E. Rosenbaum.
Composed by Vail-Ballou Press, Inc.,
in 11 point linotype Baskerville, 2 points leaded,
with display lines in Palatino.
Printed from letterpress plates by Vail-Ballou Press
on Warren's No. 66 Text, 60 pound basis,
with the Cornell University Press watermark.
Bound by Vail-Ballou Press
in Columbia Bayside Linen
and stamped in All Purpose foil.